# MEN AND IDEAS IN ECONOMICS

*A Dictionary of World Economists*
*Past and Present*

# MEN AND IDEAS
# IN ECONOMICS

*A Dictionary of World Economists*
*Past and Present*

*by*

## LUDWIG H. MAI

*Professor of Economics*
**St. Mary's University, Texas**

1975

## LITTLEFIELD, ADAMS & CO.
Totowa, New Jersey

Copyright © 1975

by

**LITTLEFIELD, ADAMS & CO.**

Library of Congress Cataloging in Publication Data

Mai, Ludwig H.
  Men and Ideas in Economics.

  (A Littlefield, Adams Quality Paperback No. 284)
  Bibliography: p.
  1. Economists—Biography. I. Title.
HB76.M3       330'.092'2 [B]      75–20243
ISBN 0–8226–0284–9

Printed in the United States of America

# CONTENTS

# PREFACE

Nobody, be he saint or sinner, lives outside the economic sphere. Man in all his acts and activities is guided by the urge to preserve himself and his kind, the urge for logical reasoning and the search for truth. In his struggle to survive and to improve his living conditions, man has always, however, faced a great variety of problems. Countless men and women have tried, and try at present, to find solutions for, or at least come closer to solving, these difficulties. Through bold actions, practical experiments, and analytical studies they have intended to show the way to a richer and better life, as can be seen from their writings or reports of their actions. Many have been far ahead of their time, have often been misunderstood, and paid for their search for the truth with loss, suffering, and even death. Whether or not we agree with their opinions, conclusions, and actions, they can still teach us much that will make our own search easier. Most of them hoped to serve their fellow men, and this deserves our respect. Even where they have erred, they still teach us a lesson. All have in some way contributed to the development of civilization.

This book in a modest way aims to introduce the reader to such people. Arranged in the form of a dictionary of brief biographical profiles, it aims to offer the opportunity to make the acquaintance of the seven hundred most outstanding figures in the development of economic thought and policy—to learn who they are; where, when, and how they lived; and what it was they did that makes them remarkable. The short profiles in this book include not only economists and academicians; they also present brief statements about men of affairs and philosophers whose actions or ideas had a profound influence on forming economic policies and trends in economic thought from ancient times on up to the present.

Although this book includes all the major economic thinkers of the past, choosing present-day economists was especially difficult and complicated, and relatively few have been included in the main body of the text. My apology to those who are not listed; to do justice to all would make an additional book necessary. In any case, facts about these current figures are readily available in directories and handbooks of professional organizations. In order to round out this book with some consideration of today's economic scene, however, without adding unduly to the length of the text, I have appended a brief list of economists currently at work all over the world.

In the main text, the biographical profiles are arranged alphabetically by name. Where there is confusion about what name to look under, cross-references have been inserted in this main alphabet. So that the key figures in each historical period and each school of economic thought can be located, there is at the end of the book an outline of economic periods and trends that lists the names that are associated with each. And in the Introduction which follows, there is a very brief summary of the major historical trends in economic thinking.

I have had to rely on the works of many to whom I am in intellectual debt. Sincerest thanks are due to Professor Francis J. Greiner, S.M., who read the complete manuscript, and to Dr. Franz H. Müller, Dr. Francisco E. Saenz, and Dr. Elisabeth Lauschmann for their help and advice. I am especially grateful to Dr. Joseph Zrinyi, S.J., of Georgetown University for his extensive contribution to this work and his friendly counsel. Thanks go also to many of my students for helping in the research.

L. H. M.

# INTRODUCTION
# The Growth of Economic Thought

Ideas of economists and political philosophers are more powerful than it is commonly understood. Indeed, the world is ruled by little else.

—John Maynard Keynes

Political economy, or economics as it is now often called, is one of the sciences connected with the study of the life of man, of his needs and wants, his activities, and his relationship to other men and to the natural environment. It specifically concentrates on the material welfare of man.

Man, the starting point and the center of all economic endeavors, is born as an individual. He is endowed with a mind and a soul; with self-consciousness; the urge and desire for survival; the quest for economic security; the desire for comfort, beauty and enjoyment; and the drive to exercise his faculties.

But, man is also a social being. At the moment of his birth he becomes a part of society, his family, his clan, his community, his nation, and, in fact, of the whole human race. Without the loving care of his parents or fellow men he would not endure the first weeks, months, and years.

This dual role of man is the root of many a problem. Men are not equal in ability and physical strength. Personal interests and desires may clash with the interests and plans of the society; and institutions, set up to facilitate the struggle for survival, may change or be changed. In fact, the final goal and purpose of economic activities may alter with changing times and circumstances. In 1885 the great English economist Alfred Marshall wrote, "Economic conditions are changing constantly," and at about the same time the German Karl Knies said, "No economic system is final." The study of the historical development of economic ideas and of the philosophy behind them proves how true these statements are.

In the Middle Ages, which made much use of the ancient economic observations of the Greeks and Romans, people lived in an entirely different world. The functional, carefully organized, substantive medieval economy had the purpose of assuring the individual's place in society and of supplying what was needed for survival in the status into which he was born. The human quest for improvements and achievements was conditioned by belief in an eternal life after death. Since preparing for an afterlife was considered the most important goal of life on earth, material progress was of little importance and economic improvements were only accidental by-products, and rarely the planned purpose, of activities. All this has changed, but the reflections of these centuries of optimism and hope, of love and devotion, of the desire to earn the kingdom of heaven are still with us.

The search for human perfection moved onto a different level and into a different direction during the Renaissance. In this era material things received more attention and men came to believe that life on earth can be made more comfortable and beautiful. They also felt that greater independence from the society could do much to improve the lot of the individual. This was the time of emerging national states, the time of Machiavelli's "strong prince." It was also the time of regulated economies under close government control—the economic system called Mercantilism. Mercantilism produced wealth and luxury for those in power, but it was largely supported by the hard work of laborers, farmers, and the peoples in the new colonies.

Although those who suffered most from these economic conditions were not strong enough to make themselves heard, educated people in high positions saw the shortcomings. A small group of such men in France took up the struggle with the vested interests of those privileged by the mercantilist system. To the king they demonstrated the interrelationship and interdependence of all within an economy. Natural law, they believed, governs economic life as well as other spheres of existence. Therefore a laissez-faire economic system—one that was allowed to function naturally and free from restriction—would produce the best results for the king and the whole society. They lost their struggle for needed reforms, and the exploited masses took in the French Revolution what the advocates of laissez-faire could not give them through orderly reforms. This small group of men, under the leadership of the royal physician, Quesnay, has been called the Physiocrats. These men were the first to visualize the economic process as a circular flow. Though it was soon to be superseded, their work remains a cornerstone in the development of economic science.

Some of the laissez-faire ideas were taken up in Britain by Adam Smith in his famous book *The Wealth of Nations* (1776). Supported by the philosopher John Locke's idea of the natural liberties of the individual, the economics of Smith and the Classical School which followed him emphasized self-reliance and unrestricted individual action to obtain economic security and equality. Through the individual's acting in his own self-interest in a situation of unrestricted competition, the economic interests of society as a whole were thought to automatically benefit. Thus economic success came to be emphasized over ethical values, economic power over political power, wealth over nobility.

Such ideas did indeed free the world for extraordinary economic progress: the Industrial Revolution, which they helped foster, increased production more than anybody had expected. Man became convinced that he could change the world to his liking; a multitude of inventions and discoveries were made, and progress reached all fields.

But the never-sated hunger to possess, to control, and to command had darker effects. The promise that an "invisible hand" would in the end bring about the best for everybody did not come true. It became clear that the interests of other individuals and of the society as a whole were in fact not being served by unrestricted individual self-interest. The rich became richer and the poor became poorer. The economically weak were ruthlessly exploited. The only freedom workers had was the freedom to accept what was offered to them or starve.

Independent men, some of them successful businessmen themselves, uneasily observed these developments. Now, basing their arguments on the same ideas of individual liberty and freedom, critics came from many quarters, condemning much of what the new liberalism had created. Nationalists objected to the cosmo-political attitude of the classical writers. Optimists requested that "the irresistible impulse toward the good" be implemented. Others attacked the methods used by the classical writers and wanted to include in the scope of economics all forces, motives, and conditions that affect the development of man within the society. A growing number of people proposed social reforms of all kinds. Some developed ideas like the cooperative movement, which is still with us. There were also those who—convinced that the new system, which they called Capitalism, could not be reformed, but must be replaced—spread Communism all over the world until it became a serious danger to the systems it criticized.

While all this was going on, many outstanding scholars produced new concepts of value, wages, income, prices, and the workings of the economic system. Many of them tried to replace moral concerns with the rationality of mathematics. Such studies became urgently needed as disturbances in the circular flow, called business cycles, became more frequent, stronger, and longer until the great crash in 1929 threatened the whole system.

It was the English economist John Maynard Keynes who developed a system of controlling business cycles. He stressed that consumption spending keeps the economy moving and noted that the spending money comes mainly from wages, thus indicating the importance of full employment. He showed that savings have to return to the circular flow by means of investment and—if this is not done—that instability, stagnation, and unemployment are the consequences. He assigned to governments the responsibility of interfering when the wheels of the economic machinery slow down and demonstrated anew the interdependence of all within an economy. Under the recommendations of Keynes, in the first three decades after the Second World War production and consumption in industrial countries reached dimensions the magnitude of which nobody had anticipated.

But new problems appeared with this phenomenal economic growth, new problems that became more pressing the faster the giant, complicated, and sensitive modern economies grew. These were the problems of human behavior in an affluent society, the control of economic power, the formation of multinational corporations, inflation, unemployment, serious energy crises threatening to stop needed economic growth, pollution of the environment, and the population explosion— not to speak of the development of sophisticated weapons that could be used by countries with adversary economic systems in a last world-wide war.

Once more, we have arrived at a time of transition. We may well be advised to go back to men and ideas of the past to find whether they have something to offer that can help us solve the problems of today.

# BIOGRAPHICAL PROFILES

## Men and Women in Economics and Selected Influential Personalities in Related Fields

Once more you hover near me, forms and faces
Seen long ago with troubled youthful gaze.
And shall I this time hold you, limn the traces,
Fugitive still, of those enchanted days?
You closer press: then take your powers and places,
Command me, rising from the murk and haze.

—Goethe, *Faust*

Dedication, Translated by Philip Wayne, The Penguin Classics

Reprinted by permission of Penguin Books Ltd.

# A

### Peter Thorvald Aarum
*Norwegian Economist*                                      *1867–1926*

Aarum was born near Oslo, where he was also educated. He joined the civil service, held various administrative offices, and became professor of economics at the University of Oslo in 1917. In his writings he followed the marginal productivity theory closely. He dealt with the economic value of labor, the cooperation problem, and with practical aspects of economics. All his works were published in Norwegian, except a contribution on Scandinavian economists which appeared in *Die Wirtschaftstheorie der Gegenwart* (4 vols., 1927–28), published in Vienna.

### Charles Francis Adams
*American Political Economist*                                *1807–1886*

Charles Francis Adams, the son of John Quincy Adams, was born in Boston. He graduated from Harvard in 1825, studied law with Daniel Webster, and was admitted to the bar in 1829. He was a Whig member of the Massachusetts legislature (1840–45), edited the *Boston Whig* (1846–48), and became a Republican member of the U.S. Congress (1858–61). He was Minister to Great Britain (1861–68), and also acted as a representative of the U.S. on the Board of Arbitrators at Geneva, which settled the Alabama Claims (1870–71). In 1837 Adams wrote *Reflections Upon the Present State of the Currency in the U.S.*, followed by *Further Reflections Upon the State of the Currency in the U.S.*

### Henry Carter Adams
*American Economist and Statistician*                           *1851–1921*

Adams, born at Davenport, Iowa, graduated from Iowa College (1874), received the Ph.D. degree from Johns Hopkins University (1878), and did postgraduate work in Berlin, Heidelberg, Oxford, and Paris (1878–80). He became a lecturer at Johns Hopkins and the University of Michigan, was chairman of the department of political economy at Cornell University (1882–87), and professor at the University of Michigan (1887). After 1888 he also was in charge of the statistical department of the U.S. Interstate Commerce Commission. He was a founder of the American Economic Association, of which he was president in 1896. In 1913 he accepted the position of an advisor to a Chinese Commission for standard railway records. Adams was one of the early opponents of laissez-faire economics and stressed the inter-relationship between political economy and ethics. Important works: *Public Debts* (1887), *Science of Finance* (1898).

**Albert Aftalion**
*French Economist*
*1874–1956*

Born in Bulgaria, Aftalion went to France and became a professor at the University of Lille and the University of Paris. His main contributions to economics were in the field of monetary and business-cycle theories. He stressed the time element elapsing until new investments became productive, and was the first to analyze what later was called the acceleration principle. All his works are in French. Representative titles are: *The Economic Work of Sismonde de Sismondi* (1899), *The Periodic Crises of Overproduction* (2 vols., 1913), *Money, Price and Exchange* (1927), *Equilibrium in International Economic Relations* (1937).

**George Agricola**
*German Scientist*
*1494–1555*

Born in Saxony, Agricola studied in Leipzig, Bologna, and Padua and earned a Doctorate in Medicine at the University of Ferrara. He practiced medicine in Joachimstal (Bohemia) and Chemnitz, the greatest mining area in Europe at that time. Agricola has been called "the father of mineralogy." In his book *De re Metallica* (1556) he also deals with economic problems. His works, written in Latin, were translated into German and English three and four hundred years later. Agricola has been called a great factor in bringing about the Industrial Revolution.

**Johan Gustav Äkerman**
*Swedish Economist*
*1888–1959*

Born in Vienna, Äkerman became a pupil of Wicksell and a professor of economics. He expanded the capital theory and dealt with problems of fixed capital, distinguishing between "forced inflation" and "voluntary or subjective inflation." His representative publications are: *Realkapital und Kapitalzins* (1923), *Om den industriella Rationalisierungen* (1931), and *Nationalekonomiens utveckling* (1951). In *Logiker und Konstrukteure mathematischer Funktionen und Archioforscher, Verfasser von Chroniken* Äkerman warned against splitting political economy into mathematical, historical and normative schools. He held that the complex theoretical-philosophical nature of economic problems has to be considered in its entirety. It is not enough that the answer is correct; it must also be true.

**Albertus Magnus**
*German Scholastic Philosopher*      *ca. 1200–1280*

Born in Lauringen, Swabia, Albertus studied in Padua and Bologna and taught in Paris and Cologne. He became a Dominican and, against his wishes, a bishop. Called Doctor of the Church, he was canonized in 1931. He wrote 45 books on philosophy, natural sciences, and social theory. Albertus taught St. Thomas Aquinas and defended the doctrines of St. Thomas after his pupil's death. Albertus called "just price" the price a commodity is worth according to the estimate of the market at the time of the contract. He held that value should be equal to labor and other costs. He condemned interest as contrary to justice, and reintroduced many of Aristotle's ideas.

**Sir Archibald Alison**
*Scottish Lawyer and Historian*      *1792–1867*

He was the son of Sir Archibald Alison who had written *Essays on the Nature and Principles of Taste* (1790), treating the possibilities and limitations of psychologistic approaches to economics. The son published in 1840 *The Principles of Population and Their Connection with Human Happiness*, in which he expressed his conviction that the population question offers no reason for distress. In the long run, he says, the invisible hand will direct men to prudence; Malthus may be right as far as savages are concerned, but civilized people will act more prudently. In 1844 he wrote *Free Trade and Protection*, arguing for the protection of agriculture.

**St. Ambrosius**
*Italian Theologian*      *340–397*

St. Ambrosius was Bishop of Milan. He taught that God had admitted private property after the Fall of Adam and Eve, with all the consequences of sadness and suffering.

**Alfred Otto Ammon**
*German Anthropometrist*      *1842–1916*

Ammon, born at Karlsruhe, Baden, remained an independent scholar, who later was honored with a Doctor of Medicine degree *honoris causa*. He developed a systematic theory of the evolution of society and was one of the founders of the anthropo-social school of sociology. Among his books, *Die Gesellschaftsordnung und ihre natürlichen Grundlagen* (1895) is of special interest.

**Alfred Amonn**
*Austrian Economist*      *1883–1962*

Amonn was born in Bruneck, South Tyrol. He became professor in Prague, Tokyo, and Bern, Switzerland. His greatest contributions to economics were in the fields of methodology, theory, and monetary economics. He tried to harmonize different theories. Amonn distinguished various orders of economic activity: individual economics (related to exchange value), political economy (dealing with social welfare), and applied political economy (including methods of reform). Of his writings should be listed: *Objekt und Grundbegriffe der Theoretischen Nationalökonomie* (1911), *Grundzüge der Volkswohlstandslehre* (1926), *Grundsätze der Finanzwissenschaft* (2 vols., 1947, 1953), *Nationalökonomie und Philosophie* (1961).

**Benjamin McAlester Anderson**
*American Economist*                1886–1949

Anderson, born in Columbia, Missouri, studied at the University of Missouri, the University of Illinois, and, under John Bates Clark, at Columbia University (Ph.D.). He taught at Missouri Valley College, Missouri State Normal School (where he was head of the department of history and political economy), Columbia University, Harvard University, and the University of California (1939–46). He was economic adviser of the National Bank of Commerce of New York (1918–20) and editor of the *Chase Economic Bulletin* (Chase National Bank, New York, 1920–39).

In spite of the fact that at the 1917 annual meeting of the American Economic Association he took the side of the critics in discussing the institutional approach to economic theory, he is widely considered to be an Institutionalist. Anderson wrote numerous articles on money and banking in the *Chase Economic Bulletin* and published *Social Value* (1911), *The Value of Money* (1917), *Effects of the War on Money, Credit, and Banking in France and the United States* (1919). *The Value of Money*, etc., found wide international attention.

**James Anderson**
*Scottish Agricultural Economist*                1739–1808

Born near Edinburgh, Anderson became a gentleman farmer and pioneer in scientific agriculture. For Prime Minister William Pitt, the younger, Anderson investigated the state of the fisheries in Scotland. He contributed through his writings to the early formation of economic theories of writers later known as the English classical school, and has been called the discoverer of the rent theory. Anderson described rent as a differential surplus. He discussed diminishing returns in relation to rent and indicated a location rent theory. His *Observations on the Means of Exciting a Spirit of National Industry* (1777) deserves special attention. It was intended chiefly to promote the agriculture, commerce, manufactures, and fisheries of Scotland. Therein he gave an excellent analysis of the phenomenon that later was called the "law of indifference." Also noted should be his *An Enquiry into the Nature of the Corn*

*Laws* (1777) and *Recreation in Agriculture, Natural History, Arts and Literature* (6 vols., 1799–1802).

**Etienne Antonelli**
*French Economist*                                              *1879–1950*

Antonelli was born in Valencia, Spain, studied in Marseilles, became a doctor of law, French provincial governor, and professor at the National Conservatory of Arts in Paris. His most important books are *Principes d'économie pure* (1914) and *Principes d'économie pure du capitalisme* (1939). Antonelli defended Walras, but admitted that a genuine social science could not be based exclusively on a mathematical approach.

**St. Antonine**
*Italian Scholastic Philosopher*                               *1389–1459*

Born Antonio Pierozzi, Antonine became archbishop of Florence, where he introduced many social reforms. In his *Summa theologica* and *Summa moralis*, he qualified and modified many of the doctrines of St. Thomas Aquinas. He recognized the impersonal forces of the market, distinguished between circulating coins and money capital, noted the uncertainties of the "just price" concept and came close to developing a capital theory. His observations and comprehensive vision of economic processes and aspects are a great source of information concerning economic developments at his time. Famous is his remark "Earn to live; do not live to earn."

**St. Thomas Aquinas**
*Italian Scholastic Philosopher*                             *ca. 1225–1274*

Son of the Count of Aquino, St. Thomas was born near Naples, studied at Monte Cassino, University of Naples and, under Albertus Magnus, in Paris and Cologne. He received a doctorate from the Sorbonne. Early, he joined the Dominican Order and became a famous teacher in Paris, Rome, Bologna, and Naples. He was canonized in 1323 and has been called "Angelic Doctor" and the most brilliant of the Scholastics. St. Thomas wrote more than sixty books, including *Summa contra gentiles* and *Summa theologica*. The latter represents a summary of all knowledge at that time, trying to synthesize Christian and Aristotelian philosophy.

In economic activities, St. Thomas saw only one of the many phases of human activity, and in the earthly life he saw only a prelude to the eternal life after death. His teaching consists of normative and metaphysical economics. He emphasized mutual obligations and services by all. He held that private property is not contrary to natural law; it is beneficial to productivity. Wealth is justified when it leads to a life of virtue and is accepted as a stewardship for which account will have to be given after death. Usury is prohibited; interest is condemned (money is barren). Just wages must enable laborers to maintain their situation of life. Just prices consider only costs, risks, and utility. Trade must be an exchange of equal values. Value is an objective quality within a thing. These ideas dominated medieval life and are of influence even today.

**Marquis d'Argenson**
*French Statesman*     *1694–1757*

D'Argenson was foreign minister from 1744–47. He believed that to rule better and more successfully it was necessary to rule less. Basically he was opposed to the absolute monarchy and thought that it would be better to divide France into a number of republics the size of Switzerland. His *Journal économique* (1751) was handed only to friends in the form of manuscripts. Argenson was in favor of improved transportation facilities, free trade, and the support of agriculture, and rejected the theory of balance of trade.

**Aristotle**
*Greek Philosopher*     *384–322 B.C.*

Son of the physician to King Amyntos II of Macedonia, Aristotle studied for twenty years under Plato in Athens, and became tutor and later counselor of Alexander the Great. He returned to Athens and established a school in the Lyceum. Prosecuted for impiety, he was forced into exile and died shortly afterwards in Chalcis.

Of his many works, it is the *Politics* and *Ethics* in which his ideas on economics are principally found. For Aristotle, economic problems were moral problems related to the establishment of the ideal state. He divided economics into the science of supply and the science of household management. He distinguished between use value and exchange value. Exchange is "just" when work involved in producing the commodity is equated in the exchange. He recognized money as a medium of exchange and a measurement and store of value, but he favored accumulation of wealth only if it served "domestic economy." He condemned interest (money does not breed), but favored private property and was opposed to community property. He had a clear concept of division of labor. Aristotle's ideas had a great influence on the teaching of the Scholastics of the Middle Ages. He was the first who tried to apply causal analysis to economic reality.

**Armack**
see Alfred *Müller-Armack*

**Armeston**
see Clement *Armstrong*

**Clement Armstrong**
**(Clement of Armeston)**
*English Mercantilist Writer*        *ca. 1490–1550*

Armstrong published *A Treatise concerning the Staple and the Commodities of this Realme* (1519 or later), explaining that different nations live under different conditions and produce different commodities. To exchange surpluses would be advantageous to all concerned.

**John Asgill**
*Irish Jurist and Politician*        *1659–1738*

Asgill wrote a great number of short essays, some of which were very progressive and outspoken. He was expelled from the Irish House of Commons in 1703 and from the British Parliament in 1707 on account of his "eccentric" pamphlets. Of interest today are *Several Assertions Proved in Order to Create Another Species of Money than Gold and Silver* (1696), and *Abstract of the Public Funds Granted and Continued to the Crown* (1715). Asgill was in favor of a land bank, where landowners could obtain loans at low interest rates, and was of the opinion that an increase of circulating medium would also increase trade and manufacture. Many of his views were more anti- than pro-mercantilistic.

**Sir William James Ashley**
*British Economic Historian*        *1860–1927*

Born in London, Ashley studied at Balliol College, Oxford, under Sir Henry Maine and Arnold Toynbee. He was a fellow of Lincoln College, professor of political economy at the University of Toronto, Canada, and professor of economic history at Harvard University, occupying the first chair of this sort anywhere. Ashley returned to England in 1901 to become professor and later dean of the faculty of commerce at the University of Birmingham. In 1917 he was knighted.

Ashley has been called the most extreme member of the Historical School, but his works do not demonstrate prejudice and narrowness. In fact, Ashley did not consider himself merely an economic historian, since he was highly interested in evolutionary economics. Later he became the supporter and academic leader of Joseph Chamberlain's campaign for protection, favored tariff "reforms," and defended the rationality of mercantilist policies. His book *Introduction to English Economic History and Theory* (2 vols., 1888, 1893) was translated into German, Russian, French, and Japanese. *The Tariff Problem* appeared in 1903 and was enlarged in 1920. Of his many articles, "The Present Position of Political Economy" (*Economic Journal*, 1907) was widely discussed.

Thomas Southcliffe Ashton
*British Economic Historian*                                    *1889–1969*

Ashton studied at Manchester University and taught at Sheffield University, Birmingham University, and the University of London, where he became professor of economic history. Of his many writings, *The Industrial Revolution* (1948), *An Economic History of England: The Eighteenth Century* (1955), and *Economic Fluctuations in England 1700–1800* (1959) deserve particular attention. According to Ashton, the Industrial Revolution started in 1790 with a sudden acceleration in the rate of output.

Willard Earl Atkins
*American Economist*                                            *1892–1971*

Born in Chicago, Atkins studied at Montana State College and the University of Chicago (Ph.D.) and taught at Albion College (Michigan), University of Chicago, University of North Carolina, and New York University, where he was professor of economics and chairman of the department. Atkins wrote on labor economics and economic behavior from the institutionalist viewpoint. Of his many contributions to economic literature, the following are well' known: *Economic Behavior* (1931), *Gold and Our Money* (1934), and his article "What is Institutionalism?" (*American Economic Review*, 1932).

Edward A. Atkinson
*American Businessman and Writer on Economics*                  *1827–1905*

Atkinson, born in Brookline, Massachusetts, was educated at Dartmouth, where he received his doctorate. He also obtained the LL.D. degree from the University of South Carolina. A man of great activities, interested in many fields, he became president of the Boston Manufacturers Mutual Fire Insurance Company, wrote many remarkable reports, and lectured extensively to learned societies and professional organizations at home and abroad. Atkinson published *Distribution of Products* (1885), *Taxation and Work* (1892), *Margin of Profits* (1902), and *Facts and Figures: the Basis of Economic Science* (1904). He advocated free trade, opposed socialism, and looked for class cooperation, hoping that improvement of industrial techniques would produce general prosperity and social progress. He expressed such concepts in *Labor and Capital: Allies Not Enemies* (1880).

Thomas Attwood
*British Banker*                                                *1783–1856*

A prominent political leader and member of Parliament (1839), Attwood was an excellent speaker and outstanding analytical writer who made great contributions to the study of monetary management and currency reform. Attwood suggested the issuing of nonconvertible paper money to offset currency deflation, which in his opinion was the cause of trade depression. He strongly influenced the passage of the franchise reform law in Britain (1832). Of his many pamphlets the following are outstanding: *On the Creation of Money, and on its Action upon National Prosperity* (1817), *Observations on Currency, Population, and Pauperism* (1818), *A Letter to the Earl of Liverpool* (1819), and *The Scotch Banker* (1828). His brother Mathias (1779–1851), also a banker and successful promoter, has been known as a bimetallist.

**St. Augustine**
*African Philosopher*                                        *354–430*

Born in Tagaste, North Africa, the son of the Christian, St. Monica, Augustine early embraced Manichaeism. While teaching rhetoric in Milan he was converted back to Christianity; after some years as a hermit in North Africa he became Bishop of Hippo. His *Confessions* are still widely read, and his *City of God* proves his analytical mind and brilliant intellect. St. Augustine exercised great influence on theology, philosophy, and the socioeconomic doctrines of the Middle Ages. He gave dignity to labor, in which he saw a way toward moral perfection. He opposed charging interest as well as the notion that the rich will be deprived of eternal bliss, but he emphasized the duty of the rich to help the poor. Trade seemed to him permissible to earn a livelihood if a "just price" is charged. In *The Trinity* he offered his famous example of the honest buyer.

**Rudolf Auspitz**
*Austrian Industrialist*                                    *1837–1906*

Auspitz was also a mathematical economist and a politician. For nearly thirty years he was a member of the Austrian Lower Chamber, where he was in favor of reform of the direct-tax system proposed by Böhm-Bawerk. He introduced the progressive tax bill and opposed cartels, notwithstanding his personal interests. As a theorist he leaned strongly toward the mathematical method and made original contributions concerning marginal demand and supply curves. Together with Richard Lieben, a relative, he wrote *Untersuchungen über die Theorie des Preises*, published in two parts (1887, 1889).

**Richard Aylesbury**
*English Civil Servant*                                  *ca. 1340–1400*

Aylesbury was an officer of the English Royal Mint during the reign of Richard II. He is still known on account of his statements to the royal commission in 1381 on the export of gold and silver. Aylesbury advised that export of coins should be prohibited, that payments to Rome should be made in kind and not in money, and that imports should be restricted. He anticipated the notion of balance of trade and the so-called "invisible items" in the balance of payments.

**Clarence Edwin Ayres**

*American Economist*                                              *1891–1972*

Born in Lowell, Massachusetts, Ayres studied at Brown University and the University of Chicago (Ph.D.). He was professor of economics at the University of Texas from 1930 and became a leading Institutionalist. His dissertation was on *The Nature of the Relationship between Ethics and Economics* (1918). Of the list of his publications, the following should be noted: *The Theory of Economic Progress* (1944), *The Industrial Economy* (1952), and *Toward a Reasonable Society: The Value of Industrial Civilization* (1961).

# B

**Franz Xavier von Baader**
*German Social Philosopher*                           *1765–1841*

Born in Munich, Baader enjoyed a very comprehensive education in medicine, engineering, mining, philosophy, and theology. He received his medical degree from the University of Vienna. Later (1792–96) he studied in England, where he fell under the influence of Godwin. He became superintendent of mines in Bavaria (1817) and in 1826, professor of philosophy and speculative theology at the University of Munich. His ideas affected the entire German Romantic movement greatly. Baader had, according to Spann, an organic concept of economic life. He was opposed to the atomistic, individualistic notions of Adam Smith, saw the social evils in the impoverishment of the masses, and felt that the machine age was based solely on money power. He believed in a corporative state and in a government of vocational organizations in which labor should be represented. A collection of his extensive writings was published in 16 volumes as *Sämtliche Werke* (1851–1860). They included his *Sozietaetsphilosophie*.

**Charles Babbage**
*English Mathematician and Economist*                 *1792–1871*

Babbage was born near Teignmouth, Devonshire, and studied at Cambridge University, where he was also professor of mathematics. Babbage was a founder of the Royal Astronomical Society and the first to have the idea for an automatic sequence-controlled digital computer. Although he had not the technology to realize his idea, he was in effect foreseeing the modern punched-card machine. He published *On the Economy of Machinery and Manufactures* (1832), which includes his remarkable definitions of machine and invention, and shows deep understanding of industrial technology, business process, and economic theory. The book was used by Marx and John Stuart Mill. He wrote on many subjects and published *Thoughts on the Principles of Taxation, with Reference to Property Tax and Its Exceptions* (1848).

**Francois Noel Babeuf**
*French Revolutionist*                                *1764–1797*

Babeuf assumed the name Gaius Gracchus. He was on the extreme left during the first episode of French socialism. Released after an arrest, he formed a secret organization of "Equals" to overthrow the revolutionary government and to set up a communist state. He was betrayed and executed. As expressed in his articles, Babeuf's ultimate aim was complete equality for all. This, he believed, should be attained slowly. He advocated community property and the suppression of inheritance rights: "The fruits of the land belong to the whole world." Everyone should work according to his ability and consume according to his wants. All community members would have to dress, live, and eat alike. Children were to be taken from the parents and placed in public institutions. All products were to be collected into common stores and distributed equally to all community members. Babeuf became an idol of 19th-century European revolutionaries.

**Sir Francis Bacon**

*English Statesman and Philosopher*                          *1561–1626*

Born in London, Bacon studied at Trinity College, Cambridge. He became lord chancellor in 1621 but was later barred from office for accepting bribes and was imprisoned. Released by the king, he lived in retirement and devoted his remaining years to philosophy and science. He introduced the inductive method of modern experimental science and advanced the doctrine of the divine right of kings. In 1627 his *The New Atlantis* appeared; in it, he described a utopia resting upon a broad concept of human relations and scientific principles. In his *History of the Reign of King Henry VII* (1622) he touched upon the fallacy of the mercantilist notion on gold and stressed agriculture as a means of increasing national wealth. He defended the charging of interest but also stated "money is not good except to be spread."

**Roger Bacon**

*English Scholastic Philosopher*                          *ca. 1214–1292*

Bacon studied at Oxford, and taught there and at the University of Paris. He became a Franciscan monk, was well known because of his scientific experiments and inventions, and has been called the Admirable Doctor. An ethical system or a moral philosophy, he believed, should determine the use of scientific knowledge.

**Baden**

see *Karl Friedrich, Margrave of Baden*

**Walter Bagehot**

*English Banker and Economist*                          *1826–1877*

Born in Langport, Somersetshire, Bagehot studied at University College, London, and was called to the bar. He joined the business of his father, who was a banker and shipowner at Langport. He married the daughter of James Wilson, the founder of the *Economist*, a London newspaper, of which Bagehot became editor (1860–77).

A brilliant writer and well-informed economist, Bagehot was inclined to follow Ricardo but with some reservations. His greatest contributions to economics are found in his book *The Lombard Street* (1873), a classic description of the English banking system. In 1880 a volume of his *Economic Studies* (collected by R. H. Hutton) appeared, which included some essays on the analysis of fundamental postulates in English economic theory. Bagehot discussed economic evolution and showed the force of customs and habits in economic behavior and their effect on competition. He came to the conclusion that competition does not always produce results that are in the best interests of mankind. Economic life in its complexity is exposed to constant changes. He criticized the writers of the English classical school as being too abstract and too devoid of verification.

Bagehot was an expert in the field of money and banking, a true scholar, and a stimulating writer. His historical approach made him one of the early members of the Historical School.

## Samuel Bailey

*English Banker*  
*1791–1870*

Sometimes called the "Hallamshire Bentham," Bailey was born in Sheffield. He found that value is relative and is the consequence of utility. Utility is therefore not the cause of value as Ricardo stated. Bailey's works include *Questions on Political Economy* (1823), *Critical Dissertation on the Nature, Measure and Cause of Value* (1825), and *A Dictionary of Political Economy* (1863).

## Alexander Bain

*Scottish Psychologist and Educator*  
*1818–1903*

Bain was born in Aberdeen, and received a doctorate of laws from Edinburgh University. He became professor of logic, was rector of the University of Aberdeen, and founded the journal *Mind*. He promoted the reform of education in Scotland, became a close friend of John Stuart Mill, and developed a utilitarian psychology, a synthesis of calculation of advantages and habits. The most important of his extensive writings were: *James Mill: A Biography* (1882) and *John Stuart Mill: A Criticism, with Personal Recollection* (1882).

## Mikhail A. Bakunin

*Russian Anarchist*  
*1814–1876*

The son of a wealthy landowner, Bakunin was educated at the St. Petersburg military school and served in the Imperial Guard until 1838. He resigned his commission to study philosophy and fell under the spell of

Hegel. In Paris he met Proudhon, who exercised a great influence on him. In 1848 he participated in the revolutions in Dresden and Prague. Arrested, he was condemned to death in Saxony as well as in Austria, but he was handed over to Russian authorities and exiled to Siberia. He escaped, and on an American ship reached Japan and the United States and finally arrived in London in 1861. He joined the socialist movement with Marx and Engels and the International Workingmen's Association (1869). In 1872, however, he was expelled from the Association because of his militant ideas, and he became an arch-foe of Marx. He went to Switzerland, planning on a new association to organize anarchist uprisings, as he had successfully done in Lyons in 1870, but soon he died in Bern. His *God and the State* appeared in 1882.

Bakunin became an idol for Anarchists, who believed that by nature man is good and the root of evil is the state. He advocated the overthrow of the existing political system by force and the formation of a new order of self-governing voluntary associations with collective property. Rejecting any form of uniformity and central authority, he saw in complete individualistic liberty the ideal life and accepted only purely voluntary cooperation.

**Thomas C. Banfield**
*English Economist*  ca. *1800–1860*

Banfield spent some years in Germany and followed closely the teachings of Hermann. He has been called the forerunner of Jevons, who quoted him in his works. He is known because of his *Four Lectures on the Organization of Industry*, delivered at Cambridge in 1844. He saw in the theory of consumption the foundation of scientific economics and remarked that the satisfaction of lower wants will always be followed by the desire for satisfaction of wants on a higher level. He compiled *The Statistical Companion* (1848–54, with C. R. Weld).

**Baranovsky**
see Mikhail Ivanovich *Tugan-Baranovsky*

**Nicholas Barbon**
*English Mercantilist*  ca. *1640–1698*

Born in London, Barbon graduated with a degree in medicine from the University of Utrecht (1661). After the great fire in London (1666) he took an active part in rebuilding the city. He was the founder of the first English fire-insurance office ca. 1681 and established, together with John Asgill, the Exeter Exchange Land Bank. With Briscoe he was one of the projectors of the National Land Bank which, however, was not a success. From 1690 to 1695 he was a member of Parliament.

Barbon was of the opinion that international division of labor would be beneficial to all. He attacked the balance of trade idea and some of the mercantilist state regulations. Of his many writings, deserving special attention is his *Discourse of Trade* (1690), in which he stated that value arises from the use of a good, which is nothing else than "the supply of the Wants and Necessities of Man . . . the Wants of the Body and the Wants of the Mind." By recognizing that both scarcity and utility are the principal factors determining the value of a good, he became the forerunner of the marginal-utility economists. He also gave an impulse in the direction of "real analysis" with his interest theory stating that interest results from the use of physical capital ("Wrought and Artificial Stock") and is a return to physical capital in the same sense in which rent is a return to land. Barbon, together with Petty, has been called a Reform-Mercantilist.

**Bargemont**
see Vicomte Alban de *Villeneuve-Bargemont*


**Enrico Barone**
*Italian Mathematical Economist*                                   *1859–1924*

Barone was trained for a military career and became colonel with the Italian general staff. Stimulated by the works of Menger and Walras, in 1907 he left the army to teach economics. He published *Principi di economia politica* (1908) and *Problèmes actuels de l'economique* (1921). A disciple of Walras and Pareto, he dealt with general equilibrium theory and particular equilibria of Marshall's type. In an article, "The Ministry of Production in the Collective State" (1908), he came to the conclusion that all changes in individual welfare can be expressed as an amount of real income and that an equation system that distributes resources and incomes satisfactorily is possible even in a socialist economy.


**John Barton**
*English Economist*                                             *ca. 1789–1852*

Barton took his place in the history of economic thought with a remarkable book, *Observations on the Circumstances which Influence the Conditions of the Labouring Classes of Society* (1817). In his opinion, capital increase would lead to an increase in new machinery and consequently to a reduction in employment of labor. He favored a relief program for the unemployed. He contradicted the Select Committee on the Poor Law in its report of 1817, which said increase in capital would automatically increase the number of workers.

Barton was criticized by Malthus and McCulloch. Ricardo, however, accepted some of his notions and included them in his theories.

**John Bascom**
*American Educator and Philosopher*                    1827–1911

Born in Genoa, New York, Bascom was educated at Williams College and Andover Seminary and taught at Williams College and the University of Wisconsin. The Civil War had created many new problems and increased the general interest in economics. The works of the English Classical School were widely read. It was Bascom who published an American book entitled *Political Economy* in 1859, with liberal and idealistic views.

**Charles Francis Bastable**
*Irish Economist*                    1855–1945

Born in County Cork, Bastable studied at Femoy College and Trinity College in Dublin. He was professor of political economy at Dublin University from 1882–1932 but also taught at Queens College, Galway. Among his publications should be noted *The Commerce of Nations* (1892), *Theory of International Trade* (1893), and *Public Finance* (1892). Bastable tried to make Ricardo's international trade theory more realistic by expanding the basic model. He also spoke about "interregional trade."

**Claude-Frédéric Bastiat**
*French Writer and Gentleman Farmer*                    1801–1850

Born near Bayonne, the son of a merchant and landowner, Bastiat was trained for business but became interested in political economy. He gave more and more of his time to these studies, and since he spoke English, Italian, and Spanish fluently he was able to become familiar with most of the economic literature. Fascinated by the free-trade movement of the Manchester School, he organized free-trade associations in Bordeaux and Paris. He opposed protectivism and socialism vehemently, and advocated complete liberty for business enterprises. He was also opposed to Malthus' pessimistic views on population and to the theory of diminishing returns. Bastiat earned the name "optimist" because he believed that the social world is in harmony with a providential order and because, as he expressed it, "God has placed within each individual an irresistible impulse toward the good, and a never-failing light which enables him to discern it." A throat-and-lung disease forced this brilliant mind and excellent speaker to restrict himself to writing during the last six years of his life. His *Sophismes économiques* (two series, 1845 and 1848) were much read and admired. His fables, such as that of the candlemakers who petitioned the government for protection against competition by the sun, are masterpieces. His *Harmonies économiques* were published posthumously but parts had already appeared as articles in 1848 and 1849. Bastiat has been called the most ardent Continental exponent of economic liberalism.

**Abbé Nicolas Baudeau**

*French Journalist*          *1730–1792*

After an extensive university education and some journalistic activities, Baudeau founded in 1765 a weekly paper, *Ephémèrides du citoyen,* favoring protectionism, attacking Quesnay's doctrines, and demanding the abolition of slavery. One year later he changed his position and became one of the strongest supporters of the Physiocrats. In 1771 he published *Première introduction à la philosophie économique,* a clear and comprehensive statement of the physiocratic doctrine. Here and elsewhere in his numerous writings, he dealt with the origin and justification of private property, the productivity of agriculture, the duties of landed proprietors, the natural order, and many other subjects. The *Ephémèrides* was suppressed at various times but reappeared in 1788 as *Nouvelles éphémèrides économiques.* Differences with Turgot finally drove Baudeau into exile. Shortly before his death he returned to France.

**Henry Joseph Leon Baudrillart**

*French Economist*          *1821–1892*

Born in Paris, Baudrillart contributed much to economic history. He became professor of political economy at the Collège de France and Ecole Nationale des Ponts et Chaussées. His many books and articles include *Jean Bodin et son temps* (1855), *Manuel d'économie politique* (1857), *Des rapports de la morale et de l'économie politique* (1860), and *Lectures choisies d'économie politique* (1884).

**Otto Bauer**

*Austrian Socialist*          *1881–1938*

Born in Vienna, Bauer became the recognized leader of the Austrian Social Democratic Party. He was a cabinet minister of the first revolutionary Austrian government. His *Sozialdemokratische Agrarpolitik* (1926) and his "Akkumulation des Kapitals" (1912–13, in the *Neue Zeit*) are still of interest. Bauer enjoyed great respect because of his exceptional ability and outstanding personality.

**Bawerk**

see Eugen von *Böhm-Bawerk*

**Richard Baxter**

*English Puritan*          *1615–1691*

Born near Shrewsbury, Baxter became a Nonconformist clergyman and was appointed a chaplain in Cromwell's army. After the Restoration, he was made one of the king's chaplains. *A Christian Directory* (1673) by him shows some similarities with the Scholastic teaching. The public should be valued over and above the individual; "Every man is bound to do all the good he can do to others." All should engage in work, even the wealthy. Labor is necessary and keeps the thoughts from vanity and sin. It is a sin to desire wealth because of fleshly lusts and pride, but it is no sin to choose a gainful profession in order to be able to do more good.

## Robert Dudley Baxter

*English Economist and Statistician*                    *1827–1875*

Baxter, born in Doncaster, Yorkshire, was educated at Trinity College, Cambridge, and became a parliamentary lawyer at Westminster. His extensive writings include *The Budget and the Income Tax* (1860), *National Income: The United Kingdom* (1868), *The Taxation of the United Kingdom* (1869), and *National Debts and the Various States of the World* (1871). The way he handled figures and estimates made him a forerunner of econometrics, and Schumpeter has called Baxter "an economist of major importance."

## Saint-Amand Bazard

*French Social Reformer*                    *1791–1832*

Born in Paris, already in his poverty-stricken youth Bazard had developed messianic ideas. In 1818 he became the founder of a secret society (Amis de la vérité) to overthrow the monarchy and establish a republic. He took part in the conspiracies of 1821 and 1822, which were unsuccessful. Bazard became an enthusiastic disciple of Saint-Simon and cooperated with Enfantin in spreading the doctrine of their master. From 1828 to 1830 he delivered popular lectures which have been praised for their remarkable clearness and were attended by many who later were influential in French politics. These lectures were published in 1830 under the title *Exposition de la doctrine de Saint-Simon*. But Bazard attacked private property much more strongly than Saint-Simon ever did, and stated that all social institutions ought to have the sole purpose of the moral, intellectual, and physical amelioration of the poor. With Enfantin he published *Manifeste aux Français*. The Chamber of Deputies denounced it for propagating the collectivism of property and women. The authors answered in a letter to the president of the Chamber in 1830, outlining ideas and programs of the Saint-Simonians. This movement developed into a kind of religious sect from which, however, Bazard withdrew shortly before his death. It was Bazard who introduced the concept of exploitation into the economic literature.

## Beaulieu

see Paul *Leroy-Beaulieu*

### August Bebel
*German Socialist*                                                    *1840–1913*

Born in Deutz, Germany, Bebel over a length of time acquired an education which was far above that of the average German worker. He studied the works of Marx and Engels and became their loyal disciple, strongly opposing the socialist revisionists. He was a founder of the Social Democratic Party in Germany and became its sole leader after the death of Liebknecht. Bebel was a member of the Reichstag from 1871–1913 with only a few interruptions, and editor of the newspaper *Vorwärts*. Of special interest are his *Der Deutsche Bauernkrieg* (1892), *Die Frau und Der Sozialismus* (1883), *Christentum und Sozialismus* (1892), and *Aus Meinem Leben* (1910). Bebel was an excellent orator who knew how to enthrall and influence working men.

### Cesare Bonesana, Marchese di Beccaria
*Italian Administrator*                                               *1738–1794*

Born in Milan as the son of a wealthy and noble family, Beccaria was educated at the Jesuit College in Parma. For a short time he was professor of law at the Palatine University, Milan, lecturing also in economics. He was appointed magistrate in Milan (1771) and a member of the commission for the reform of civil and criminal justice (1794).

The first of his extensive writings was *On Crimes and Punishments* (1764), translated into English in 1767 and read by Bentham. The book was a great success in France, England, and Russia. It denounced capital punishment and recommended the prevention of crime through education. One of his articles deals with smuggling. Beccaria tried with the help of algebra to figure out the total quantity a smuggler must move to come out even. His lectures on economics were published in 1804 under the title *Elementi di Economia Pubblica* (*Elements of Political Economy*). Beccaria stood for free trade, saw in agriculture the only productive industry, spoke about the division of labor and the determination of wages, and formulated a theory of capital. He has been called the Italian Adam Smith but had expressed his views before the *Wealth of Nations* was written. He was also one of the Continental precursors of utilitarianism who clearly formulated the normative principle of the system ("la massima felicità divisa nel maggior numero"; translation: the greatest happiness shared by the greatest number).

### Johann Joachim Becher
*German Cameralist*                                                  *ca. 1635–1682*

Born in Speyer, Becher first became professor of medicine and court physician at Mainz but soon turned to administration and finally was appointed economic adviser to Leopold I of Austria and manager of state-owned enterprises. He strongly influenced Austrian economic policy. Becher favored state-sponsored and state-regulated trading companies for foreign trade and a state board of commerce to supervise money, banks, state factories, and the execution of all economic-policy regulations. He recognized that consumption is the "soul of economic life," and, as a mercantilist, advocated measures stimulating high-level mass consumption. Taxes should be paid by the rich rather than by the poor. Special attention should be given to agriculture, because food will be needed for an increasing population in a growing economy. His economic concepts, demonstrated in his *Political Discourse* (1668), made Becher one of the cameralists. In this tract he observed the rudiments of income-flow analysis, stating that one man's expenditure is another man's income; and he seems to be the first to realize the principle's theoretical possibilities.

**Max Beer**

*American Journalist*                                              *1886–1965*

Beer, born in Vienna, was educated in Germany and France (Ph.D., University of Würzburg), taught briefly at L'Ecole Libre des Hautes Etudes in France, and came to the U.S. in 1940. He was a reporter for various newspapers, and became dean of the United Nations correspondents. He served for three years in the Secretariat of the League of Nations. Of his many articles and books, the following should be noted: *The Life and Teaching of Karl Marx* (1921), *Early British Economics from the XIIIth to the Middle of the XVIIIth Century* (1938), and *Inquiry into Physiocracy* (1939).

**Edward Bellamy**

*American Writer and Social Theorist*                    *1850–1898*

Born in Chicopee Falls, Massachusetts, he studied law at Union College. However, he was more interested in journalism and founded, with his brother Charles, the *Springfield Daily News* (1880) and became editor of periodicals, including *The New Nation* (1889–91). Some of his novels are of great interest: *Equality* (1897) and *Looking Backward* (1888); the latter was a tremendous success, was translated into many languages, and exercised a great political influence. This utopian story shows the society in the year 2000 in a socialist state where all factors of production and all resources are nationalized. Bellamy, however, called his program not socialistic but patriotic and nationalist, realizing that under the prevailing conditions only with such a label would it be acceptable.

**John Bellers**

*English Philanthropist*                                          *1654–1725*

Bellers was a Quaker who proposed the establishment of "a College of Industry, and of all useful Trades and Husbandry for the profit of the rich, the better living of the poor, and through good education, for the advantage of the government." In 1699 he published a tract, *Essays about the Poor, Manufactures, Trade.*

**Friedrich Bendixen**
*German Banker*                                          **1864–1920**

Born in San Francisco, Bendixen studied at Heidelberg and Leipzig, became a banker in Hamburg, and made notable contributions to monetary theory. He saw in money a note to obtain goods. As production increases, the circulation of such notes must remain in the same ratio to goods. To assure stable values and prices, money supply should not increase faster than production.

**Jeremy Bentham**
*English Social Philosopher*                             **1748–1832**

Bentham, son of a wealthy lawyer, was born in London. He studied at Oxford and Lincoln's Inn. He was called to the bar (1772), but his interest turned toward social philosophy, and he founded the *Westminster Review.* His *A Fragment on Government* appeared in 1776. It was followed by *An Introduction to the Principles of Morals and Legislation* (1789), which won little attention at first but since has become a classic. Bentham devoted all his life to the study of the welfare of man and to writing. He gave special attention to prison reform, even developing a model prison, on which he spent a good part of his fortune. He found little support from the British government for this project.

Bentham can hardly be called an economist, but his influence on the development of economic thought and theory was very great. He hoped to be able to develop a science of human behavior applicable in law, economics, politics, and education. The forces controlling this behavior he found to be pleasure and pain. The central problem in his utilitarian system became "the greatest good for the greatest number." This goal was to be attained through the application of the hedonistic calculus: the balance between pleasure and pain. He established his "principle of utility" and noted the feature of diminishing utility. Bentham called himself a disciple of Adam Smith, but he did not accept Smith's moral philosophy. He presumed that men act rationally in all situations, deciding on actions to be taken after weighing and calculating pleasure against pain. Among his works on economics the following should be mentioned: *Defense of Usury* (1787), *Protest against Law Taxes* (1795), *Observations on the Poor Bill of Mr. Pitt* (1787), and *Manual of Political Economy* (1798). Many of his manuscripts remained unpublished for a long time. Sponsored by the Royal Economic Society and edited by W. Stark, *Jeremy Bentham's Economic Writings* was published in 1952.

Bentham was the leading philosopher of his day and an intimate friend of David Ricardo and James Mill. He strongly influenced John Stuart Mill, who, along with men like Francis Place, Samuel Romilly, James Mackintosh, and Henry Edgewood, propagated Bentham's ideas actively. These men were known as the "Philosophical Radicals" and, supported by allies in Parliament, exercised great influence on legislation. They demanded social reforms, but they desired a middle-class reform under the leadership of learned people.

**George Berkeley**
*Irish Philosopher and Economist*                      *1685–1753*

Born near Thomastown, Berkeley studied at Trinity College, Dublin, where he became a Fellow. In 1724 he was appointed dean of Derry and in 1734 bishop of Cloyne. The economic plight of Ireland awakened his interest in economic problems. In a publication called *The Querist* (1735) he made some significant suggestions. He stated that addition to the money circulation would employ the people that are idle. He asked, "Whether the true idea of money, as such, be not altogether that of a ticket or counter." He established a loan bank to encourage investment in industrial enterprises.

**Adolf Augustus Berle, Jr.**
*American Lawyer*                                        *1895–1971*

Born in Boston, Berle studied at Harvard University and was the youngest student receiving the Bachelor of Laws degree. He practiced law but also taught at Harvard and Columbia universities. Berle had close connections with Franklin D. Roosevelt and was chairman of a task force set up by John F. Kennedy to study Latin-American problems. He was treasurer of the City of New York, assistant secretary of state, and U.S. ambassador to Brazil. Berle's main interest, however, was the study of modern corporations and in particular the problem of separation of ownership and control. Of his books, the following are of special interest: *The Modern Corporation and Private Property* (1934, with Means), *The 20th-Century Capitalist Revolution* (1954), *Power without Property* (1959), and *The American Economic Republic* (1963).

**St. Bernardin of Siena**
*Italian Scholastic*                                     *1380–1444*

St. Bernardin has been called the best economist of the Middle Ages. The fact is that he had very progressive economic ideas, far ahead of his time. In his *Summa theologica* he expressed the opinion that just price is the value of a good commonly accepted at a given market. He also introduced the concepts of rarity and risk.

*Swiss Mathematician*

**Daniel Bernouilli**
*1700–1792*

Born into a family of mathematicians which included his uncle, Jacques Bernouilli (1654–1705), the first to develop the theory of probability, the basis of statistical method, and his father, Jean Bernouilli (1667–1748), known for work in integral and exponential calculus, Daniel Bernouilli became both a mathematician and a physician. In 1738 he published *Specimen theoriae novae de mensura sortis* (*Exposition of a New Theory on the Measurement of Risk*). For the first time, calculus was used in the analysis of a probability that would result from games of chance.

Bernouilli's hypothesis has interesting applications not only in business practice in the area of risks and investment, but also in the field of marginal utility analysis. Keynes discussed Bernouilli in "The Application of Probability to Conduct" (*A Treatise on Probability*, 1921), pointing out that one of his theorems was "the first explicit attempt to take account of the important conception known to modern economists as the diminishing marginal utility of money—a conception on which many important arguments are founded relating to taxation and the ideal distribution of wealth."

*German Socialist*

**Edward Bernstein**
*1850–1932*

Born in Berlin, Bernstein first became a bank clerk, but his main interest was politics. He joined the Socialist Democratic Party in 1872 and became contributor to and editor of several socialist newspapers. Bismarck's anti-socialist laws forced Bernstein to move to Switzerland, from where he was expelled. He went to London and became a friend of Engels and of members of the Fabian Society. Returning to Germany, he was elected to the Reichstag in 1902 and 1912, and remained a member from 1920–28.

Bernstein became a leader of Socialist Revisionism, an evolutionary form of Marxism. Of his many articles and books, one is of particular significance. Translated into English as *Evolutionary Socialism* (1911), this book makes Bernstein's disagreement with Marx explicit. Bernstein pointed out that Marx erred in expecting the early fall of capitalism. Class differences sharpen only slowly, people become stockholders in corporations, and many small business enterprises survive. Bernstein argued that the labor movement would be better off using the tools of political democracy rather than the revolutionary approach; thus the movement could attain its aim step by step. This attitude of course met strong opposition from the orthodox socialists, but in the end it was accepted by the Social Democratic Party.

**Christoph Besold**
*German Cameralist*                                                    *1577–1638*

Besold was born in Tübingen, where he later became law professor at the University. He wrote more than 90 books, all in Latin, of which *Synopsis politicae doctrinae* (1623) is of special interest. Besold denied the sterility of money, was in favor of interest, advocated the continuation of the guild system, and felt that public revenue should be collected mainly from the wealthy. He pointed to the danger of concentrating land property in the hands of a few by eliminating small farms. Many of Besold's students became German statesmen and administrators.

**Béthune**
see Maximilien de Béthune, Duc de *Sully*

**Sir William Henry Beveridge**
*British Economist*                                                    *1879–1963*

Beveridge was born in Rangpur, Bengal, India, and studied at Balliol College, Oxford. He was in government service and served as director of the London School of Economics and Political Science for 18 years. Beveridge proposed a comprehensive system of state social insurance, parts of which were enacted into law. He wrote *Unemployment, a Problem of Industry* (1909, rev. ed., 1931), *Insurance for All* (1924), *British Food Control* (1929), and *Pillars of Security* (1943). In an article in *Economica* he attacked Keynes: "Mr. Keynes' Evidence for Overpopulation" (1924).

**Nicholas Biddle**
*American Banker*                                                      *1786–1844*

Biddle was born in Philadelphia and studied at the University of Pennsylvania and Princeton University. He became a state senator in Pennsylvania and was later in the diplomatic service (Paris and London). In 1822–36 he was president of the second Bank of the United States. Biddle was an authority on international law and trade regulations, and made a considerable contribution to the theory of banking and money. Well-remembered is his *Letters to the Hon. J. Q. Adams* (1828), giving the history of the recharter of the Bank of the United States and "a view of the present condition of the currency."

**Gabriel Biel**
*German Scholastic Philosopher*                                        *ca. 1430–1495*

Biel was born in Speyer, and became professor at the University of Tübingen. A disciple of Oresme, Biel has been called the last of the Scholastics. He gave a summary of all the economic writings of his time and wrote a tract on the utility of money which was translated into

English in 1930. He denounced the debasement of currency, stated that the equality of goods exchanged should be based on utility, and advised that price fixing should consider human needs and scarcity of goods and labor.

**Count Otto von Bismarck**
*German Statesman*                                              *1815–1898*

Bismarck was born at Schönhausen, Prussia, studied law at Göttingen and Berlin, joined the civil and later the diplomatic service. He has been called the founder of imperial Germany and became its first chancellor in 1871. He introduced in the 1880's a nearly complete social security system with sickness, accident, and old-age insurance which became the model of similar programs in other countries. Whether this was done for humanitarian reasons or as a political move to counter the growing socialist influence is debatable.

**Jean Louis Blanc**
*French Socialist*                                              *1811–1882*

Blanc was born in Madrid, where his father was inspector of finances for King Joseph, brother of Napoleon Bonaparte. He was educated at the Collège Royal de Rodez, Madrid, and in Paris. In France he gained prominence with his book *Organisation du Travail* (1840), was elected to the provisional government (1848), and became president of a commission for the discussion of labor problems. He forced the government to adopt the principle of employment-guarantee for workingmen. Accused of conspiracy, he had to flee to England, where he remained for 22 years and wrote his outstanding work, *Histoire de la Révolution Française* (12 vols., 1847–62). He returned to France in 1870, was elected to the National Assembly and in 1871 to the Chamber of Deputies, where he was a member until he died. Highly respected, he was given a state funeral.

Blanc was the first to declare "the right to work" and has been called the father of State Socialism. He saw in competition the cause of poverty, crime, prostitution, depressions, and war. Liberty and equality, he felt, could only be obtained under a strong central government. Everyone should have the opportunity to work and be paid according to his needs and wants. To provide employment, there would be state workshops, which were to be financed by credits, without interest. The managers at first would be chosen according to ability; later they would be elected by the workers. After all costs were paid, revenues earned by the workshops were to be divided into 3 parts: one to the workers as a bonus, one to the aged and sick workers, and one to be reinvested.

The national workshops failed, partly because the assigned director, Emile Thomas, opposed the scheme. But Blanc never abandoned the idea. He believed in state planning for employment, and saw in the state the regulator of industry and the banker of the poor. He was convinced that work-associations would attract the best workers so that laissez-faire capitalism would fade away. Yet, Blanc was opposed to class war and even trade unionism. He hoped for the development of each man's personality and the brotherhood of man. *A Catechism of Socialism* (1849) describes his attitude toward the state.

**Jerome Adolphe Blanqui**
*French Economist*      *1798–1854*

Born in Nice, Blanqui studied philosophy and political economy in Paris, and became the successor of his teacher, J. B. Say, at the Conservatoire National des Arts et Métiers (1833). In 1838 he was appointed director of Ecole Spéciale de Commerce. For the Académie des Sciences Morales et Politiques he studied the economic and cultural conditions of most of the European countries and reported about his experiences and observations in the *Journal des économistes*, of which he was the chief editor. Blanqui was the first to write on the history of political economy (1838) and also published a history of commerce and industry (1826). He was especially interested in the welfare of the working classes and suggested government action for their protection. It has been said that Blanqui was the first to use the term "industrial revolution."

**Louis Auguste Blanqui**
*French Socialist*      *1805–1881*

Brother of Jerome Adolphe Blanqui, Louis Auguste was an active communist who participated in all French uprisings and revolutions from 1830 on up to the Paris Commune of 1871. In spite of the fact that he doubted the ability of the masses to overthrow the masters he had a great influence also on Marx. He was in jail from 1871 to 1879.

**Maurice Block**
*French Writer and Economist*      *1816–1901*

Block was born in Berlin but became a citizen of France. From 1843–61 he worked in the statistical department of the French Ministry of Agriculture, Industry, and Trade. He was the editor of *Annuaire de l'économie politique et de la statistique* (1856–1900). Among his prolific writings the following should be listed: *Le progrès de la science économique depuis Adam Smith* (1890) and *Les Finances de la France* (1865). He also wrote for the *Journal des économistes*. Block saw in economics a pure science. He rejected any form of government intervention in economic affairs and bitterly criticized the new German historical school of economics.

*Italian Economist*

**Gerolamo Boccardo**
*1829–1904*

Born in Genoa, Boccardo began his career as a journalist. Later he became president of the Technical Institute of Genoa, senator, and councilor of state. He was editor of the *Biblioteca dell'economista* and published *Trattato teorico-pratico di economia politica* (1853). Leaning closely toward the English classics, Boccardo was in favor of free trade. He utilized mathematics in teaching value and price problems. He opposed any form of poor relief, was influenced by Spencer, and admired John Stuart Mill.

*French Political Philosopher*

**Jean Bodin**
*1530–1596*

Bodin was born in Angers, and studied law at the University of Toulouse, where he lectured for 12 years. Later he went to Paris and served at the court of Henry III. In his *Six libres de la République* (1576) he described the supreme power of the state, which is unique and absolute, subject only to the principles of divine and natural law. Bodin made significant contributions to the quantitative theory of money and the study of inflationary prices. Answering in 1568 to M. Malestroit (the controller of the Mint), he pointed out that price inflation is caused by the abundant inflow of gold and silver, which reduces the value of the precious metals. In *Discours sur le rehaussement et la diminution des monnaies* (1578) he expressed these ideas again. He accepted the mercantilist notion of balance of trade but stated that trade can be beneficial for both partners and that the gain made by one does not necessarily need to be a loss for the other.

*Austrian Economist*

**Eugen von Böhm-Bawerk**
*1851–1914*

Born in Moravia, where his father was vice-governor, Böhm-Bawerk studied law and political economy at the German universities of Heidelberg, Leipzig, and Jena under Knies, Roscher and Hildebrand. He also studied at the University of Vienna. He taught at the universities of Innsbruck and Vienna and alternated university teaching with government service. Three times he became finance minister and he promulgated the great Austrian tax reform which became law in 1896.

His basic theory was formulated during his stay in Innsbruck, where he became full professor at the age of 37. His first work, *Geschichte und Kritik der Kapital Zinstheorien* (1884), was translated by William Smart into English as *Capital and Interest* (1890). Böhm-Bawerk also published *Grundzüge der Theorie des Wirtschaftlichen Güterwertes* (1886), *Positiv Theorie des Kapitals* (1889), *Zum Abschluss des Marxschen Systems* (1890) and many articles in European and American journals. He criticized the Marxian ideas sharply. In his works Böhm-Bawerk followed the teachings of Menger and his close friend Wieser but presented an even more complete theory of value. He distinguished between subjective and objective value and divided subjective value into subjective use-value and subjective exchange-value. Concerning price determination he introduced his "marginal pairs" and found that objective exchange-value, expressed as price, depends upon individual evaluation. Outstanding were his contributions to the theory of interest, which led to the discount or agio theory. He came to the conclusion that "the interest problem in its last resort is a problem of value."

## Pierre le Pesant, Sieur de Boisguillebert
*French Administrator and Economist*                                  *1646–1714*

Born in Rouen, Boisguillebert served there as lieutenant-general (1690–1714). His sharp critical remarks about the economic and financial system prevailing during the reign of Louis XIV brought him into disgrace and he was exiled for six months.

Boisguillebert favored direct taxes over indirect taxes and proposed a 10% tax on all incomes. He stressed laissez-faire as the key to liberty but favored protection of agriculture. For him, wealth consisted of goods and not of money. Money was only a title for future transactions, and he saw in hoarded money the "Moloch of the world" which has done more harm than good, calling it the "criminal thing." He found that the coin in the hand of a small trader will be spent much faster than the coin in the hand of the rich. Land property, in his opinion, was only the consequence of power and violence.

Boisguillebert stressed solidarity of all economic classes. The welfare of a country cannot be improved by administration if active support and cooperation of all are not secured. Incentives to such action are freedom and non-interference. His contributions to economic theory are considerable. Noteworthy are his anonymously published *Le Détail de la France* (1696), which was translated into English under the title *The Desolation of France* (1697), *Factum de la France* (1707), and *Traité dissertation sur la nature des richesses, de l'argent et des tributes* (1710), re-edited in 1843 by Eugène Daire. Marx makes him the originator of the classical school in France.

## Albert Sidney Bolles
*American Economist*                                                    *1846–1939*

Bolles was born in Montville, Connecticut, studied law privately, and was admitted to the bar. He was editor of *The Bankers' Magazine*, professor of banking at the Wharton School of Finance and Economics, University of Pennsylvania, and chief of the Pennsylvania Bureau of Industry Statistics. He published *The Conflict between Labor and Capi-*

*tal* (1876), *Industrial History of the United States* (1878). His book *Practical Banking* (1889) saw six editions.

**James Bonar**
*Scottish Economist*                    *1852–1941*

Bonar was born in Collace, near Perth, and studied at the University of Glasgow and in Leipzig and Tübingen in Germany (Ph.D.). He became an examiner in the Civil Service Commission and deputy master of the Royal Mint (Ottawa branch). He published *A Catalogue of the Library of Adam Smith* (1894), *Parson Malthus* (1881), and *Malthus and his Work* (1885), but his main work was *Philosophy and Political Economy* (1893). Referring to Adam Smith, he wrote, "The system of natural liberty would not lead to perfect economy unless men are, for the sake of the argument, supposed to be infallible in judging their interests and single-minded in pursuing them." One of Bonar's last publications was *Theories of Population from Raleigh to Arthur Young* (1931).

**Bonesana**
see Cesare Bonesana, Marchese di *Beccaria*

**Bonnot de Condillac**
see Etienne Bonnot de *Condillac*

**Bonnot de Mably**
see Gabriel Bonnot de *Mably*

**Charles Booth**
*English Social Writer and Investigator*                    *1840–1916*

Born in Liverpool, Booth became a wealthy businessman and shipowner. Highly interested in statistics, he was elected president of the Royal Statistical Society (1892–94). He attempted to demonstrate statistically the problems of poverty in London and pioneered the concept of social surveys investigating urban conditions. He succeeded in bringing the plight of the destitute to the eyes of the public and was instrumental in the passage of the Old Age Pensions Act of 1908. Booth published several pamphlets and headed the group that published *Life and Labor of the People of London* (17 vols., 1891–1903).

**Jakob Bornitz**
*German Cameralist*                    *(approx.) 1570–1630*

Bornitz was born in Torgau, Saxony. He became the first systematizer of fiscal policy and recommended state monopoly of the coinage yet warned against debasement. He also argued for close supervision of private industry by the state and for importation of raw materials, but with the restriction of the import of expensive finished commodities. In money he saw only a medium of exchange. Of his tracts, the best-remembered are *De numis in republica percutiendis et conservandis* (1608), and *Tractatus politicus de rerum sufficientia in republica et civitate procuranda* (1625).

**Ladislaw van Bortkiewicz**
*German Statistician*                                      *1868–1931*

Bortkiewicz was born in St. Petersburg, Russia, and served for seven years in the Ministry for Transportation and Communication of that country. Trained as mathemetician, physicist, and statistician, he taught at the University of Strassburg, Germany, and was professor in Berlin from 1907. His contributions to economics were mostly in the form of critical analyses published in leading German journals. These articles dealt mostly with aspects of the theories of Böhm-Bawerk, Marx, and Rodbertus. His main works were *Die mittlere Lebensdauer* (1893), *Das Gesetz der Kleinen Zahlen* (1898), and *Bevölkerungswesen* (1919).

**Giovanni Botero**
*Italian Writer*                                         *ca. 1543–1617*

Botero was born in Piedmont and became a member of the Jesuit order. An able fact-finder and analyst, he wrote about economics, public administration, and political thought. He opposed Machiavelli. His main contribution to economics was on the population question. Two centuries before Malthus he came to the conclusion that an increase in population would lead to an increase in misery. This pessimistic outlook was based on the assumption that the nourishing power of the earth is limited to a fixed quantity. Among his writings the following are noteworthy: *Della ragion di stato* (1589), *Relazioni universali* (1591–1596), *Delle causa della grandezza delle città* (1598).

**Leon Victor Auguste Bourgeois**
*French Statesman and Social Philosopher*                  *1851–1925*

Born in Paris, Bourgeois was educated at the Lycée Charlemagne. He was of great influence during the years of the Third Republic, holding many high offices: minister of the interior, premier of France, president of the Chamber of Deputies, minister of foreign affairs, minister of labor, and president of the Senate. He headed the French delegation to the Hague Peace Conference in 1899 and 1904 and became a member of the Permanent Court of Arbitration at the Hague. In 1920 he was awarded the Nobel peace prize.

Bourgeois was the founder of the French school of Solidarism, which was opposed to liberalism and the principle of competition, but he also opposed exploitation, expropriation, and revolutionary socialism. Bourgeois favored social reforms, social insurance, and labor legislation. He supported health programs and the protection of the unemployed. Social justice should be established through an extensive intervention of public authority, he believed. In 1897 he published *La Solidarité*, a collection of his articles which had appeared in *Nouvelle Revue*. The book saw seven editions. Deserving of mention also is his *Essai d'une philosophie de la Solidarité* (1877). In 1895 an association was founded to propagate the new ideas of Solidarism and in 1900 an international congress was held in Paris; but this, it seems, was the high point of the movement.

*French Economist*

**Maurice Bourguin**
**1856–1910**

As professor of political economy at the universities of Lille and Paris, Bourguin made excellent contributions to the theories of value, money, and comparative economic systems. In his studies of Marxism and State Socialism he came to the conclusion that the collective doctrines are impractical and unacceptable. However, guided by the desire to help the working classes, he recommended a procedure that would evolve democratic and progressive goals. His articles in *La Revue d'Economie Politique* and his book *Les Systèmes socialistes et l'évolution économique,* (1904) were highly praised.

*American Economist and Philosopher*

**Francis Bowen**
**1811–1890**

Bowen was born in Charlestown, Massachusetts, and was educated mainly at Harvard College, where he graduated with highest honors (1833). He taught at Phillips Exeter Academy and became professor at Harvard, retiring at the age of 74. For over ten years he was editor of the *North American Review*.

Bowen published *The Principles of Political Economy Applied to the Condition, the Resources, and the Institutions of the American People* (1856). A later edition was simply entitled *American Political Economy* (1870). The book has been recognized as a masterpiece in using liberal doctrines to support conservative (even reactionary) arguments in defense of what he saw as the American system. He admired the English classics but opposed the free-trade idea of Smith and the rent theory of Malthus and Ricardo. Bowen rejected Darwin's doctrines. He defended laissez-faire by making God the regulator through His general laws.

**Sir Arthur Lyon Bowley**
*English Statistician*                                          *1869–1957*

Born in Bristol, Bowley was educated at Cambridge and taught at the London School of Economics and at the University of Reading. He became the first holder of the chair in statistics at London University and was for a time director of Oxford University's Institute of Statistics. In 1950 he was knighted.

Most of his numerous works present excellent statistical material. Several are notable: *Wages and Income in the United Kingdom Since 1860* (1937), *The Division of the Product of Industry* (1920), *Mathematical Groundwork of Economics* (1924), and *The National Income in 1924* (1932, with Stamp). Fourteen articles published 1898–1906 in the *Journal of the Royal Statistical Society* on "Statistics of Wages in the United Kingdom During the Last Hundred Years" should also be mentioned. His daughter, Marian Bowley (born 1911 in Reading) gained recognition with an excellent doctoral dissertation, *Nassau Senior and Classical Economics* (1937) and became professor at the University of London.

**John Brand**
*English Clergyman*                                          *ca. 1750–1808*

Born in Norwich, Brand studied at Caius College, Cambridge, and became a vicar in Suffolk. His pamphlets on national debts (1796), the termination of the average price of wheat, and comparative views on the role of the state are noteworthy.

**Victor Brants**
*Belgian Economist and Historian*                                          *1856–1917*

Born in Antwerp, Brants earned the degree of Ph.D. and Doctor of Law at Leyden at the age of 22. He was a professor at the Catholic University of Louvain, the founder of the Société Belge d'Economie Sociale (a counterpart of the Le Play Society in France), and one of the founders of the Association Internationale pour la Protection Légale des Travailleurs.

He accepted Leo XIII's teaching as found in *Rerum novarum*, rejected the economic-man idea of the classics, and questioned the validity of the so-called economic laws. Economic behavior, according to Brants, should be based on moral law and religious norms. Unemployment and exploitation are the consequences of making economic activity an end in itself instead of serving as a tool for the improvement of human welfare. Brants exercised considerable influence in intellectual circles and on the Belgian government, stressing the welfare of farmers and handicraftsmen and the support of small business. He preferred a regulated economic system similar to the system of the Middle Ages.

Among his writings the following deserve attention: *Les Grandes lignes de l'économie politique* (1901), *La Petite industrie contemporaine* (1902), and *La Législation comparée et internationale du travail* (1903), which brought him to international reputation. Among his historical works must be listed *L'Economie politique au Moyen Age* (1895).

**Karl Braun**
*German Economist and Politician*
*1822–1893*

Braun, born in Nassau, studied at the universities of Marburg and Göttingen and practiced law until he became member of the Nassau Landtag (1849), the Prussian Lower House (1867–79), and the German Supreme Court. Braun was one of the leaders of the free-trade movement; he opposed government interference in economic affairs and favored the repeal of the legal maximum-interest charges. He cooperated in the formation of the Congress of German Economists, of which he was president for many years, and in the foundation of the quarterly *Vierteljahrschrift für Volkswirtschaft, Politik und Kulturgeschichte*, in which most of his writings appeared. Braun took an active part in the unification of Germany under Prussian leadership (1870).

**John Francis Bray**
*American Socialist*
*1809–1895*

Bray was born in Washington, D.C., but in 1822 with his father he went to England, where he remained for 20 years. Bray was a painter, printer, and journalist. Under the signature "U.S.," he published five *Letters for the People* in which he dealt with natural rights and equality. Associated with the Leeds Working Men's Association, he gave public lectures, which appeared in book form under the title *Labour's Wrongs and Labour's Remedy, or, The Age of Might and The Age of Right* (1839; reprinted 1921 by the London School of Economics). Returning to the United States, Bray remained active in labor movements.

Bray anticipated Marx. He thought that equality can exist only if the accumulation of property is prohibited, if private property is abolished, and if justly-earned rewards are no longer withheld from the worker. In his opinion, labor was the only value-creating force and should be rewarded according to the labor time expended. The capitalist system cannot be reformed; the whole system must be changed, but not by force, which can only overthrow the political institutions, but not inaugurate a new social order.

**(Ludwig Joseph) Lujo Brentano**
*German Economist*
*1844–1931*

Born in Aschaffenburg, Brentano was educated at various German universities and in Dublin. He became professor at the universities of

Breslau, Strassburg, Vienna, Leipzig, and Munich (1891–1914). An excellent teacher, he drew students from all nations. He together with several of his friends have been called "Kathedersozialisten" (academic socialists or "socialists of the chair"). This started as an insult and developed into a title. Basically a member of the Historical School, he started with Schmoller, Wagner, Hildebrand, and others the Verein für Sozialpolitik (1873). Brentano favored free trade, rejected the wage-fund theory, opposed rigid laissez-faire, and believed in social evolution. Among his many writings, all in German, the following should be noted: *History and Development of the English Guilds* (1870), *The Economic Man in History* (1923), *Ethics and Economics in History* (1901), and *The Development of Value Theory* (1908). Brentano was a champion of social reform and for many years the leading pacifist in Germany. In 1927 he received the Nobel peace prize.

**Constantino Bresciani-Turroni**
*Italian Economist*                                   *1882–1963*

Bresciani studied at the University of Padua and became professor at the universities of Palermo, Genoa, Bologna, and Milan. He taught at the Egyptian University of Cairo after he expatriated himself during the Fascist regime. Later he was appointed director of the International Bank for Reconstruction and Development and became minister of foreign trade. He wrote *The Economics of Inflation* (1932), *Some Methods of Measuring the Inequality of Income* (1938), *Introduzione Politica Economia* (1942), and *Corso di Economica Politica* (1962). His essay, "The Theory of Saving" (*Economica*, 1936) was widely read.

**Breuning**
see Oswald von *Nell-Breuning, S.J.*

**Goetz Antony Briefs**
*American Economist*                                  *1889–1974*

Born in Eschweiler, Germany, Briefs studied at Munich, Bonn and Freiburg. He taught at Freiburg, at the Technical University Berlin, and (from 1937) at Georgetown University, Washington, D.C. He made remarkable contributions to social economics and wrote *The Proletariat* (1937) and *Between Capitalism and Syndicalism* (1952).

**John Bright**
*English Statesman*                                   *1811–1899*

Born in Rochdale, Lancashire, son of a Quaker cotton miller, Bright had only elementary education but showed great energy and shrewdness and developed himself into an eminent orator. He joined the Anti-Corn

Law League, cooperated with Cobden, was for nearly 45 years a member of Parliament, and became president of the Board of Trade (1868–70). As an important member of the Manchester school of economics, he was for free trade and laissez-faire and defined his viewpoints thus: "I was opposed to all legislation restricting the work of adult men and women."

**Carl Brinkmann**
*German Economist* *1885–1954*

Brinkmann, born in Tilsit, became a pupil of Schmoller and taught mostly at Heidelberg and Tübingen. He attempted to relate the historical approach in economics to economic theory and succeeded in making a considerable contribution to economic analysis through his studies of social changes. Much attention was given by the public to his *Wirtschaftstheorie* (1948). His collected writings appeared under the title *Wirtschaftsformen und Lebensformen* (1944).

**Albert Brisbane**
*American Social Reformer* *1809–1890*

Born in Batavia, New York, Brisbane spread the ideas of Fourier in the United States and participated in the Brook Farm experiment at West Roxbury, Massachusetts. He published *Social Destiny of Man* (1840), *Association* (1843), and *General Introduction to Social Science* (1876).

**John Briscoe**
*English Writer on Economics* *1652–1728*

Briscoe deserves attention because he was possibly the first to demonstrate the equation of exchange as the stock of money equals price times real income. But there have been arguments that Briscoe plagiarized Chamberlen and that Barbon and Asgill plagiarized Briscoe. Obviously, it was quite generally understood that economic growth will be the consequence of increased monetary supply. Briscoe published *Discourse on the Late Funds* (1694).

**Jacques Pierre Brissot de Warville**
*French Girondist* *1754–1793*

Brissot, born at Quarville (near Chartes), studied law in Paris, advocated the spread of republican ideas in Europe, and became the leader of the Girondists. He incurred the enmity of Robespierre because he opposed the condemnation of the king, and, with other Girondists, was executed.

During a stay in the United States he studied the problems of slavery. He believed that Negroes should have all the rights of ordinary citizens. In 1788 he formed the Société des Amis des Noirs. He also advocated the reform of the penal laws.

Of his books, one is of special interest: *Recherches philosophiques sur le droit de propriété et sur le vol* (1780). Here he maintained that the property right is the outcome of want. The right disappears when the want is satisfied. Brissot did not attack private property as such, for he found it to be necessary to assure economic growth.

**Carlo Antonio Broggia**
*Italian Merchant*                                           *approx. 1683–1763*

Broggia, living in Naples, wrote *Trattato de tributi e del governo politica della sanità* (1743). He asserted that the wealth of a country depends upon the turnover of business, and favored indirect taxation, untaxed business funds, and moderate customs duties, low enough not to interfere with business. A pamphlet, published in 1754, resulted in his exile to Palermo because of critical remarks concerning the Neapolitan ministry.

**(Baron) Henry Peter Brougham**
*British Jurist and Statesman*                                   *1778–1868*

Born and educated in Edinburgh, Brougham was admitted to the English bar in 1808, became member of the House of Commons (1810) and lord chancellor (1830). He was one of the founders of the University of London. Brougham had outstanding dialectical skill and was a prolific writer. He collaborated with the Philosophical Radicals, favored abolition of slavery, called for improvement of the penal code, better administration of justice, and for public education. His *Life and Times* appeared in 1871 (3 vols.).

**David M. Buchanan**
*Scottish Journalist and Economist*                              *1779–1848*

Buchanan was born in Montrose, and became editor of the *Caledonian Mercury* (1810–27) and the *Edinburgh Courant* (1827–48). He published an annotated edition of Adam Smith's *The Wealth of Nations* (Edinburgh, 1814), to which he added an auxiliary volume, *Observations on the Subjects Treated of in Dr. Smith's Inquiry*, in which he criticized Smith's work. In 1844 his *Inquiry into the Taxation and Commercial Policy of Great Britain* appeared, criticizing the British tax system and supporting free trade. He stressed that a taxation of labor would result in demand for higher wages only.

**Karl Bücher**
*German Economist*                                             *1847–1930*

Bücher was born in Kirberg near Wiesbaden and studied at Bonn and Göttingen. He belonged to the German Historical School and was professor of economics at the University of Leipzig. Still of interest among his extensive writings is *Die Entstehung der Volkswirtschaft* (1893), translated into English under the title *Industrial Evolution* (1901). The book was an inspiration for J. R. Commons. In it Bücher described three stages of economic development (house, town, and national economics) and showed the rise of social classes. *Arbeit und Rhythmus* (1896) also merited wide attention.

**Philippe Joseph Benjamin Buchez**
*French Reformer*                                              *1796–1865*

Buchez was born in Matange, now in Belgium, studied natural science, and received a doctoral degree in 1825. He cooperated with Bazard in the formation of a secret society (the Carbonari) and came close to being condemned to death in 1822. Until 1829 he was an active member of the Saint-Simon movement. Being a Catholic, he tried to combine some of Saint-Simon's ideas with Catholicism and published *Essai d'un traité complet de philosophie au point de vue de Catholicism et progrès* (3 vols., 1838–40). He argued in favor of labor associations, which should assume control of the tools of production and of raw materials. He also published works on medical science and history. His *Traité de politique et le science social* appeared after his death.

Buchez was president of the Assemblée Constituante and with his outstanding courage and dignity he distinguished himself by the fulfillment of his duties under difficult situations.

**Georg von Buguoy**
*German Industrialist and Economist*                           *1781–1851*

Buguoy, whose full title was Freiherr von Vaux, Graf von Buguoy, was born in Brussels and studied at various colleges in Switzerland, France, and Italy. He managed his industrial enterprises and lived at his estates in Bohemia. A follower of Adam Smith, Buguoy turned, in his *Theorie der Nationalwirtschaft* (1815), against the misuse of mathematics in economic research. Algebra should only help to unveil the economic laws, he felt, not try to impose mathematical solutions on the entire complex economic structure.

**Nikolai Ivanovich Bukharin**
*Russian Communist*                                            *1888–1938*

Born in Moscow, Bukharin studied at the University of Moscow and became a member of the Central Committee of the Communist Party, a member of the Politburo, and head of the Third International. He edited *Pravda* until 1928. After Lenin's death Bukharin was for a few years the chief theoretician of the Communist Party. Being opposed to forceful collectivization of peasant holdings, however, he became suspected of supporting Trotsky. He fell into disgrace, and was purged and executed in the treason trials of 1936–38.

In 1914 Bukharin wrote a provocative book entitled *Economic Theory of the Leisure Class*, in which he maintained that the marginal utility theory is relativistic and is an ideology of the unproductive bourgeoisie. He also stated that "the psychology of the consumer is characteristic of the rentier." An English translation of the book appeared in 1972. In 1926 he wrote *Imperialism and the Accumulation of Capital in Germany*, in 1929, *Imperialism and World Economy*, and in 1932, *The Soviets Plan Science*.

**Charles Jesse Bullock**
*American Economist*                    *1869–1941*

Bullock was born in Boston and studied at Boston University and the University of Wisconsin (Ph.D.). He taught at Cornell University, Williams College, and Harvard University, and was a member of the Massachusetts Taxation Commission. Of his contributions to economic studies, the following deserve mention: *The Finances of the United States, 1775–1789* (1895), *Introduction to the Study of Economics* (1897), *Essays on the Monetary History of the United States* (1900), *Finances of Massachusetts, 1789–1905* (1907), *Economic Essays* (1936), and *Politics, Finances, and Consequences* (1939).

**Antoine Eugene Buret**
*French Economist*                    *1810–1842*

Buret, born in Troyes, became known because of his book *De la misère des classes laborieuses en Angleterre et en France* (2 vols., 1841). He also wrote many articles in the *Journal des économistes* and in *Courier Français*. He drew a gloomy picture of the conditions of labor and strongly favored the suffering working classes, but he was opposed to the rising socialist school.

**Burghley**
see William *Cecil*

**Jean Buridan**
*French Scholastic Philosopher*                    *ca. 1300– after 1358*

Born in Béthune in Artois, Buridan studied in Paris under Occam, became professor of philosophy and in 1327 rector of the University of Paris. It has been said that he was one of the students who were lured to the Tour de Nesle by the queen of France and thrown into the river Seine in sacks. But Buridan survived.

In his many books he treated economic values as subjective values depending upon the intensity of demand and desire. The greater the need, the greater the value. He also described the value-price relationship. His theory of volition brought out the paradox illustrated in his well-known story of a perfectly rational ass who has the choice between two equally attractive bales of hay. Not being able to decide which bale should be consumed first, he starves to death. The story illustrates the inability of the will to act when faced with two equally powerful motives.

**Edmund Burke**
*Irish Political Writer*                                                               *1729–1797*

Burke was born in Dublin and studied there at Trinity College. He opposed the French Revolution and defended conservative concepts. He was a good friend of Benjamin Franklin. Of his numerous writings, noteworthy are his *Thoughts on the Present Discontent* (1770), *Plan for Economic Reform* (1780), *Reflections on the Revolution in France* (1790), and *Thoughts on Scarcity* (1795). He initiated *The Annual Register*, a yearly survey of world affairs. Often quoted is his remark, "The age of chivalry is gone; that of sophists, economists, and calculators has followed."

**Theodore Elijah Burton**
*American Economist*                                                               *1851–1929*

Burton was born in Jefferson, Ohio, and studied at various colleges and universities, including New York University. He practiced law, became a member of Congress, and then a senator, serving on the monetary and foreign debt committees. Of his writings, *Financial Crises and Periods of Industrial and Commercial Depression* (1902) and *Corporations and the State* (1911) should be noted.

**Georges Marie Butel-Dumont**
*French Diplomat*                                                               *1725– ca. 1795*

Butel was secretary at the French embassy in St. Petersburg and published *Théorie du Luxe* (1771), an apologetic defense of luxury. Of interest is his *Histoire et commerce des colonies anglaises dans l' Amérique* (1755). Basically he presented mercantilist ideas.

# C

**Etienne Cabet**
*French Socialist*
*1788–1856*

Born in Dijon, Cabet studied medicine and law and received a doctorate in law in 1812. He joined the party of the Carbonari. In 1830 he was appointed general secretary to the Ministry of Justice and soon became attorney general of Corsica, but was removed from this position because of critical attitudes toward the French government. He founded the newspaper *Le Populaire*, which had a wide circulation among workers. New denunciations brought him a prison sentence, but he fled to England, where he remained 1834–39. In London he wrote *Voyage en Icarie* (1839), the story of a utopian city-state in which land and industry were to be owned collectively and the products were equally divided among the workers. Cabet knew Fourier well, admired Robert Owen, and met Marx in Paris. With hundreds of followers, he went to America in 1848 to establish Icarian communities in Texas and Illinois. But he had to face many difficulties. The Texas plan failed; the community in Nauvoo, Illinois, survived until 1898, but in 1856 Cabet was forced to leave the settlement together with 200 loyal followers. He went to St. Louis, where he soon died.

Cabet's ideas were basically communistic, but he did not propose revolution and destruction. Rather, he believed that his utopia must be founded on morality and sincere cooperation. In fact, he said, "The communists will never gain much success until they have learned to reform themselves. Let them preach by example and by the exercise of social virtues, and they will soon convert their adversaries." He published *Colonie icarienne aux États-Unis d' Amérique* in 1856.

**John Elliot Cairnes**
*Irish Economist*
*1824–1875*

Born at Castle Bellingham, Cairnes studied at Trinity College, Dublin, and was admitted to the bar. In 1856 he won the Whetely professorship of political economy at the University of Dublin, and in 1859 he was appointed professor of political economy and jurisprudence at Queen's College, Galway. From 1866 on, he taught at University College, London, until ill health forced him to resign in 1872. At the time of his death he was generally regarded as the leading British economist and the last defender of the classical school.

Cairnes defined economics as a science of production and distribution of wealth. He distinguished four occupational groups: unskilled labor, artisans, dealers, and business executives (including professional men). Movements from the labor group to one of the others seemed to him nearly impossible, but otherwise he believed that the "non-competing industrial groups" experience a constant passing up and dropping down. He tried to revive the wage-fund theory. According to Cairnes, economic actions are the causes determining historical developments, and political economy should deal only with what actually is and not with what ought to be. He advocated the use of the deductive method.

Of his many writings, these are of particular interest: *The Character and Logical Method of Political Economy* (1856), *Essays in Political Economy, Theoretical and Applied* (1873), and *Some Leading Principles of Political Economy Newly Expounded* (1874). In his *The Slave Power* (1862) he offered a forceful defense for the northern American states during the Civil War.

**John Calvin**
*French Theologian and Reformer*                                    *1509–1564*

Calvin was the first to allow, under certain conditions and within limitations, the charging of interest. He felt that every man has a duty to work but also the duty to abstain from unnecessary consumption. Thus, the accumulation of wealth became permissible and wealth itself became a sign of divine favor. Max Weber saw in Calvin's theology the roots of modern capitalism.

**Tommaso Campanella**
*Italian Philosopher*                                               *1568–1639*

Born in Stilo, Calabria, Campanella studied in Naples and Cosenza and entered the Dominican Order. For heresy he was imprisoned for a few months; for his political activities he was sentenced to life imprisonment. Released after more than 24 years, he fled to France, fearing rearrest.

Campanella wrote about philosophy and political problems. Of interest is his *Città di sole* (1623), describing a utopian society much like that in Plato's *Republic*, except that it did not know slavery. Property was collective, and life was regulated in accordance with religious and ethical concepts. This little book has seen reprints in many countries, including Soviet Russia.

**Pedro Rodriguez, Count Campomanes**
*Spanish Economist and Statesman*                                   *1723–1802*

Campomanes was prominent during the reign of Charles III and influenced the king's reform programs leading to economic liberalism. Educated in law and economics, he demonstrated great abilities in applied economics. In *Respuesta fiscal* (1764) he wrote about grain trade, and in 1774 he published *Discurso sobre el fomento de la industria popular*. He advocated three kinds of taxes: progressive income taxes, luxury taxes, and taxes on products but not on property.

**Nicolas François Canard**
*French Economist*                                                ca. *1750–1833*

Canard won a prize offered by L'Institut National for the best discussion on the single-tax doctrine. His *Principes d'économie politique* (1801) developed the diffusion theory of taxation. Canard distinguished between natural labor (necessary to sustain existence), acquired labor, and superfluous labor, and called the result of fixed labor applied to land or industry "rente fonciere," to which he added "rente industrielle," and "rente mobilière" (commerce). All taxes must be paid from one of these three rents, i.e., all taxes are shifted until every buyer and seller bears an equal share of the burden.

**Edwin Cannan**
*British Economist*                                                *1861–1935*

Cannan was born on the island of Madeira and studied at Balliol College, Oxford. He wrote *A History of the Theories of Production and Distribution in English Political Economy from 1776 to 1848* (1893) and taught at Oxford part-time until he became the first lecturer at the London School of Economics. He retired in 1926 and published what has been regarded as the standard edition of Adam Smith's *Wealth of Nations*. Among his writings there should also be listed *Wealth, A Brief Explanation of Wealth and Welfare* (1914), *The Economic Outlook* (1922), *An Economist's Protest* (1927), *Balance of Trade Delusions* (1931), *Money* (1932), and *Economic Scares* (1933). Cannan's main contributions were in the field of monetary theory.

**Richard Cantillon**
*Irish-born Banker*                                                ca. *1680–1734*

Little is known about the early years of this remarkable man who left the most complete and systematic statement on economics before Adam Smith's *Wealth of Nations*. Cantillon was born in Bally-Heigh, Ireland, appeared later as a successful London merchant, and moved to Paris, where he established a banking house. Speculating against John Law's promotional schemes, he made a fortune but had to leave France. Returning to London, from where he directed his extensive financial transactions covering most of Europe, he was murdered by a discharged servant, probably his cook, who stole manuscripts and set fire to the house to hide the crime.

The only essay left was written originally in English in 1730. It had been translated into French by Cantillon himself to please a friend, and was published in 1775 as *Essai sur la nature du commerce en général*.

It was rediscovered in 1881 by Jevons, who called it the first treatise on economics. Therein Cantillon showed a comprehensive grasp of economic subjects. He discussed wealth, value, wages, prices, money, exchange, interest, population, social classes, and foreign trade, as well as credit and banking. Land was seen as the source of wealth, and labor as productive force. The value theory was a cost-of-production theory, but influences of supply and demand on the market value were also indicated. In his view, normal price is determined by cost (the quantity of land and labor that enter into production of a commodity), while market price is determined by supply and demand. A subsistence wage theory was developed, and the effect of inflation on international trade was carefully described. While mercantilist concepts were dominant, many of the author's ideas were rather modern, or at least well ahead of his time. He also had a clear conception of the functions of entrepreneurs, the risk-bearing directors of production and trade. He seems to be the first to draw an economic table depicting clearly and vividly the circular flow of economic life.

**Diomede Carafa**
*Italian Statesman*                                    *ca. 1406–1487*

Carafa, Duke of Maddaloni, was a Neapolitan administrator who favored a balanced budget (including all welfare expenditure) and moderate taxes which would not oppress labor or drive capital out of the country. He thought that commerce should be free, industry and agriculture should be encouraged, and that labor is the source of wealth. His book entitled *De rigis et boni principis officio* was an important contribution to economic analysis. He covered political, military, and administrative problems, and dealt with public finance. Carafa was the first to write about the role of economics in the state.

**Jacob Newton Cardozo**
*American Writer and Editor*                            *1786–1873*

Cardozo was born in Savannah, Georgia, but spent most of his life in Charleston, South Carolina. His small book, *Notes on Political Economy* (1826), was a highly abstract and analytical work in which he criticized Ricardo's rent theory and Malthus' population doctrine. But he advocated free trade strongly. For him the New World was a better place than the Old World to study economic problems, because the New World was closer to the natural order of things while the Old World suffered from "vicious social organization."

**Henry Charles Carey**
*American Economist*                                    *1793–1879*

Born in Philadelphia, the son of Matthew Carey, Henry Charles entered his father's business at the age of 24 and thus became junior partner at

Carey, Lea, and Carey, the leading publishing house in the U.S. He had little formal education but a good mind, a dominating personality, and good looks. Growing rich from his business transactions, he retired at age 42 to devote himself to writing. He wrote many newspaper articles, over 3,000 pages of pamphlets, and 13 books covering many fields. These were widely translated and well received, especially in Germany. Most popular were: *Essay on the Rate of Wages* (1835), *The Principles of Political Economy* (3 vols., 1836–40), *The Past, the Present, and the Future* (1843), *The Harmony of Interests* (1851), *The Principles of Social Science* (1858), and *Social and Moral Science* (1872).

Carey's optimistic ideas reflect the environment in which he lived (the great opportunities offered in the New World, the seemingly unlimited natural resources) and his belief in the laws of nature set by a benevolent Creator. He contradicted Malthus' population theory because he was convinced that production will always outrun population growth. He held that the position of the laboring class will continue to improve, and that a harmony of interests of men will be a reality. Utility was for him the measure of man's power over man; value was the measure of nature's power over man. Both move in opposite directions. As one increases the other decreases. He regarded only capital and labor as production factors and thought them equal claimants to the wealth they produce. In land he saw only a commodity. He rejected the classical law of diminishing returns and stated that Ricardo's rent theory was wrong because in real life land cultivation did not start with the richest or best soil but with the poorer soils on sides of hills. Originally he accepted free trade concepts but finally he became a protectionist and nationalist. Utopian notions can be found in his late speeches and writings. At the famous "Carey Vespers" in Philadelphia he discussed such ideas with his followers.

**Matthew Carey**

*American Publisher and Writer*          *1760–1839*

Matthew Carey, the father of Henry Charles Carey, was born in Dublin. He was an Irish immigrant who had served a prison term for his critical attitude toward the British government. In Philadelphia he became a printer, publisher, and editor of journals. He was a charter member, and later president, of the "Society for the Promotion of National Industry" founded by Alexander Hamilton. In the long list of his writings, of special interest is his *Essays on Political Economy* (1822). His speeches and writings were major contributions to the nationalist economic thought of his time. He called for protective tariffs, encouragement of manufacturers, and development of the domestic markets.

**Caritat**
see Marie Jean Nicolas de Caritat, Marquis de *Condorcet*

*German Economist*

**Ernst Ludwig Carl**
*1682–1743*

Carl, born in Öhringen, South Germany, studied at Halle and entered the service of the Count of Bayreuth and Ansbach. In 1720 he went to Paris to study and observe the efficiency of the mercantilist system. Here he wrote: *Traité de la richesse des princes et de leurs états, et des moyens simples and naturels pour y parvenir* (3 vols., 1722–23), building his whole economic system on division of labor, stressing that prosperity can be achieved only within a well established order of collaboration. His well organized, systematic work deserves attention since, later on, Adam Smith, too, emphasized the importance of division of labor.

*Italian Scientist*

**Count Gian Rinaldo Carli**
*1720–1795*

Carli, born in Capo d'Istria, became professor of astrology in Padua but moved in 1753 to Milan where he was made president of the Council of Finance in 1771. This made it possible to enforce his proposals stated in his *Osservazioni preventive al piano intorno alle monete de Milano* (1766) and to carry out a complete reformation of the coinage system. He had already published other works on the monetary question and strongly objected to the balance-of-payments concepts. Also interesting are Carli's observations in regard to methods of property evaluation and his efforts to use index numbers. In 1780 appeared his *Della Lettere Americane* (which was expanded to four volumes in 1786), showing his concern with economic and political developments in America.

*American Economist*

**Frank Tracy Carlton**
*1873–1961*

Born in Mantua, Ohio, Carlton was educated at Case Institute of Technology and at the University of Wisconsin. He taught at Albion College, DePauw University, Case Institute, and the University of Wisconsin. His main contributions were in labor economics. He published *Education and Industrial Evolution* (1908), *Organized Labor in America* (1920), and *Labor Problems* (1933).

*British Writer*

**Thomas Carlyle**
*1795–1881*

Born in Ecclefechan, Scotland, Carlyle became one of the most influential writers of his time. An outspoken critic of British society, he attacked the new industrial order and the classical school of economics. He ridiculed the concept of the economic man, denounced the laissez-faire philosophy, and called political economy the "dismal science." He felt that the power of the government should be exercised in the public interest. He described the role of government assigned by the classical school as an "anarchy plus the policeman." Of his numerous books, *Past and Present* (1843) deserves special attention from a socio-economic standpoint.

**Thomas Nixon Carver**

*American Economist*                *1865–1961*

Born in Kirkville, Iowa, Carver studied at Iowa Wesleyan College and the universities of Southern California, Johns Hopkins and Harvard (Ph.D.). He taught at Oberlin College and Harvard. His works include *Distribution of Wealth* (1904), *Principles of Rural Economics* (1911), *Principles of Political Economy* (1914), *Essays in Social Justice* (1915), *The Essential Factors of Social Evolution* (1935), and *The Economics of Freedom* (1948). Carver made adjustment to the environment a major point in economics. In his later writings he stressed the problems of materialism and proposed that we should train our consciences to approve whatever makes the state survive.

**Karl Gustav Cassel**

*Swedish Economist*                *1866–1945*

Cassel was educated at Uppsala University and at the University of Stockholm (Ph.D.) where he was professor of political economy and financial science 1904–33. Widely recognized as an expert in international monetary affairs, he advised the League of Nations on currency problems, the Banking Committee of the U.S. House of Representatives on the stability of the dollar (1928), many European governments on monetary problems after World War I, and the Soviet Union in 1922.

He wrote numerous articles, papers, and books. In his early writings such as *Elementary Theory of Prices* (1899) and *The Nature and Necessity of Interest* (1903) he dealt with free competition. But he also wrote *Social Policy* (1902) and *Theory of Social Economy* (1918). With his *Memorandum on World Monetary Problems* (1920) he acquired an international reputation. Cassel's Rhodes lectures at Oxford were published as *The Crises in the World's Monetary System* (1932), and *The Downfall of the Gold Standard* (1936). In 1935 his *Quantitative Thinking in Economics* appeared, which made him an early econometrician, even if he avoided mathematical demonstrations in his own writings. While Cassel's contributions were often normative his theoretical works cannot be overlooked. He wrote on business cycles, developed a purchasing power parity theory of international exchange rates, and a price theory based on scarcity of supply. The term "value" had no real meaning for him, who taught "value-free" economics.

**Marcus Porcius Cato**

*Roman Statesman*       *234–149 B.C.*

Cato, known as Cato the Elder, rose from very modest circumstances to great wealth and the high offices of Roman consul, tribune, and censor. All his life he denounced luxury and extravagance. He strongly advocated agriculture and the agricultural population as the sources of morality and strength for the state. His little book *De agricultura* discusses economic problems in agriculture.

**Paul Louis Cauwès**

*French Economist*       *1843–1917*

Cauwès studied law and political economy at the universities of Nancy and Paris. Influenced by the German historical school he was opposed to the individualistic and cosmopolitan attitudes of the classics. A nationalist, he argued in favor of protectionism as a safeguard of industry, a stimulus for production, and a prerequisite for the harmonious development of the national economy. For Cauwès, economics was the art of social well-being. His most important contribution was *Cours d'économie politique* (2 vols., 1879).

**William Cecil**

*English Statesman*       *1520–1598*

The son of a small landowner, Cecil became the trusted minister of Queen Elizabeth, serving her for 40 years, and the first Baron Burghley. Cecil was largely responsible for the execution of Mary, Queen of Scotland. He was one of the strongest supporters of mercantilist policy, and his activities were designed to help and assist industry and commerce. Famous are his words, "Nothing robbeth the realm of England more than when more merchandize is carried in than is coming forth."

**Giovanni Ceva**

*Italian Mathematician and Engineer*       *1647–1734*

Ceva was born in the province of Milan, and was an engineer in Mantua, but most of his life was spent as a professor at Mantua University. His *De re nummaria* (1711) was one of the first works on mathematical economics. He stressed the need for theoretical models "to get out of the dark night of unmanageable complexes." He used what he called "geometry" for economic reasoning and for an explanation of economic problems.

Thomas Chalmers

*Scottish Social Reformer*                                   *1780–1847*

Chalmers, born in Fife, studied mathematics, physics, political philosophy, and theology at St. Andrews University in Edinburgh. The Scottish church had to dispense with the minimum-age requirements to license Chalmers as preacher in 1799. He became a professor of moral philosophy and political economy at St. Andrews, and later a professor of divinity in Edinburgh. He is regarded as the founder of the Free Church of Scotland. Of his writings on economics, *Political Economy* (1832) and *Enquiry into the Extent and Stability of National Resources* (1808) deserve attention. Chalmers favored voluntary, church-administered relief for the poor, and opposed tax-paid public relief. He was convinced that moral concepts and behavior would lead to the economic improvement of society. In his opinion, the study of value as well as the importance of foreign trade were overemphasized. He strongly criticized Say's Law.

Hugh Chamberlen

*English Financial Projector*                                *1664–1728*

Son of a court physician, Chamberlen studied at Trinity College, Cambridge, and became an obstetrician. He advocated the establishment of a Land Bank that would grant loans to landowners at favorable terms and would, he hoped, earn more money for the government than the Bank of England did. The Scottish Parliament rejected the idea, but the English House of Commons in 1696 was more favorably inclined. When the date fixed by the act of foundation arrived, however, subscriptions for funds were not completed, and the project was dropped. Chamberlen then went to Holland. Two later attempts were no more successful, in spite of support from Barbon, Asgill, Briscoe, and John Law. All these men believed that an increase in the quantity of the circulating medium would have a favorable effect on trade and manufacture since, as Barbon said, money has a value made by law.

Edward Hastings Chamberlin

*American Economist*                                         *1899–1967*

Born in La Conner, Washington, Chamberlin studied at Iowa State University, the University of Michigan, and Harvard University, and taught at the last two. His dissertation, *The Theory of Monopolistic Competition*, was published in 1933 and became a classic. Besides many articles, Chamberlin also wrote *Toward a More General Theory of Value* (1957) and *The Economic Analysis of Labor Union Power* (1958).

**Antoine Elisée Cherbuliez**
*Swiss Lawyer and Economist*                                    *1797–1869*

Born in Geneva, Cherbuliez studied and practiced law but became interested in politics and economics and joined the faculties in Geneva and Zurich as professor of political economy. He wrote *Riche ou Pauvre* (1840) and in 1862 a book on pure economics and its applications: *Précis de la science économique et de ses principales applications*. Cherbuliez had been influenced by Say and was one of the first writers dividing economics into theory and policy/application. The concepts and style of his later book have been highly praised.

**Michel Chevalier**
*French Economist*                                              *1806–1879*

Chevalier was born in Limoges, and studied engineering at the Ecole Polytechnique. He became an active member of the Saint-Simonian movement and was imprisoned with others of this group, charged with forming an illegal association. On the request of Adolphe Thiers, who was minister of the interior, his penalty was reduced.

In 1840 he was appointed professor of political economy at the Collège de France and subsequently became one of the most eminent economists of his time and a great influence on the economic policies of France. Chevalier negotiated and successfully concluded the French-English commercial agreement in 1860, followed by similar treaties with other countries. He foresaw the importance of railways for economic development and also the opportunities of the Suez Canal project, and predicted as early as 1857 the decline in the value of gold. He advocated industrialization and free trade and insisted that special attention be given to labor problems. He shared the optimism of Adam Smith but declared that reliance on competition as the only regulating factor is illogical and irrational. Governments should not hesitate to act whenever the general public interest requires it, he felt. Among his many publications, of special interest are *Cours d'économie politique* (1842–44), and *Monnaie* (1850). His *Letters on North America* (1839) should also be mentioned.

**J. J. Emile Cheysson**
*French Economist*                                              *1836–1910*

Cheysson was born in Nîmes, and studied engineering at the Ecole Polytechnique in Paris. As a public servant he became interested in economic problems and published *Statistique géometrique* (1887). He operated with cost and revenue curves, and wrote about profit maximization, location problems, transportation rates, product variation, and choice of raw material. He dealt with sales as functions of wages, and presented clearly econometric concepts. Cheysson influenced social legislation greatly.

**Sir Josiah Child**

*English Merchant and Economist*      **1630–1699**

Born in London, Child rose to become director and governor of the East India Company and the richest man in England. He was knighted in 1678. His *Observations concerning Trade and the Interest of Money* (1668) and *A New Discourse of Trade* (1693) recommend solutions to many problems.

Child defended joint-stock companies as bringing the aristocrats and merchants together. Basically he was in favor of free trade and believed that low interest rates should be used to stimulate commerce and industry. Bullion, he thought, adds less to the wealth of a nation than the import of raw materials. The balance of trade seemed to him an uncertain and doubtful instrument, and in money he saw only a commodity. He recognized that emigration to colonies reduces the domestic labor force, and he advocated the confinement of colonial trade to the motherland so that both countries would grow into a single market serving the same purpose.

**Marcus Tullius Cicero**

*Roman Orator and Philosopher*      **106–43 B.C.**

Cicero became a consul and one of the most influential figures in the intellectual life of Rome. Later, however, he was exiled and murdered. His economic ideas are found in *De res publica*. He wrote about division of labor, made a list of respectable professions, praised agriculture, strongly favored private property, and was against interest and free trade. His opinion of retail merchants was highly unfavorable, as he felt that they can succeed only by deceiving others.

**Sir John Harold Clapham**

*English Economic Historian*      **1873–1946**

Clapham, born in Broughton, taught at Cambridge and the University of Leeds. He wrote *The Economic Development of France and Germany 1815–1914* (1921), *An Economic History of Modern Britain* (1938), *The Bank of England* (1944), and *A Concise Economic History of Britain* (1949). In 1922 he published an article, "On Empty Economic Boxes" (reprinted in *Readings in Price Theory*, American Economic Association, 1952), in which he attacked Marshall and Pigou and questioned the realism of some of their theories.

**John Bates Clark**

*American Economist*      **1847–1938**

Born in Providence, Rhode Island, Clark studied at Brown University and Amherst College and, in Europe, at the University of Heidelberg (under Knies) and the University of Zurich. He taught at Carleton,

Smith, and Amherst colleges, and at Columbia University from 1895 until he retired in 1923. He was a founder of the American Economic Association and its president in 1894–95.

His first book, *The Philosophy of Wealth* (1885), was largely a collection of previously published articles. He criticized the classical notion of the economic man, whom he wanted to replace by the complete man motivated by ethical principles and not just by desire for material improvements. He felt that the relation between ethics and economics was not stressed sufficiently, that society is not a sum of individuals but an organism in itself, that capitalistic competition is dangerous, and that the economic future should be built upon cooperative institutions. In 1888 he wrote *Capital and Its Earnings*. But the great breakthrough came with *The Distribution of Wealth* (1899), which made him the first American theorist of international reputation. Clark related marginal utility analysis to the field of distribution. He searched for analytical tools to connect the pricing process with social justice, and arrived at a wage for the marginal worker that is equal to the value of the marginal product. In a just society, he felt, men should get all that they produce or at least a fair share of it. He went on to determine the wage level that assures full employment, developed marginal utility as a value theory, and finally arrived at a full-scale distribution theory. Thus, Clark became the leading exponent of the marginal productivity theory of distribution. His analysis was based on static conditions, but he saw that in a dynamic economy five types of changes may occur: changes in population, tastes, capital, techniques, and the structural form of industrial organization. His efforts in pure theoretical analysis were unique and original, and have hardly been surpassed by any other American economist. In *Essentials of Economic Theory* (1907) Clark dealt with "social economic dynamics" and came closer to dealing with practical economics.

**John Maurice Clark**

*American Economist*                                    *1884–1963*

He was born in Northhampton, Massachusetts, son of John Bates Clark, and studied at Amherst College and Columbia University (Ph.D.). He taught at Colorado College, Amherst College, the University of Chicago, and Columbia University. He received the Francis A. Walker Award of the American Economic Association, of which he was president in 1935. Clark was managing editor of the *Journal of Political Economy*, and served as consultant to various national agencies.

Of his numerous writings, the most important are: *Social Control of Business* (1925), *Strategic Factors in Business Cycles* (1933), *Economics of Planning Public Works* (1935), *Preface to Social Economics* (1937) and *Competition as a Dynamic Process* (1961). Clark did not hesitate to express value judgments and to consider social policy matters aimed at welfare maximization.

**Henry Clay**

*English Economist*                                                    *1883–1954*

Clay was educated at Oxford, where he became a lecturer before he was appointed professor at the University of Manchester. He served the government on various committees and in the ministry of labor. Labor problems, especially unemployment questions, received his special attention but he also wrote about currency. He devoted time to labor education and with this intention wrote *Economics for the General Reader* (1916). His numerous writings include *The Problem of Industrial Relations* (1929), *The Post-War Unemployment Problem* (1929), and *War and Unemployment* (1945). His *Lord Norman* (1957), dealing with the banking system and currency problems, appeared posthumously.

According to Clay, the goal of economic studies must be social welfare. Ethics must be considered an essential part of such studies, and purely individualistic attitudes should be excluded. He denied Pigou's statement that high real wages can be the cause of unemployment.

**Clement of Armeston**
see Clement *Armstrong*

**William Cobbett**

*English Reformer and Pamphleteer*                                    *1763–1835*

Cobbett was born in Surrey, the son of a small farmer. He joined the army in 1783, but sailed to Philadelphia in 1792 to avoid prosecution for pamphlets on army abuses. He returned to England in 1800, where he soon ran into difficulties again, but was able to found the *Register*. Denouncing the flogging of soldiers, he was convicted of sedition. He nevertheless found ways to edit the *Register* from prison. He was released in 1812 but had to flee to the U.S. in 1817, fearing new imprisonment. He rented a farm on Long Island and continued writing for the *Register*. He returned to England and published books and pamphlets on a variety of subjects, and became a radical labor leader and champion of agriculture. After passage of the Reform Bill of 1832, for which he had agitated, he was elected to Parliament. In economics, his most effective contribution was an attack on paper money, *Paper against Gold* (1811). Noteworthy also are his *Surplus Population and Poor-Bill, a Comedy in Three Acts* (1835), and *Legacy of Labourers* (1835).

**Richard Cobden**

*English Statesman*                                                    *1804–1865*

Cobden was born in Sussex, the son of a small farmer who died early. He entered his uncle's warehouse business in London, but, eager to learn, ambitious, and observant, he started a cotton textile factory in

Manchester with two friends in 1828, and it brought him a fortune. He traveled to Europe and America and used every opportunity to study economic conditions and problems in various countries. He joined the Manchester Anti-Corn Law Association and, together with John Bright, soon became its driving force. Elected to Parliament, he finally succeeded in having the corn laws repealed. For this victory he paid with great financial losses and with the loss of his health; however, subscriptions and donations restored £80,000 to him. He continued his fight for free trade and successfully negotiated the reciprocal tariff treaty with France (Cobden-Chevalier Treaty, 1860), followed by similar agreements with other countries. Knowledge and logic, the ability to speak convincingly, a pleasing personality, and pleasant manners made Cobden a political leader of great stature. He supported many domestic reforms and favored universal elementary education. He wrote many newspaper articles and published *England, Ireland, and America* (1835) and *Russia* (1836).

### Gustav Cohn
*German Economist*     1840–1919

Cohn, born in Marienwerder, studied at the universities of Berlin and Jena. He taught at the polytechnic institutes of Riga and Zurich and at the University of Göttingen. His special interests were transportation problems and public finance. He spent some years in England, mainly to study railroad policy, and in 1900 published *Zur Geschichte und Politik des Verkehrswesens*, followed in 1905 by *Zur Politik des deutschen Finanz-Verkehrs und Verwaltungswesen*. He strongly favored government ownership of railways. His theoretical contributions are found in *System der National-Ökonomie* (3 vols., 1885–89) and in *Finanzwissenschaft* (1889). Both have been translated into English. In all his writings Cohn stressed social-psychological observations and ethical factors.

### Roger Coke
*English Mercantilist Writer*     ca. 1626–1696

Coke, born in Suffolk, was educated at Queens College, Cambridge, and became a well-known writer on economic problems. He made many suggestions for the improvement of commerce and trade, for the use of idle workers in reclamation of wasteland, for a plentiful money supply to increase prosperity, and for free import of raw materials. He published *A Discourse of Trade* (1670), *England's Improvements* (1675), and *Reflections upon East Indy and Royal African Companies* (1695).

### Jean Baptiste Colbert
*French Statesman*     1619–1683

Born in Rheims, Colbert was the son of a merchant and protégé of Cardinal Mazarin, whose personal intendant young Colbert became.

With the recommendation of the cardinal, he was appointed to the court of Louis XIV, where he proved himself an efficient administrator and rose to the rank of controller-general and secretary of state.

Colbert applied all concepts of mercantilism to such an extent and so completely that "Colbertism" was a synonym for what has later been called mercantilism. He was a great financial reformer who introduced protective tariffs, strict regulations of commerce and industry, and close supervision of the colonies. He improved transportation, building roads and channels to stimulate domestic commerce. The policies of Colbert were very nationalistic and pragmatic, and in many ways narrower than the English mercantilist policies. He never hesitated to use the power of the state in enforcing economic and financial policies designed by him to make France the most powerful and prosperous nation on the Continent. He brought the guilds under state control, opposed trade restrictions between provinces, and controlled the export of grain to assure a cheap and abundant food supply; and to free France from dependence on foreign manufacturers, he induced craftsmen to immigrate to France.

**George D. H. Cole**
*English Economist*
*1889–1959*

Cole was born in Cambridge, studied at Balliol College, Oxford, and became a Fellow of Magdalen College, Oxford. He taught at London University and at Oxford. He was a prominent member of the Fabian Society, serving as president in 1952, and the leader of a movement advocating "guild socialism." Guilds, organized by producers, would manage the industrial enterprises. Every worker would be a partner in the business organization in which he worked; this would eliminate the division between capital and labor. Consumers, too, would have their associations and, under government supervision, would decide on the overall economic policy. A partnership of equals would be formed between producers and consumers. The movement remained chiefly English.

The author of some 50 books, Cole deserves special attention for: *The World of Labor* (1913), *Studies in World Economics* (1934), *What Marx Really Meant* (1934), *Principles of Economic Planning* (1935), *The British Common People, 1746–1938* (1939), *The Meaning of Marxism* (1948), and *History of Socialism* (1953). He also wrote biographies of Cobbet and Owen and a great number of popular detective stories and articles in the *New Statesman and Nation*.

**Samuel Taylor Coleridge**
*English Poet, Philosopher and Writer*
*1772–1834*

Coleridge, born in Ottery St. Mary, Devonshire, and educated at Jesus College, Cambridge, exercised great influence on many outstanding men, including Lord Shaftesbury, John Stuart Mill, Gladstone, and

Disraeli. He criticized utilitarianism because of its philosophical and psychological inadequacies, and the classical economists because of their abstractness. Coleridge declared that individualism and laissez-faire economics could not serve as remedies for unemployment and poverty, which are both consequences of industrialism. He planned a utopian community in Pennsylvania based on "pantisocracy," which failed. His political writings include the periodical *The Watchman* (1796) and *Constitution of Church and State* (1829).

**Jean Hippolyte, Baron de Colins**
*Belgian Social Reformer*                                    *1783–1859*

Colins, a Belgian baron, served under Napoleon as a volunteer, was exiled after the restoration, went to Havana in 1819 as a physician, and returned to Paris in 1830. Here he developed his social reform system known as "rational socialism," advocating land nationalization. In his opinion, all men should have access to the soil. Therefore, land and most of the capital goods should be owned collectively, though they should be worked privately. Thirty-year rent contracts should be issued and the rent received used for social purposes. Among his writings, notable are *Socialisme rationnel* (1851), *Qu'est ce que la science sociale?* (4 vols., 1851–54), and *La science sociale* (1857).

**Gerhard Colm**
*American Economist*                                         *1897–*

Colm was born in Hanover, Germany, and studied at the University of Freiburg. Before coming to the U.S. he was a statistician in the German federal service and a professor at the University of Kiel, where he was also research director at the Institute of World Economics. In 1933 he was appointed professor at the New School for Social Research, New York. He became fiscal adviser in the Department of Commerce (1939), department chief of the Bureau of the Budget (1940), and senior economist in the Council of Economic Advisers (1946). In 1952 he joined the National Planning Association. Colm published *Economic Theory of Public Finance* (1927), *The Economy of the American People* (1960, with Geiger), and *Essays in Public Finance and Fiscal Policy* (1955).

**Clement Colson**
*French Public Servant*                                      *1853–1939*

Colson was born in Versailles and served in the Ministry of Public Works. Originally trained as an engineer, he switched to teaching but soon became a public servant. He published *Transports et tarifs* (1890) and *Cours d' économie politique* (1901), which won wide attention for its mathematical demonstration of supply and demand.

**Lucius Junius M. Columella**
*Roman Agronomist*                                    *First Century A.D.*

Born in Cadiz, Spain, Columella had a career as a Roman tribune in Syria and was also active in politics and law. In Italy he became an experienced, enthusiastic, and successful farmer. One of the first works on agriculture, his *De res rustica* (12 bks.) is a rich source of information on rural life and deals with the techniques and economic problems of farming.

**Stephen Colwell**
*American Lawyer, Industrialist, and Economist*                    *1800–1872*

Born in Brocke County, Virginia (now West Virginia) and educated at Jefferson College, Cowell spent most of his life in Philadelphia, where he amassed a fortune in the iron business. Influenced by Henry Charles Carey, he made extensive studies in political economy. In 1865 he became a member of the U.S. commission for revision of the revenue system. He published *Domestic Production and International Trade* (1850), *The Ways and Means of Commercial Payment* (1859), and *The Claims of Labor and Their Precedence to Claims of the Trade* (1861). Remarkable are his studies on tariffs, excise taxes, and tax duplication. In his opinion, the quantity theory of money offers no explanation for price movements.

**John Rogers Commons**
*American Economist*                                    *1862–1945*

Commons was born in Hollandsburg, Ohio, studied at Oberlin College, and did graduate work at Johns Hopkins University. He taught at Oberlin, Indiana University, Syracuse University, and from 1904–32 at the University of Wisconsin. He was often on leave to serve the federal government, and he led the "brain trust" of Wisconsin governor Robert M. La Follette. He was connected with and served as director of the National Bureau of Economic Research, and in 1917 he was president of the American Economic Association.

Of his many publications, particularly notable are *The Distribution of Wealth* (1893), *The Legal Foundations of Capitalism* (1924), and *Institutional Economics* (1934). With others, he published *Documentary History of American Industrial Society* (10 vols., 1910) and *History of Labor in the United States* (4 vols., 1919–35).

An institutionalist, Commons was a great synthesizer of the social sciences. He was especially interested in the nature of capitalism, legal aspects of economies, labor affairs, and public utility regulations. He advocated a greater role of the government in economic life and felt that the government should be the mediator whenever economic interests conflict, as between labor and management, between business and the public interest, and between welfare and the market forces. His writings were in many instances instrumental toward a better understanding of industrial relations, and he drafted much of the reform legislation on civil service, public utility, workmen's accident compensation, and unemployment insurance.

**Auguste Comte**
*French Philosopher*     *1798–1857*

Comte, born in Montpellier, studied at the Ecole Polytechnique, Paris, where he later became a tutor and examiner. In 1818 he met Saint-Simon and until 1824 contributed to his publications. In economics Comte saw only a part of a broader master-science, which he called sociology. His extensive writings are based on a philosophical system that rejects metaphysics completely and relies exclusively on positive scientific methods. Comte hoped to reform society so that all men live in harmony. His most important work is *Cours de philosophie positive* (1842). Positivism was a great influence in the further development of economic thought. In particular, John Stuart Mill, who corresponded with Comte but never met him, accepted many of Comte's philosophical ideas.

**Charles Arthur Conant**
*American Banking Expert*     *1861–1915*

Born in Winchester, Massachusetts, Conant was financial reporter for the Boston *Post* and the New York *Journal of Commerce*. He wrote *Principles of Money and Banking* (1905), *A History of Modern Banks of Issue* (1909), and reports on the monetary system of the Philippines and on the National Bank of Nicaragua. Conant assisted in the reforms of the currencies of Nicaragua and Cuba.

**Etienne Bonnot de Condillac**
*French Philosopher*     *1714–1780*

The son of the Vicomte de Mably, Condillac was born in Grenoble. He became an ordained priest but was primarily interested in philosophy. Among his friends were Rousseau, Diderot, and Duclos. His contributions to French philosophy were widely discussed and caused his election to the Berlin Academy and to the French Academy of Sciences. Worthy of special note are his books *Traité des sensations* (1754) and *Le commerce et le gouvernement* (1776). Condillac saw the center of economic problems in the concept of value. The source of value was for him utility; but utility is not a quality of a good; rather it is attached to the good by individuals in accordance with their needs and wants. He said "Our needs give rise to value; our exchanges give rise to price." Utility increases with scarcity and declines with abundance. Exchange transactions are possible only because the utility and the value of the goods are different for each of the exchange partners. Condillac became the forerunner of the modern school of subjective value. Although he avoided an open break with his physiocrat friends, he argued that utility and value are also produced by industry and commerce and not exclusively by agriculture, as the physiocrats stated.

### Marie Jean Antoine Nicolas de Caritat, Marquis de Condorcet
*French Mathematician and Philosopher*                           *1743–1794*

Condorcet was born in Ribemont, studied at the College of Navarre, and early made himself a name in mathematics, with valuable contributions to the theory of probability. At 26 he was made a member of the Academy of Sciences and at 39 a member of the Académie Français. He was a member of the National Assembly and supporter of the revolution until his protest against the persecution of the Girondists forced him into hiding. Here he wrote his famous philosophical work, *Esquisse d'un tableau historique des progrès de l'ésprit humain* (1794), on the progressive evolution of man, which would finally lead to absolute equality of rights. He left his hiding place to avoid embarrassment for his host, was soon arrested, and died mysteriously on the night of his arrest.

Condorcet believed that the optimum happiness and prosperity of mankind would be reached through science and the incessant perfecting of human reason. All differences in wealth, inheritance, and education would disappear. He was in favor of wide distribution of property, free education, and social security. A league of all nations would outlaw war. Condorcet realized that greater affluence would increase population, but he was convinced that science would find ways to produce more food on the same land and that reason would keep the population growth in check.

During his lifetime he was befriended by Voltaire, Thomas Jefferson, Benjamin Franklin, Adam Smith, and Turgot, whose economic concepts he accepted and of whom he wrote his *Vie de M. Turgot* (1786).

### Carlo Angelo Conigliani
*Italian Economist*                                              *1870–1901*

Conigliani studied at Salerno and became an outstanding professor of political economy at the University of Modena. He wrote numerous articles on profit, exchange, and capitalism, but his greatest contributions are in the field of taxation. He was also interested in labor problems, unemployment questions, and aid to the laboring classes. He wrote *La riforma delle leggi sui tributi locali* (1898), *Teoria generale degli effetti economici delle imposte* (1890), and *Saggi di economica politica e di scienza finanze* (1903).

**Johannes Conrad**
*German Economist and Statistician*     *1839–1915*

Born at Gut Borkau, Conrad studied at the universities of Berlin and Jena and became professor at the University of Halle. An outstanding teacher, he appealed to many Italian and American students and was well known internationally. He was a founder of the Verein für Sozialpolitik and editor of *Jahrbücher für Nationalökonomie und Statistik*. His *Grundriss zum Studium der politischen Ökonomie* (1900) was the textbook which for 30 years enjoyed widest use in German-speaking countries. It was divided into 4 parts: national economy, economic policy, finance, and, as a distinct branch of economics, statistics. Conrad was chiefly interested in problems of agrarian policy and statistics.

**Hermann Conring**
*German Cameralist and Scholar*     *1606–1681*

Conring was born in East Friesland and studied medicine in Helmstadt. He has been called the first professor to teach specialized courses in public administration. He dealt with monetary and fiscal policies, statistics, and population problems. Conring pointed out that commodity transactions are more important than money itself. In 1662 he published *Examen rerum publicarum totius orbis*.

**Victor Prosper Considérant**
*French Social Reformer*     *1808–1893*

Born in Salins, Considérant studied at the École Polytechnique. He was an intellectual leader of Fourier's supporters and popularized his doctrine restlessly. In 1848 he was elected to the National Assembly. From 1852 to 1854 he attempted to establish a phalanstère in Texas but failed. He returned to France working for Fourier's ideas until he died. Considérant published in 1847 *Principes de socialisme* and in 1848 *Le socialisme devant le vieux monde*, a comparative survey of socialist systems demonstrating the superiority of Fourier's teachings.

**Charles Horton Cooley**
*American Social Scientist*     *1864–1929*

Cooley was born in Ann Arbor, Michigan, studied at the University of Michigan, and was a professor of sociology there until his death. He was especially interested in studies of the nature of the society and of social progress. Through his outstanding works he has enriched all social sciences. He published *Human Nature and the Social Order* (1902), *Social Organization* (1909), and *Social Process* (1918).

**Cooper**
see Anthony Ashley Cooper, 3rd Earl of *Shaftesbury*
Anthony Ashley Cooper, 7th Earl of *Shaftesbury*

**Thomas Cooper**
*American Writer and Economist*                                    *1759–1839*

Cooper was born in London and studied law at Oxford and later medicine in London and Manchester. After some experience as a lawyer in Lancashire, he came to America in 1795 and established himself as a physician and lawyer in Northumberland, Pennsylvania. He soon became involved in politics, and was a frequent contributor to newspapers and a vigorous pamphleteer. His writings finally brought him a prison term for sedition. A man of many talents, he served as a state judge in Pennsylvania and as a professor of chemistry at Dickinson College and the University of Pennsylvania. In 1820 he went to the University of South Carolina, where he established the first department of political economy and where he was president until 1834.

Cooper had a great ability to change his mind and to adjust himself to new affiliations. He wrote against slavery and later defended it. He advocated protective tariffs for infant industries and later denounced the protectionists. He criticized the Bank of the United States and later came to its defense. In his *Lectures on the Elements of Political Economy* (1826) he expounded the doctrines of Adam Smith and Ricardo. But here again, he first rejected Ricardo's rent theory only to change his viewpoint with changed environment. In the competitive system he saw a divine manifestation for the benefit of deserving individuals. The wealth of the community he found in the aggregate wealth of its individual members.

**Nicholas Copernicus**
*Polish Astronomer*                                               *1473–1543*

Well known for his contributions to science, Copernicus, during the political struggle concerning coinage in the old German empire, in vain suggested the adoption of a uniform currency. In 1526 he wrote *Monetae cudendae ratio*.

**Luigi Cossa**
*Italian Economist*                                               *1831–1896*

Cossa was born in Milan and studied at the University of Pavia and in Germany (under Roscher). He became professor of political economy at the University of Pavia and was responsible for the revival of the scientific study of economics in Italy. He made Pavia the center of economic research, and was the first modern Italian economist to gain international recognition. His *Guida allo studio dell'economica politica* (1876) was translated into many languages and appeared in English under the title *Introduction to the Study of Political Economy* (1880) He dealt with the scope and methods of economics. Cossa divided economics into pure theory (science) and practical economics (art) and found that Oriental economic thought could be reduced to a few moral concepts. He largely followed the classic doctrines, but his contributions to the science of finance demonstrated his own independent thinking. He wrote *Primi elementi di scienza delle finanze* (1876), and *Saggi di economica politica* (1878). As a brilliant scholar and excellent teacher, he exercised great influence.

**Jean Gustave Courcelle-Seneuil**
*French Economist*                                                  *1813–1892*

Born in Seneuil, Courcelle-Seneuil became the most distinguished leader of a group of scholars who dominated the Collège de France and the *Journal des économistes* and did not allow opposition to their laissez-faire attitudes. Courcelle was also briefly professor at Santiago, Chile. He wrote *Le crédit et la banque* (1840), *Traité théorique et pratique d'économie politique* (1858), *Liberté et socialisme* (1868), and *Traité théorique et pratique des operations de banque* (1858). He argued for a pure science of economics, which he called "plutology," whereas he named applied economics "ergonomy."

**Antoine Augustin Cournot**
*French Mathematician and Economist*                                *1801–1877*

Cournot was born in Gray and became professor of mathematics and physics at the University of Lyons. He made recognized contributions to probability theory and epistemology. Later he was rector of Grenoble and Paris and became inspector of schools.

In 1838 he published *Recherches sur les principes mathématiques de la théorie des richesses*, which went unnoticed for years. Not a single copy was sold. Omitting the algebraic formulae, he offered in 1863 a simplified edition and finally, in 1876, a still more elementary form of the original under the title *Revue sommaire des doctrines économiques*. The result remained moderate. Shortly before his death, however, interest in his work was awakened through the tribute that Jevons paid him for his great contribution to economics.

Cournot has ever since been recognized as a great economist. He was the first to make important use of symbols and mathematical analysis in the study of economic theories. He supplied many original ideas on pure and imperfect competition, duopoly, and monopoly. He explained price determination under various market conditions, and the concept of elasticity. He found that demand is a function of price and that supply is related to price. He demonstrated supply and demand curves, advocated macroanalysis, criticized the theory of free trade, spoke about profit maximization instead of utility, and was concerned with partial equilibrium analysis. He dealt with shifting of taxes, which he treated as changes in production costs. Cournot asked whether the competitive system is superior to all other systems and concluded that no satisfactory answer could be given. This does not prevent the search for improvement of the existing system, which does not necessarily depend on private initiative alone. Private and public interests may collide; the state may have the duty to intervene; no economic principle prohibits the control of business management by the state. Cournot observed that the organic gives way to the mechanical as civilization progresses: the calculable substitutes for the spontaneous, the rational for the intrinsic, and logic and mathematics for disorderly movements in life.

**Trench Coxe**
*American Public Servant*                          *1755–1824*

Born in Philadelphia, Coxe became a member of the Continental Congress, assistant secretary of the treasury (1790), and commissioner of revenue (1794). It has been said that he was the ghost writer of Alexander Hamilton's report on manufactures. Coxe published in 1787 *An Inquiry into the Principles on which a commercial system for the United States of America should be founded; to which are added some political observations connected with the subject*, and in 1794 *A View of the United States*, which represented a survey of the nation's economic prospects with supporting statistical material.

**John Craig**
*Scottish Economist*                          *approx. 1780–1850*

Very little is known about Craig's life. He was elected to a fellowship in the Royal Society of Edinburgh in 1818 and published *Elements of Political Science* (1814) and *Remarks on Some Fundamental Doctrines in Political Economy* (1821). He argued against the classical wage and rent theories, rejected Smith's distinction between productive and unproductive labor, and denounced Ricardo's ideas of the inevitable opposition between profit and wages. Craig offered original observations in regard to utility and value and analyzed utility and value with increasing supply. He also made original contributions to the theory of public finance and developed the equal-sacrifice and capitalization theories of taxation.

**Benedetto Croce**
*Italian Philosopher and Political leader*                          *1866–1952*

Born in Pescasseroli, Aquila, Croce studied at the University of Rome. He founded a periodical called *La Critica* in which he published his writings. In 1910 he became a senator and in 1920 minister of education. His anti-Fascist manifesto (1925) was well known to Mussolini, who, however, never exiled the world-renowned author. Croce was throughout his life a leader of liberal forces. In 1943 he reestablished the liberal party and named himself the party's president. Again he became a minister and a member of the consultative council. Croce was also a leader of the "New Idealism" philosophical movement and presented his philosophy in *Filosofia della spirito* (4 vols., 1902). In the last 2 volumes he wrote about practical philosophical concepts, economics, and ethics. He attacked Marxian materialism and objected to the use of mathematical methods. He wrote *Materialismo storico Marxistica* (1900) and *Reduzione della filosofia del diritto alla filosofia dell'economia* (1907). In addition, Croce made important contributions to the historical study of Italian culture and the philosophy of history.

**Oliver Cromwell**
*English Lord-Protector*                                            *1599–1658*

In 1651 Cromwell issued the Navigation Act, whereby only British ships were permitted to bring goods of non-European countries to England. Goods from European countries had to be transported either by British ships or ships of the country of origin.

**Sir Thomas Culpeper**
*English Economic Writer*                                          *1578–1662*

Culpeper, a country gentleman in Kent, was much concerned with bringing to England the same prosperity that he had observed in Holland. In his opinion, this required a lower interest rate, and he argued that 10 percent, the legal rate at the time, was too high for commerce as well as for morality. He expressed these ideas in *Tract against the High Rate of Usurie* (1621), asking for a reduction to 6 percent. In 1624 Parliament lowered the rate to 8 percent. Later, in 1641, Culpeper presented the same tract again, urging a further reduction of the interest rate to 5 or 6 percent, which was done in 1651. Culpeper's requests were based on economic considerations alone. He was convinced that England's economic development was depending on what was later called "cheap money." His son, **Thomas Culpeper** (1621–1697), who was also knighted, became Governor of Virginia but was convicted of corruption in 1683. In 1668 he reprinted his father's tract. He himself wrote *The Necessity of Abating Usury Reasserted* (1670), *Brief Survey of the Growth of Usury in England with the Mischiefs Attending It* (1671), and several other pamphlets. In 1754 the physiocrat Gournay translated these tracts into French.

**William Cunningham**
*British Economic Historian*                                       *1849–1919*

Born in Edinburgh, Cunningham studied at Edinburgh University and at the University of Tübingen, Germany. He taught economic history at Cambridge University and later at King's College, London. His many works include *The Growth of English Industry and Commerce* (1882), *Western Civilization in Its Economic Aspects* (2 vols., 1898–1900), and *Progress of Capitalism in England* (1916). Cunningham favored protective tariffs and defended the mercantilist system, through which, he thought, national regulations replaced the moral dominance of the Middle Ages.

**Pietro Custodi**
*Italian Lawyer and Economist*                    *1771–1842*

Born in Piedmont, Custodi was arrested by Napoleon but freed after the establishment of the Kingdom of Italy and appointed secretary-general of the finance department in Milan. Later he was made a baron and became a state councilor. His greatest contribution to economics was the compilation of 50 volumes of Italian essays and articles on political economy, *Scritori classici italiani di economia politica* (1803–16). Many of these papers, written from the earliest times to the beginning of the 19th century, had not been published before. In 1824 Custodi founded a magazine, *Italian Economic Review*, which was discontinued in 1871.

**Vito Cusumano**
*Italian Economist*                    *1843–1908*

Cusumano studied in Germany under Adolf Wagner, became a professor at the Palermo Technical Institute and later at the University of Palermo, and wrote *Le Scuole economiche della Germania in rapporto alla questione sociale* (1875). The book was widely discussed and stimulated the further development of economic thought in Italy. In his historical writings Cusumano showed an inclination toward state socialism.

# D

**Eugène Daire**
*French Economist* | **1789–1847**

Daire, born in Paris, started as a tax collector and became a capable financier and distinguished economist. He published *Les Physiocrates* (1846), two volumes of selected works on Physiocracy. Daire also collected and published *Les Economistes-financiers du XVIII siecle* (15 vols., 1843), a compilation of the works of the great economists of the 18th century, and wrote biographies of Turgot and Say.

**Adolf Damaschke**
*German Land Reformer* | **1865–1935**

Damaschke, born in Berlin, became a teacher in the poorer districts of Berlin. Here he became aware of the social significance of the housing problem. He became president of Flürscheim's land-reform association, which in 1898 had had its name changed to Bund Deutscher Boden-reformer. He succeeded in drawing wide attention to the movement. Damaschke was against nationalization of land but favored a value-added tax on land and protection for homestead owners. His most important book was *Die Bodenreform* (1923).

**D'Argenson**
see Marquis d'*Argenson*

**Joachim George Darjes (Daries)**
*German Cameralist* | **1714–1791**

Darjes was born in Frankfurt-an-der-Oder. He became professor at Jena and later professor and rector at the University of Frankfurt-an-der-Oder. He taught administrative science and wrote *First Principles of Cameral Science* (1756, in German). Here he demonstrated a comprehensive understanding of economic interrelationships. For the prince of the land to reach an optimum income, his subjects must have high incomes. Justice and security must be assured. All people must apply themselves in useful occupations and should be encouraged and aided in these efforts. The well-being of the subjects and that of the prince are inseparable. A large population is a source of wealth for the country. To guard the State's interests, the prince may intervene in the affairs of the people at any time and at any place. Darjes was not in favor of general trade restrictions. He felt rather that such decisions, including those on the export of gold, should be made as required by the interests

**65**

of the state and should be made shrewdly. Besides his *Erste Gründe der Cameralwissenschaften* mentioned above, Darjes wrote *Discurs über Natur und Völkerrecht* (3 vols.).

**Charles Robert Darwin**
*English Naturalist*                                    *1809–1882*

Born in Shrewsbury, Darwin studied medicine but later became a naturalist. In his *Origin of Species* (1859) he proposed the concepts of evolution, the struggle for survival, and natural selection, which were taken up by social scientists to support both individualism and socialism.

**Bernardo Davanzati**
*Italian Mercantilist*                                    *1529–1606*

Davanzati was born in Florence, became a merchant and classical scholar who translated Tacitus, and wrote a history of the Reformation in England. Two short essays assure him a permanent place in the history of economic thought: *Lezione delle monete* (1588), in which he related the mass of commodities to the mass of money, and *Notizia dei cambi* (1581), in which he described the fluctuations of foreign exchange rates between the gold points. Even the notions of velocity of money, the utility theory of value, and a simple formulation of the quantity theory of money can be found in his writings. He said, "The money in a country is worth all the goods, for no one wants money for its own sake."

**Charles Davenant**
*English Public Servant*                                    *1656–1714*

Davenant was born in London and studied at Balliol College, Oxford, but left without graduating. He was elected to Parliament 3 times and later was appointed commissioner of excise and inspector general of export and import. Davenant defended many mercantilist concepts but rejected others. He favored import restriction, but was convinced that trade, free by nature, could find its own channels. According to him, the wealth of a country is determined by its production and not by gold and silver. There may be too much or too little gold in a country's treasury; much more important is how the precious metal is used. Davenant was in his time an authority on public finance and understood the significance of "the art of reasoning by figures upon things relating to the government." He wrote *Ways and Means of Supplying the War* (1695), *Essay on the East India Trade* (1696), *Discourses on the Public Revenues, and on the Trade of England* (1698), *Essay on the Probable Means of Making People Gainers in the Balance of Trade* (1699), and other essays. His writings demonstrate high ethical ideals.

**Herbert Joseph Davenport**
*American Economist*                                      *1861–1931*

Davenport, born in Wilmington, Vermont, had an exceptional career. He earned a fortune in real estate and went abroad to Leipzig and Paris to study. In the panic of 1893 he lost his money and had to accept the position of high-school principal. He was well into his thirties when he enrolled as a freshman at the University of South Dakota and obtained his bachelor's degree in one year. His struggle for survival went on for several years until he received a fellowship from the University of Chicago, where he earned his Ph.D. in two years (1898). He became professor and dean of the School of Commerce at the University of Missouri and, in 1916, professor of economics at Cornell University.

Davenport, who saw in economics a study of the private pursuit of monetary gain, gave special attention to the competition among gain-seeking entrepreneurs, the process of price determination, and distributive payments. Property in any form was for him capital. The price system, he felt, is central to all economic studies. He tried to separate all ethical notions from economics, and the social organism was for him an idea for a "social insane asylum." In spite of all this, he encouraged many young liberal economists and gave Thorstein Veblen a place to stay when all other academic administrators had turned him away. Among Davenport's works, of special interest are *Outlines of Economic Theory* (1896), *Value and Distribution* (1908), *Economics of Enterprise* (1913), and *Economics of Alfred Marshall* (1925).

**David Davidson**
*Swedish Economist*                                       *1854–1942*

Born in Sweden, Davidson studied at Uppsala where he was appointed professor of economics and public finance in 1890. He was always a close friend of Wicksell, in spite of the many arguments they had together. In 1899 he founded what is now the *Swedish Journal of Economics*, in which many of his 250 articles were published. In his writings he dealt mainly with equilibrium analysis and monetary economics (specifically, inflation). He distinguished various types of inflation; some he called beneficial, others harmful.

**Daniel Defoe**
*English Writer*                                          *1660–1731*

Born in London, Defoe was educated at Morton's Academy at Stoke Newington and became a wholesale merchant. Known for his novels such as *Robinson Crusoe*, this brilliant, prolific writer also authored a systematic presentation of mercantilist views, *A Plan of English Commerce* (1728), and hundreds of other economic and political tracts. He was an early writer on business cycles and described the stages of fluctuation. He dealt with the problem of state credit and recommended the establishment of national banks. Though he favored child labor, he was concerned about poverty, unemployment, old-age problems, and discrimination against women and advocated high real wages to improve the position and performance of labor.

**De Groot**
see Hugo *Grotius*

**De Laveleye**
see Emile de *Laveleye*

**Delitzsch**
see Franz Hermann *Schulze-Delitzsch*

**Alexander Del Mar**
*American Economist*     *1836–1926*

Born in New York City, Del Mar was trained as an engineer but soon became interested in monetary history. He wrote *Gold Money and Paper Money* (1862), *A History of the Precious Metals from the Earliest Times to the Present* (1880), *The Science of Money* (1885), *Money and Civilization* (1886), and *History of Monetary Systems* (1895). In 1865 he was appointed director of the Bureau of Statistics in the Treasury Department and participated in the organization of the Bureau of Commerce, which later became the Department of Commerce and Labor. For many years Del Mar edited the *New York Social Science Review*, for which he wrote numerous articles.

**De Lugo**
see Juan de *Lugo*

**Gustavo Del Vecchio**
*Italian Economist*     *1883–1971*

Del Vecchio was born in Lugo. An outstanding leader in political economy as well as an expert on economic policies, Del Vecchio taught at the universities of Trieste, Bologna, Geneva, and Rome. He was president of the statistical commission for war damage at the Ministry of Reconstruction, member of the National Council of Economics and Work, minister of the treasury, and governor of the International Monetary Fund. Among his many publications, the following should be listed: *Prodotto netto e monopolio* (1905), *Economia pura* (1939), *Capital e interesse* (1956), and *Economia generale* (1960).

**De Martiis**
see Cognetti de *Martiis*

## De Molina
see Louis de *Molina*

## De Molinari
see Gustave de *Molinari*

## Edmond Demolins
*French Educator and Writer*                                   *1852–1907*

Demolins was born in Marseilles and studied at the Jesuit College in Mongre. In 1873 he went to Paris, intending to write a history of France showing that the common people had contributed extensively to the greatness of the country. He cooperated for a short while with the Le Play movement and founded a magazine, *Réformes sociales,* which he renamed *Science sociale* after he left the movement. Among his books, *La Supériorité des Anglo-Saxons* (1897) was instrumental in leading to educational improvements in France. In 1901 he published *Les grandes routes des peuples.* It was Demolins who said, "No social phenomenon can ever be explained if it is taken out of its own setting."

## Bernard William Dempsey, S. J.
*American Economist*                                           *1903–1960*

Father Dempsey was born in Milwaukee, Wisconsin, and studied at St. Louis University, Harvard University (Ph.D.), and at the Gregorian University in Rome. He taught at St. Louis and Marquette universities. Dempsey, widely known as an authority on medieval economic doctrines, wrote many articles on the economics of the Scholastics. His *Functional Economy* (1958) is perhaps the best description of Catholic economic concepts in modern times. Noteworthy also is his book *Interest and Usury* (1943).

## Hector Denis
*Belgian Economist & Philosopher*                             *1842–1913*

Denis was born in Braine-le-Comte. He became a professor of ethics and political economy at the University of Brussels and for 20 years was a member of the Belgian Chamber of Representatives. He believed in the organic concept of society and related the historical tendency of political economy to the positivist philosophy of Comte. In the parliament he argued in favor of labor movements, which he described in many articles. He hoped that the existing political system could be replaced by a system of vocational representation. In *L'impôt sur la revenue* (1881) he offered interesting data on the collection of taxes, and in *L'impôt* (1889), a public finance and taxation theory. In 1895 he published *Le dépression économique et sociale et l'histoire des prix* and in 1897 *Histoire des systèmes économiques et socialistes.*

**Thomas De Quincey**
*English Writer*                                             *1785–1859*

De Quincey was born in Manchester, attended Worcester College, Oxford, and became a famed writer of essays, including a great many magazine articles on economics. He was ever a loyal supporter of Ricardo, and his "Dialogues of Three Templars" (*London Magazine*, 1824) is a brilliant defense of the Ricardian theory of value. In 1844 his book *The Logic of Political Economy* appeared, from which John Stuart Mill quoted generously.

**De Roover**
see Raymond Adrian de *Roover*

**René Descartes**
*French Philosopher*                                          *1596–1650*

Descartes studied at the Jesuit school at La Flèche and the university of Poitiers. He served in Maurice of Nassau's army until he retired in 1628 to Holland for research and writing. A mathematical genius, he introduced analytic geometry. Descartes got the notion that the mechanism of the universe could be described in mathematical terms and attempted to use mathematical methods in philosophy. He refined Scholastic arguments in regard to the existence of God, whom he saw as the link between senses and mind. His teaching has been called Cartesian and his influence on modern thought was and is immense. Of special interest is his *Essais philosophiques* (1637).

**Antoine Louis Claude Destutt, Comte de Tracy**
*French Philosopher and Economist*                            *1754–1836*

Born in Bourbonnais, Destutt, an important intellectual leader during the time of Napoleon, had been a member of the States-General (1789) and the Senate. Besides philosophical works influenced by Condillac, he wrote *Traité d' économie politique* (1823). Production meant for him a change in form or place. Value, he said, must be expressed in units of value, but he himself did not recommend a specific unit of measurement. Thomas Jefferson made the American people acquainted with Destutt de Tracy's works.

**De Uztariz**
see Gerónimo De *Uztariz*

**Ely Devons**
*English Economist and Statistician*                          *1913–1967*

Devons, the son of a rabbi, first studied theology. He changed to economics after graduating from Manchester University, and worked for the Cotton Board. During World War II he served in the Statistical Office of the British cabinet and later in the new Ministry of Aircraft Production. In 1948 he returned to Manchester University as professor of applied economics and became dean of the faculty of economics and social studies. In 1959 he accepted an appointment as professor of international trade at the London School of Economics. His extensive writings include *Planning in Practice* (1950), *An Introduction to British Economic Statistics* (1956), and *Essays in Economics* (1961).

**John Dewey**
*American Philosopher*                           *1859–1952*

Born in Burlington, Vermont, Dewey became professor of philosophy at Columbia University. He advocated a form of philosophic pragmatism. Dewey exercised great influence and was in the forefront of many social movements. Dewey's influence on his students Mitchell and Veblen had an effect on the institutional movement. Among his publications, *Human Nature and Conduct* (1922) and *The Quest for Certainty* (1929) are of special interest.

**Karl Diehl**
*German Economist*                           *1864–1943*

Diehl, born in Frankfurt-am-Main, studied at Berlin, Vienna, and Halle and became professor at the University of Freiburg. He was especially interested in the social and legal foundations of economic systems. He has been called an institutionalist, particularly in regard to historical relativity concepts, but his theories were rooted in the classics and especially in Ricardo's teaching. Of Diehl's many works, *Theoretische Nationalökonomie* (1927) deserves attention; he also wrote on Proudhon.

**Karl F. W. Dieterici**
*German Economist*                           *1790–1859*

Dieterici, born in Berlin, was director of the Prussian Statistical Bureau and professor of political economy at the University of Berlin. He pointed to the need for scientific economics. His published lectures show that he also stressed the historical aspects of economic developments. His *Der Volkswohlstand im preussischen Staate* (1846) and *Arbeit und Kapital* (1848) deserve special attention.

**Karl August Dietzel**
*German Economist*                           *1829–1884*

Born in Hanau, Dietzel became professor at Heidelberg and Marburg. His greatest contributions are found in the field of public finance, the credit system, and taxation. He emphasized socio-economic rights and obligations in his *Die Volkswirtschaft und ihr Verhältnis zu Gesellschaft und Staat* (1864).

**Karl Heinrich Dietzel**

*German Economist*                                                                    *1857–1935*

Dietzel was born in Leipzig, studied at Heidelberg and Berlin, and was a professor at the University of Bonn. He is remembered mainly because of his controversy with Böhm-Bawerk and because of his *Theoretische Sozialökonomie* (1895). Dietzel distinguished between theoretical and practical economics and spoke about the natural character of the economy, which remains always the same, and of social influences, which depend on changing historical and political factors. He thought the value theory superfluous.

**Diocletian**

*Roman Emperor*                                                                           *245–313*

Born of humble parents at Salona, Diocletian became a Roman army commander who was chosen emperor in 284. He abdicated in 305 and retired to a splendid castle at Salona. Inflationary pressure and agricultural supply problems caused his price-edict in 301, prescribing price ceilings for a great number of commodities and wage controls. It was no success.

**François Divisia**

*French Engineer and Economist*                                            *1889–1964*

Born in Algeria, Divisia went to France and became engineer of bridges and roads, professor of industrial economics and statistics at the Conservatoire Nationale des Arts et Métiers, and professor of political and social economics at the Ecole Polytechnique. Among his publications, *Economie rationelle* (1928) and *Traitement économétrique de la monnaie, l'intérêt, l'emploi* (1962) won much attention.

**Thomas Doubleday**

*English Economic Writer*                                                          *1790–1870*

Doubleday, born in Newcastle-on-Tyne, is known for his objections to Malthus' population theory, stating that in an ill-fed and poor community population increases, whereas in a rich and well-fed community population decreases. He published *The True Law of Population, Shown to be Connected with the Food of the People* (1841), and *Financial, Monetary, and Statistical History of England from 1688 to the Present* (1847), the latter being in the form of letters to a young man.

**Patrick Edward Dove**
*British Philosophical and Political Writer*     1815–1873

Born in Lasswode, near Edinburgh, Dove made significant contributions to political science. He published *Elements of Political Science* (1854), in which he stated that land has been given to man by God as the property of all the people. He thought that the whole concept of landed property was outdated and grew out of the feudal system at a time when landowners had military duties to the lords and received land only in exchange for such services. This obligation had long been removed, but the new landowners remained and the common people were taxed to support the state. Dove advocated nationalization of land and a single tax on land which would be easy to collect and would stimulate maximum production. It was only land that Dove wanted to see repossessed by the state. Otherwise, he believed in a natural right to liberty, which should be confirmed by legislation, and in free individual enterprise.

**François Xavier Joseph Droz**
*French Economist and Historian*     1773–1850

Born in Besançon, Droz became a follower of Sismondi. His *Economie politique, ou principes de la science des richesses* (1829) contains the widely-quoted remarks, "Certain economists seem to think that products are not made for men, but that men are made for products" and "Capital left to itself is an idle toll." Of his historical writings, *Histoire du regne de Louis XVI* (1839) is well known.

**Eugen Karl Dühring**
*German Economist*     1833–1921

Born in Berlin, Dühring, a lawyer, became totally blind. With vigor he embarked on an academic career, studying mathematics, physics, economics, and philosophy, and making outstanding contributions to these fields. He was on the faculty of the University of Berlin. An admirer of List and Henry Carey, he tried to combine the ideas of both. Among his publications, outstanding are: *Kapital und Arbeit* (1865), *Kritische Geschichte der Nationalökonomie und des Sozialismus* (1871), and *Kursus der National-und Sozialökonomie* (1873). Dühring developed a system of social reforms and an anti-Marxian theory. Harsh in his criticism of those he opposed, he was also aggressive against people who came to his assistance, and made many enemies.

**Dumont**
see Georges Marie *Butel-Dumont*

Charles Dumoulin
*French Lawyer* 1500–1566

Born in Paris, Dumoulin adopted the Latin name Carolus Molinaeus and enjoyed an international reputation. After his conversion to Calvinism and his attacks upon the Catholic church he was forced to go to Germany. He opposed feudalism, was in favor of royal authority, and contended that divine law does not forbid usury. He openly defended the practice of interest-taking. His tract on commerce, money, and interest (1546) attracted wide attention.

Charles Franklin Dunbar
*American Economist* 1830–1900

Born in Abington, Massachusetts, Dunbar studied at Harvard University (LL.D.). He became professor of political economy, dean of the Harvard faculty, and the first dean of arts and sciences at Harvard. Dunbar was the first editor of the *Quarterly Journal of Economics* (1886). Interested mainly in the study of money, banking, and credit, he wrote *Chapters on the Theory and History of Banking* (1885) and *Laws of the United States Relating to Currency, Finance and Banking from 1789–1891* (1891). Some of his articles were reprinted in *Economic Essays* (1904; ed. by O. M. W. Sprague).

Charles Dunoyer
*French Writer and Economist* 1786–1862

Dunoyer was born in Caramac (Lothringen). His full name was Barthelemy Charles Pierre Joseph Dunoyer. He studied law in Paris and became a strong supporter of laissez-faire and of Malthus' views on population. He opposed any form of social legislation to improve the conditions of labor and the poor. Ignorance, vice, and apathy among the lower classes were in his opinion the causes of their wretched condition, and were also the reasons that the upper classes had exploited and dispossessed laborers and farmers for centuries. The lower classes are therefore largely responsible for their own ills, he felt, and have to help themselves. Free labor would improve its own position and efficiency because labor is in fact the only productive factor, and all value is the result of labor activities. No government interference could improve the lot of the laboring class. The only way to true liberty is competition. Only competition can solve the social problems, he thought, and if shortcomings are obvious, this is the consequence of the imperfect character of competition. He published *L'industrie et la morale considérées dans leurs rapports avec la liberté* (8 vols., 1825), and *De la liberté du travail* (1845).

**John Duns Scotus**
*Scottish Scholastic*
*1265–1308*

Born in Scotland, Duns, a Franciscan, taught in Paris and Cologne and was well known as a philosopher. He recognized the importance of the merchant class and held a more practical outlook on buying and selling than other scholastics had. He related just price to cost and spoke about competitive equilibrium. Duns was concerned for public welfare and came close to the social-contract theory of the state. His progressive ideas were severely criticized by later scholastics.

**Claude Dupin**
*French Economic Writer*
*1684–1769*

Dupin was born in Chateauroux. He wrote *Oeconomiques* (1745), was the first in France to advocate a more liberal policy on the corn trade, and criticized Montesquieu's view on trade and finance. Many of his works were suppressed by the French press. It has been said that Dupin had some influence on F. List.

**Pierre Samuel Dupont de Nemours**
*French Economist*
*1739–1817*

Born in Paris, Dupont became a member of the States-General, president of the National Assembly, advisor to Turgot, and commissioner-general of commerce. He barely escaped execution during the French Revolution, fled to the U.S. (1799), but returned to France (1802), and in 1814 became secretary of the provisional government of Louis XVIII. Upon the return of Napoleon he left France again and founded the Dupont industrial empire at Wilmington, Delaware. Dupont was a loyal follower of Quesnay and propagated the doctrine of physiocracy, which he praised as the natural system of government, offering the greatest advantages to the human race. He wrote *La Physiocratie* (1768), which represents perhaps the best description of this system. Herewith he gave Quesnay's movement the name that is still used to identify it. In 1783 he negotiated recognition of the newly independent U.S.

**Charles Dupont-White**
*French Writer*
*1807–1878*

Born in Rouen, Dupont-White became a barrister and general secretary at the Ministry of Justice. Among his books, these titles should be specially mentioned: *Essai sur les relations du travail avec le capital* (1846), *L'Individu et l'état* (1856), and *La Centralisation* (1860). He argued in favor of a strong central government, but a state that would not threaten individual development. The state has the duty to bring moral sentiment and distribution into equilibrium and can use the tax system to secure the desired redistribution of income and wealth. Dupont-White showed strong inclinations toward State Socialism.

**Arsène Jules Etienne J. Dupuit**

*French Economist and Mathematician*      *1804–1866*

Dupuit was born in Piedmont and became an engineer in the public works department. Interested in economic problems, he wrote many articles, especially on utility and monopoly. He developed the notions of diminishing marginal utility, consumer surplus, and monopolistic discrimination, and pioneered in psychological and mathematical approaches to hedonistic economics. Dupuit has also been credited with the first use of supply and demand curves, with the first use of the term "final utility," and with powerful originality in analytical works. Some of his articles appeared in the *Journal des économistes*. He also made important contributions to the development of waterworks and highways and wrote about the utility of public works.

**Emile Durkheim**

*French Philosopher and Sociologist*      *1858–1917*

Durkheim, born in Alsace, was a professor at the University of Bordeaux and at the Sorbonne, Paris. He wrote *De la division du travail social* (1893) and expressed the hope that trade unions, associanists, or some types of solidarists would be able to create a new moral order, because to remain stable a society must have a common value system.

# E

**Sir Frederic Morton Eden**

*English Businessman*                                             *1766–1809*

Eden was born in Ashtead, Surrey, was educated at Christ Church, Oxford, and became the founder of the Globe Insurance Company. He is remembered for his *The State of the Poor, or A History of the Labouring Classes in England from the Conquest to the Present Periods* (3 vols., 1797). Outstanding in its scope and its excellent statistics, it is based on careful research work.

**Francis Ysidro Edgeworth**

*British Economist*                                                 *1845–1926*

Born in Longford County, Ireland, Edgeworth studied at Trinity College, Dublin, and Oxford University. He taught at King's College, London, and Oxford, where he was elected a Fellow of All Souls College. Here he remained for the rest of his life. Edgeworth was one of the founders of the Royal Economic Society, president of the Statistical Society, and editor of the *Economic Journal* (1891–1926). He published *Mathematical Psychics* (1881), and in 1925 many of his articles and papers appeared under the title *Papers Relating to Political Economy.*

Edgeworth accepted utilitarian principles, was a pioneer in using the indifference curve, and wrote on probability and statistical theory. Of special interest are his studies in the determination of monopoly pricing under various conditions, and his studies on marginal analysis for determining profits. He defined mathematical psychics as the problem of measurement applied to economics and other social sciences. He distinguished the measurement of utility or ethical value, the diagrammatic determination of equilibrium, the measurement of probability, and the measurement of evidence or statistics. In addition, he wrote about economic value measurement and index numbers. Edgeworth tried to add mathematical precision to the ideas of Bentham. Of importance are his contributions to the duopoly studies. Modest and absent-minded, Edgeworth was a poor speaker, yet his writings secure him a place in the development of economic thought.

**Richard Ehrenberg**

*German Businessman and Economist*                        *1857–1921*

Ehrenberg was born in Wolfenbüttel. He became a bank clerk and later studied at Tübingen, Munich, and Göttingen, earning his Ph.D. Joining the academic profession at age 40, Ehrenberg taught at the University of Rostock and introduced what has been called the "exact historical method." He founded the Society for Exact Economic Research, the Archives for Exact Economic Research and a journal, *Archiv für exakte Wirtschaftsforschung*. Ehrenberg devoted himself to the historical study of large business enterprises, stressing the importance of the entrepreneur and the harmony of interests between capital and labor. To make economics an exact science, he applied methods used in keeping business records and felt that the study of business enterprise is essential to understanding the modern body of economics and the community. His *Zeitalter der Fugger* (2 vols., 1896) came out in English as *Capitalism and Finance in the Age of the Renaissance* (1928). He also wrote *Der Handel* (1897), and *Handelspolitik* (1900).

**Luigi Einaudi**
*Italian Economist and Statesman*                          *1874–1961*

Einaudi was professor of public finance at the University of Turin (1902–42), senator (1915–45), governor of the Bank of Italy (1945–48), and president of Italy (1948–55). Conservative in his economic views, he nevertheless favored social reforms and advocated European unity. He credited the Physiocrats with the pure theory of taxation. He wrote more than 30 books on economics, including a study on land reform, *Studi sugli effetti delle imposti* (1902).

**William Elder**
*American Writer*                                          *1806–1885*

Elder, born in Pennsylvania, advocated a political economy national in concept. He may be called a follower of Matthew Carey. Nationalistic attitudes are found in many of his numerous newspaper articles. He published *The Debts and Resources of the United States* (1863) and *Conversations on Political Economy* (1882).

**Howard Sylvester Ellis**
*American Economist*                                       *1898–*

Ellis, born in Denver, studied at the University of Iowa, the University of Michigan, and Harvard University (Ph.D.), and abroad at Heidelberg and Vienna. He was connected with various government offices, taught at the University of Michigan and, from 1938, at the University of California at Berkeley. He published *Exchange Control in Central Europe* (1941), *A Survey of Contemporary Economics* (1948), *The Economics of Freedom* (1950), *Approaches to Economic Development* (1955, with Buchanan), *Economic Development for Latin America* (1961), and *Industrial Capital in Greek Development* (1964).

**Richard Theodore Ely**
*American Economist*     *1854–1943*

Ely was born in Ripley, New York, and studied at Columbia University and abroad at Geneva, Halle, Heidelberg (Ph.D.), and the Royal Statistical Bureau in Berlin. He taught at Johns Hopkins and Wisconsin universities and became research professor at Northwestern University. He was a founder of the American Economic Association, its secretary for the first 7 years and its president in 1900–01. He was also the founder of the American Institute for Industrial Research (1904), president of the American Association for Labor Legislation (1907–08), founder and president of the Institute for Economic Research, and a member of the Maryland Tax Commission (1886–88). Ely saw in economics a science of human relations and was especially interested in labor economics, monopoly, public utility, and land economics. His many articles and books include *Introduction to Political Economy* (1889), *Monopolies and Trusts* (1900), *Studies in the Evolution of Industrial Society* (1903), *The Great Change* (1935), and *Land Economics* (1940). He stressed institutional economics, defended the labor movement, and criticized "big business" and the classics.

**Ralph Waldo Emerson**
*American Writer and Philosopher*     *1803–1882*

Born in Boston, Emerson was educated at Harvard College, received his doctorate from Harvard Divinity School, and became a Unitarian clergyman. He called for intellectual freedom, took part in the so-called literary revolt against materialism and modern industrialism, and supported the establishment of the Brook Farm community near Boston in 1841. Among his publications, *Essays* (1842 and 1844), *Representative Men* (1850), and *The Conduct of Life* (1860) should be particularly noted.

**Barthélemy Prosper Enfantin**
*French Social Reformer*     *1796–1864*

Born in Paris, Enfantin was trained for the banking business and studied at the Ecole Polytechnique in Paris. A meeting with Saint-Simon changed his life. He not only became a disciple of Saint-Simon but one of the most outstanding members of the movement. He founded the magazine *Producteur*, which had only a short life but made many converts. Therein Enfantin published most of his economic papers. He advocated the reform of private property, to which he was opposed. He disliked the term profit and described the earnings of the entrepreneur as the price for his labor, and he rejected any justification of interest and rent. Together with Bazard, Enfantin became co-director of the newly founded Ecole Saint-Simon. But differences in regard to free love, which Enfantin advocated, brought this relationship to an end. Bazard withdrew and Enfantin retired with 40 followers to his estate to live there as a religious organization of "brothers" under the guidance of "Father" Enfantin. They were charged with illegal association and affronts to public morality, and were imprisoned. When released, Enfantin took active part in financial and industrial schemes. He helped to found the Paris-Lyons Railway, of which he was a director, and he was also the first to float a company for building the Suez Canal. With other followers of Saint-Simon, he established credit associations, anticipating the important role of credit in modern economies. Enfantin himself gave a definition of credit which has been called the best ever given. He expressed his economic ideas in *Economie politique et Politique* (1832) and offered a logical presentation of Saint-Simon's teaching coupled with philosophical notions of his own, which were not beneficial to the movement.

**Ernst Engel**

*German Statistician and Economist*     *1821–1896*

Engel was born in Dresden and studied engineering at Freiburg and Paris. He became head of the statistical department of the government of Saxony and later head of the Prussian Bureau of Statistics. He studied the cost of rearing children, designed a new measure of consumption, and stated that the percentage of expenditure on food is a decreasing function of income (Engel's Law, 1857). He published *Die Industrie der Grossen Städte* (1866) and the first volume of *Der Wert des Menchen* (1883), a work which was never completed.

**Friedrich Engels**

*German Businessman and Socialist*     *1820–1895*

Born in Barmen, Engels became partner and director of a textile firm established by his father in Manchester, England. A successful businessman, he retired at age 40 to devote himself to writing and political activities. He had met Marx in Paris and became a close collaborator, supporter, and friend. Engels was convinced that all social and political institutions are conditioned by economic facts. His highly intelligent, pleasant personality had an extraordinary influence on the development of the socialist movement. He argued that social changes will occur, that the capitalist system will be replaced, and that the human race will progress toward a new society of equals. Together with Marx he wrote the *Communist Manifesto* (1848) and after Marx's death edited the second (1885) and third (1894) volumes of Marx's *Kapital*. He published *Condition of the Working Class in England* (1845), *Landmarks of Scientific Socialism* (1878), and *The Origin of the Family, of Private Property and of the State* (1884), and defended Marx against Dühring's attacks in *Dühring's Revolution in Science* (1878).

**George Ensor**
*Irish Political Writer*                                   *1769–1843*

Ensor was born in Dublin and educated there at Trinity College. He advocated political reforms and attacked the English government. He refuted Malthus and blamed the miseries of the poor on society and not on an excess of population. He wrote *An Inquiry Concerning the Population of Nations* (1818), *Radical Reform, Restoration of Usurped Rights* (1819), *The Poor and Their Relief* (1823), and *Of Property and of its Equal Distribution as Promoting Virtue, Population, and Abundance* (1843).

**Epicurus**
*Greek Philosopher*                                   *341–270 B.C.*

Born in Samos, Epicurus taught in many Greek cities and founded a school at Athens. He identified happiness with intellectual pleasure and serenity and defined philosophy as the art of making life happy. He said: "The flesh cries out to be saved from hunger, thirst and cold," but also "Nothing satisfies a man who is not satisfied with little." The "eat, drink, and be merry" philosophy that was later attributed to him is opposite to his actual views. Only fragments of his many works were saved.

**Ludwig Erhard**
*German Economist and Statesman*                                   *1897–*

Born in Fürth, Bavaria, Erhard studied in Nuremberg and Frankfurt, became director of the Institute for Industrial Research, and taught in Nuremberg, Munich, and Bonn, where he was professor of economics. He was appointed state minister of economic affairs in Bavaria (1945–47), was with the Office for Currency and Credit, director of the Administration for Economics, member of the Bundestag, minister of economics of the Federal Government, vice-chancellor (1957–63), and chancellor (head of the West German government, 1963–66). He was also German governor of the World Bank. Erhard held many doctorates *honoris causa*, several from foreign universities. Among his numerous publications, of special interest is *Wohlstand für Alle*, which appeared in English as *Prosperity through Competition* (1958). Erhard has been called the father of the German Wirtschaftswunder and father of the Social Market Economy, a type of neo-liberal economic system that sets the welfare of all as the goal of all economic activities.

**Walter Kurt Heinrich Eucken**
*German Economist*                                   *1891–1950*

Born in Jena, Eucken became professor of economics at the universities of Tübingen and Freiburg. He tried to construct a universally valid economic theory and paid little attention to evolutionary aspects. Eucken distinguished only two types of economic systems: the centrally planned economy and the market economy. He gave special attention to the problem of price determination. His best-known book, *The Foundations of Economies* (German ed., 1940), was translated not only into English but also into Spanish and Italian.

**Sir George Augustus W. Schuckburgh-Evelyn**
*English Scientist*                                                    *1751–1804*

Schuckburgh-Evelyn was born in Limerick and educated at Balliol College, Oxford, was a member of Parliament for 25 years, and was noted for his scientific work on devices for measuring heights of mountains and measures of weight. In 1798 he presented a paper to the Royal Society in which he dealt with the depreciation of money, using index numbers to prove his case.

**Alexander Hill Everett**
*American Statesman and Economist*                                    *1790–1847*

Everett was born in Boston, graduated from Harvard with highest honors, and studied law in the office of John Quincy Adams. He taught at Exeter, went to Russia with Adams as his private secretary when Adams was minister to the court of the tsar, and after Adams became President served at the American legation at The Hague and as minister to Spain from 1825–29. Returned, Everett became editor of the *North American Review*, in which he published many of his essays, and then member of the Massachusetts legislature from 1830–35. He undertook a diplomatic mission to Cuba in 1840, and to China in 1847, where he died in Macao.

Of special interest is his book *New Ideas on Population with Remarks upon the Theories of Malthus and Godwin* (1832). In it, he argued that an increase in population and skill would cause abundance, not scarcity, and would create a greater division of labor. These ideas were novel at the time. Everett discussed them with Malthus, who, however, never made use of them.

# F

**Julius Faucher**
*German Journalist and Politician*                                    *1820–1878*

Born a member of a French Huguenot family living in exile, Faucher studied in Berlin, where he spent most of his life as a journalist except for a few years in London where he served as secretary to Cobden. He became a follower of Bastiat and with Prince-Smith founded a free-trade association in Berlin. Important among his many writings are: *Systems of Land Tenure in Different Countries* (8 vols., 1870), *Die Vereinigung von Sparkasse und Hypothekenbank* (1845), and *Die Handelspolitische Grenzzollfrage* (1876). Faucher founded the *Vierteljahreschrift für Volkswirtschaft und Kulturgeschichte* in 1863 and was the editor until he died.

**Francis Fauquier**
*English Statesman and Financial Writer*                             *1704–1768*

Fauquier was born in London, son of a director of the Bank of England. He became director of the South Sea Company, a Fellow of the Royal Society, and the lieutenant governor of Virginia (1758). He wrote *Essay of Ways and Means of Raising Money for the Support of the Present War without Increasing the Public Debts* (1756), in which he proposed a tax on houses. Obviously this idea was not very well received, because in the second edition he changed his suggestion to an income tax and pointed out that he merely tried to find the revenue to pay all charges as they occur. Under no circumstances should the poor be taxed, he stated, because such taxes would be shifted to the rich by way of higher money wages.

**Henry Fawcett**
*English Statesman and Economist*                                    *1833–1884*

Born in Salisbury and educated at Cambridge, Fawcett became totally blind after an accident but nevertheless decided to study economics. He was for 20 years professor of political economy at Cambridge, and later a member of Parliament and postmaster-general. His helpful, frank, and friendly personality won him friends even among his political opponents. A monument to him was erected in Westminster Abbey after his death. He wrote *A Manual of Political Economy* (1836) to make the work of John Stuart Mill briefer and easier to understand. It was a text in British and American colleges for many years, and an abridgment, titled *Political Economy for Beginners* (1870), was published by his wife, Millicent Garrett Fawcett (1847–1929), a leader of the women's suffrage movement. She helped him in his university and public work. Fawcett's other works include *The Economic Position of the British Labourer* (1865), *Pauperism: Its Cause and Remedies* (1871), *Free Trade and Protection* (1878), and *Labour and Wages* (1884). He strongly opposed socialism, objected to government interference in industry and business, and favored free trade. He was also an advocate of social and political equality for women.

**Gustav Theodor Fechner**
*German Physicist*                                               *1801–1887*

Fechner was born in Gross-Särchen and became professor of physics at Leipzig. He found that there is a quantitative relationship between material and mental forces. His bold and imaginative speculations led to the notion of an experimental and quantitative method in psychology, and this had considerable impact on economic thought. He was the founder of psychophysics.

**William John Fellner**
*American Economist*                                                 *1905–*

Born in Budapest, Fellner studied at the University of Budapest, at the Luros Federal Institute of Technology (Ph.D.), and at the University of Berlin. In 1929 he became a partner in a manufacturing enterprise in Budapest but in 1938 he left Hungary. In the U.S. he taught at the University of California at Berkeley and later at Yale University. He was a consulting expert for the U.S. Treasury Department and for the National Security Resources Board. In 1968 he was president of the American Economic Association. Fellner is the author of numerous articles and books including *Competition among the Few* (1949), *Trends and Cycles in Economic Activity* (1955), *Emergence and Content of Modern Economic Analysis* (1960), and *Probability and Profit* (1965).

**Adam Ferguson**
*Scottish Social Philosopher*                                    *1723–1816*

Born in Perthshire, Ferguson studied at the universities of St. Andrews and Edinburgh. He was appointed chaplain to the Black Watch regiment in 1745 but left the clerical profession in 1757 to succeed his friend David Hume in the chair of moral philosophy at Edinburgh, where he stayed until 1785, when poor health forced him to resign. In 1778–79 he was in Philadelphia at the request of Lord North to negotiate the disputes between the American colonies and England. In *An Essay on the History of Civil Society* (1767) Ferguson found that human actions are motivated by subrational drives, and that man finds self-realization in social activity and constantly strives for perfection. In *Institutes of Moral Philosophy* (1769) he dealt also with "public economy" and the problems of taxation, and warned against unnecessarily burdening people and trade.

**Francisco Ferrara**

*Italian Statistician and Economist*
1810–1900

Born in Palermo, Ferrara has been considered the outstanding Italian economist of the last century. He was professor of political economy at the universities of Turin and Pisa, director of the Bureau of Statistics for Sicily, member of the Chamber of Deputies, senator, minister of finance, and director of the Royal School of Commerce at Venice (1868). Ferrara was a very effective teacher and had a remarkable influence on the development of modern economics in Italy, but never wrote a comprehensive independent economic work. His statistical writings appeared in 1890 under the title *Annali di statistica*. He also wrote excellent introductions to *Biblioteca dell'economista* (1850–70), a collection of contributions by leading Italian and foreign economists. He published *Importanza dell'economia politica* in 1849. Anti-Ricardian, Ferrara was a great admirer of Henry Carey, but at the same time a supporter of the free-trade doctrine. In all economic phenomena he saw value problems, and in utility and reproduction cost, the determinants of value.

**Carlo Francesco Ferraris**

*Italian Economist and Statistician*
1850–1924

Ferraris studied at the University of Turin and also in Germany and England. As a professor at the universities of Pavia and Padua he introduced the science of social administration into Italy and also applied statistics to economic problems, in particular to monetary problems. He became a member of the Chamber of Deputies and later of the Senate. He was also briefly a member of the Italian cabinet. His chief works are *Saggi di economia, statistica e scienze dell'administrazione* (1880), *Principi di scienze bancaria* (1862) and *Il materialismo storio e lo stato* (1897).

**Frank Albert Fetter**

*American Economist*
1863–1949

Fetter was born in Indiana and educated at Indiana and Cornell universities. He also studied in France at the Sorbonne and in Germany at the University of Halle (Ph.D.). He taught at Cornell and Princeton universities.

In his *Principles of Economics, with Application to Practical Problems* (1904) Fetter hoped to introduce an entirely new concept of economics, replacing the pleasure-pain calculus theory by a volitional psychology which stated that instinctive choices may come before valuation. He divided value into "value of material things" and "value of human services." But he never incorporated the new theory into the whole of economics. Later he became more interested in trust and corporation problems, and in 1931 published *The Masquerade of Monopoly*, exposing monopolist elements in American business, especially the steel industry.

## Ludwig Andreas Feuerbach
*German Philosopher*      *1804–1872*

Feuerbach was the man who tried to make out of Hegel's metaphysics a purely materialistic philosophy. His ideas are summed up in his saying, "Der Mensch ist was er esst" ("What he eats makes the man"). His philosophy was violently attacked by Karl Marx.

## Johann Gottlieb Fichte
*German Philosopher*      *1762–1814*

Fichte was born in Saxony, studied at Schulpforta, Jena, and Leipzig, and taught at the universities of Jena, Erlangen, and Berlin. At Berlin he was rector of the university. He was a teacher who exercised great influence and a writer who through his books carried this influence into later generations.

Best-known is his *Reden an die deutsche Nation* (1808). In it, he emphasized the freedom of the will and the moral aspect of human nature. He viewed individuals as organically interrelated parts of the society and not merely as atoms making up the society by simple addition. For economists, his *Der geschlossene Handelsstaat* (1800) is of importance. Here he proclaimed that every nation should control its own economic life. What he in fact proposed was a socialist planned economy with a foreign-trade monopoly and a guild-like regulated professional organization. He did not, however, intend to eliminate private property or to regulate consumption.

## Irving Fisher
*American Economist*      *1867–1947*

Fisher was born in Saugerties, New York, studied at Yale University (Ph.D.), and at Yale was appointed assistant professor in mathematics. Later he taught political economy and became a professor in 1895. He was president of the American Economic Association in 1918. His contributions to economics are outstanding, chiefly in the fields of capital and price theories. In general, he followed the Austrian school but introduced mathematical formulae and data which have been widely used. Besides many important articles, he published *Mathematical Investigations in the Theory of Value and Price* (1892), *The Nature of*

*Capital and Income* (1906; dealing with fundamental aspects of wealth), *The Rate of Interest: Its Nature, Determination and Relation to Credit, Interest and Crises* (1911; together with H. G. Brown), *The Making of Index Numbers: A Study of Their Varieties, Test, and Reliability* (1922), *The Theory of Interest as Determined by Impatience to Spend Income and Opportunity to Invest It* (1930), and *100% Money* (1935). In the last-mentioned work he proposed to abandon the reliance of the monetary system on the gold standard, using bank reserves instead. Of the many notable ideas he added to economic theory, his purchasing-power-of-money equation is perhaps best remembered.

**Theodore Fix**
*French Economic Writer*                                            *1800–1846*

Fix was born in Switzerland but immigrated to France and became a follower of Sismondi. He worked as a land surveyor and developed an interest in economic problems after the translation of German economic books into French. His *Une Mémoire sur l'association des douanes allemandes* (1840), which became an Academy prize paper, and his *Observations sur l'état des classes ouvriers* (1846) are well remembered.

**Michael Flürscheim**
*German Land Reformer*                                            *1844–1912*

Flürscheim was born at Frankfurt-Main. He was in the United States from 1867 to 1872. Returned to Germany he founded an iron-work in Baden, which was a success. He retired to Lugano, Switzerland. Stimulated by Henry George's books, in 1884 Flürscheim wrote *Auf friedlichem Wege* and in 1888 founded an association for land-property reform. He advocated a first-hand right of the state to buy land for sale at a price which would remain stable all the time. He felt that the state should rent out the land and receive the rent revenue.

**A. W. Flux**
*English Economist*                                            *1867–1942*

Born in Portsmouth and educated at St. John's College, Cambridge, Flux was a disciple of Marshall and one of the more important members of the Cambridge School. A Cobden Lecturer in Political Economy at Owen's College, Manchester, he was also professor of political economy at McGill University, adviser to the Board of Trade, and member of the Board of the Statistical Department. His chief contribution to economics lies in his strong efforts to introduce quantitative approaches. In his *Economic Principles* (1904) and in articles in the *Economic Journal* he emphasized marginal utility. He also wrote *The Foreign Exchange* (1924).

**Carl Föhl**
*German Economist*                                              *1901–*

Föhl was born in Krefeld and studied at the Technische Hochschule, Karlsruhe, and the Wirtschaftshochschule, Berlin. He was connected with business enterprises, became honorary professor at the University of Tübingen, and in 1961 was elected president of the Bundesverband deutscher Volks-und Betriebswirte. He was appointed professor of economics and director of the Institue for Economic Theory and policy at the Free University of Berlin in 1963.

Föhl's book *Geldschöpfung und Wirtschaftskreislauf* (1937), the manuscript of which was completed before Keynes' *General Theory* appeared, contains many ideas and propositions found also in Keynes, but with a different approach. It had great influence in German-speaking countries. Föhl also published *Kreislauf analytische Untersuchungen der Vermögensbildung in der Bundesrepublik und der Beeinflussbarkeit ihrer Verteilung* (1964), and many articles.

**Follette**
see Robert M. *La Follette*

**François de Forbonnais**
*French Businessman and Civil Servant*                          *1722–1800*

Born at Le Mans, Forbonnais was appointed general inspector of currency in 1756. He was a leading neomercantilist, reacting against physiocratic ideas. He denied that trade and industry are sterile; he wanted only a reasonable tax on land, rejected the idea of free trade, and expressed the need for free competition among the crafts. He discussed money, prices, inflation, and foreign exchange rates, and produced useful historical facts and observations. He was one of the first users of mathematical symbols in proving his points. He wrote *Eléments du commerce* (1754) (in which he criticized the *Tableau économique* of Quesnay). Disagreements with Madame de Pompadour caused his restriction to his estates until the Revolution.

**Samuel Fortrey**
*English Mercantilist Writer*                                   *1622–1681*

Fortrey, born in London, the son of a merchant, served at the court of Charles II, and in 1663 published *England's Interest and Improvement*, favoring high import duties and coinage reform. He tried to prove his case with the help of spurious trade statistics.

**Charles Fourier**
*French Socialist*                                              *1772–1837*

Fourier was born in Besançon to a wealthy merchant family who later set him up in business in Marseilles. After the business failed he became a civil servant in Lyons. In 1816 he inherited some money and so was able to write full-time, and in 1823 he settled in Paris. His major works include *Théorie des quatre mouvements et des destinées générales* (1808), *Le Nouveau monde industriel et sociétaire* (1829–30), and *La Fausse industrie morcelée, répugnante, mensongère, et l'antidote: L'Industrie naturelle, combinée, attrayante, véridique donnant quadruple produit* (2 vols., 1835–36).

Commerce was to Fourier corrupt and his antipathy to large-scale production became an obsession. He formed a sweeping picture of the social order reflecting the natural order, with its laws such as gravity, as described by Newton. Fourier saw both orders as evolving in 8 ascending and 8 descending steps, with the civilization of his day (not far above barbarism) as the fifth ascending step. In order to reach the apex of development, a state of ideal harmony, he proposed organizing "phalansteries," basic social units of a certain optimal size, mixture of age groups, and mixture of activities. These communities would contain a general dining hall, an entertainment center, and private apartments, and were planned for 5 classes at different costs, with a free table in addition. He was convinced that by living under the same roof people would learn to appreciate one another, and a new type of man and society would develop, with individuals free, mature, and highly organized. He believed in the natural goodness of human nature, and felt that instead of being repressed the emotions should be put to use. He believed that the family unit should be replaced by free love. Through the phalanx, he maintained, united action would increase productivity per person to such an extent that under a properly arranged division of labor a man would produce enough in a few years to permit comfort and leisure during his remaining life.

Despite his utopian ideas and his radical reputation gained in part from his ideas on free love, Fourier was not a revolutionist. He opposed the ideas of Owen and Saint-Simon, and Marx called him scathingly a "utopian socialist." Others have described him as a "bourgeois socialist." Though he criticized capitalism, he supported the right of inheritance and stated that property must remain because of God's order. He believed that his social system would work under the monarchy of his day, and awaited a wealthy and powerful benefactor who would help him put his ideas widely into practice.

In fact, his ideas did result in a number of mid-19th-century communal experiments, particularly in France and the U.S. Under Considérant, Fourierist ideas briefly entered the political arena in France, and they also influenced the cooperative movement, which arose in the 19th century and continues to the present day, particularly in developing countries.

**Alfred de Foville**
*French Economist and Statistician*     *1842–1913*

Foville studied at the Ecole Polytechnique and entered the civil service in the Department of Finance. He taught at the Conservatoire des Arts and at the Ecole des Sciences Politique. Later he became the permanent secretary of the Academie des Sciences Morales et Politiques and director of the Mint. He published many articles, mainly on statistics and finance, in the *Economiste Française* and in the *Journal of the Royal Statistical Society*. His most noted works were *La France economique* (1887–90), and *La Monnaie* (1907).

**Herbert S. Foxwell**
*English Economist*                                                 *1849–1936*

Born in Shepton Mallet, Somerset, Foxwell received his B.A. from the University of London, and a scholarship for the study of international law. He was director of economic studies at St. John's College, Cambridge, and became professor of political economy at the University of London and the London School of Economics. He was one of the founders of the British Economic Association (now the Royal Economic Society) and served as its president from 1929–31. A charming, hard-working man, Foxwell devoted himself to the formation of economics libraries in many institutions of higher learning, including Harvard Business School.

Foxwell was of the historical school, and saw economics not as a self-contained science, but rather as part of a wider study of the institutional patterns of society. His main interest was banking, but he was also concerned with the cyclical unemployment problem. He wrote many articles and, with Mrs. Jevons, edited Jevons' works in the field of money and business cycles, a work which came out under the title *Investigations in Currency and Finance*.

**Benjamin Franklin**
*American Statesman*                                               *1706–1790*

Born in Boston, Franklin was self-educated. First a printer, he became internationally known because of his diplomatic activities, his contributions to philosophy and science, and his devotion to public affairs. He was a member of the Continental Congress of the United States and was a signer of the Declaration of Independence and the Constitution. Franklin deplored the evils of mercantilism, and declared that the only honest way for a nation to acquire wealth was to strengthen and develop agriculture. Commerce, he felt, is cheating, and war is robbery. His economic thoughts were expressed in *A Modest Inquiry into the Nature and Necessity of Paper Currency* (1729), *Observations Concerning the Increase of Mankind and the Peopling of Countries* (1751), and many papers.

**John Fullarton**
*English Economist*                                                *1780–1849*

A surgeon serving in India, Fullarton became a partner of a bank in Calcutta, earned a fortune, returned to England, and in 1844 wrote

*On the Regulation of Currencies.* He opposed the Bank Charter Act and participated in the controversy over the nature and purpose of bank notes. Fullarton defined money as an easily salable commodity. Bank notes serve as money, but also as a medium of credit, whereas paper money issued by governments can be used only as a medium for payment transactions. No overissue of bank notes would be possible, since the quantity issued depends upon demand for credit and the coverage available for the bank. He accepted the metallist doctrine.

# G

Gaius Gracchu
see François Noel *Babeu*

**Abbe Ferdinando Galian**
*Italian Economist*
*1728–178*

Born in Chieti, Galiani received holy orders but, influenced by Vicc became interested in economics and politics. For 10 years he was wit the Neapolitan embassy at Versailles, where he became a leading figur in the French Enlightenment. Galiani published *Della moneta* in 175 at age 22. In it, he proved himself a sparkling, intelligent writer with deep understanding of economic concepts. Called the best book o money before Ricardo, it deals with the nature of money, its value, th interest rate, public debts, and exchange. Galiani showed the sam analytical capacity in his other writings, of which *Dialogues sur l commerce des blés* (1770) should be noted. Here he attacked physioc crat doctrines with great wit and style, making them appear ridiculou: The physiocrats mustered their best men for a refutation, but with ver little success.

Galiani was not opposed to laissez-faire, but he refused the concep of complete freedom. He felt that time, place, and circumstances re quire some form of regulation for any economic order. He stressed th variability of man and institutions and showed that economic measure applied in different countries lead to different results. He attacked th excessive generalization in the new doctrine of the physiocrats an pointed to the relativity of economic notions. Galiani's name is als associated with utility analysis. More than anyone else he had deve oped the concept of utility value as opposed to that of cost value anc more specifically, labor value. He argued that value is a ratio of utilit (degree of satisfaction) and scarcity. What separates him from Jevo and Menger is that he lacked the concept of marginal utility.

**Charles Ganil**
*French Economist*
*1758–183*

Born in the Cantal district, Ganilh held public office during the Revolution and Napoleon's time. He published *Systèmes d'économie politiqu* (1809) and *Théorie de l'économie politique* (1815), which contained number of original ideas and terms. In *Systèmes* he offered a historic development of economic thought. Basically, Ganilh was a mercantilis but he offered important modifications. His works have been quoted by many writers, including Daniel Raymond.

**Clement Joseph Garnier**
*French Economist and Writer*                                    *1813–1881*

Garnier studied at the Ecole Supérieure du Commerce in Paris, where he also taught until he became the first professor of political economy at Ecole Nationale des Ponts et Chaussées. From 1845–81 he was chief editor of the *Journal des économistes.* He wrote *Eléments de l'économie politique* (1845) (later renamed *Traité*), *Du Principe de population* (1857), *Eléments des finances* (1858), and *Eléments de statistique,* all highly respected books. Garnier was a much-admired teacher, capable administrator, and successful writer. He was a pupil and friend of Blanqui, became a member of the Academie des Sciences Morales et Politiques, and was a founder of the Société d'Economie Politique.

**Gävernitz**
see Gerhart von *Schulze-Gävernitz*

**Joshua Gee**
*English Mercantilist Writer*                                    *approx. 1700–1750*

Gee published a number of pamphlets between 1725 and 1750. Well known is his *Trade and Navigation of Great Britain* (1729), which was later translated into French. Gee advocated protection of trade and industry to absorb the supply of labor. In all of his tracts he took a protectionist stand in viewing the employment problem. All goods and services that the kingdom could produce, at home and in the colonies, should be protected from foreign imports, but no English goods should be exported if they are needed at home.

**Antonio Genovesi**
*Italian Economist*                                    *1712–1769*

Born near Salerno, Genovesi studied for the priesthood and received holy orders in 1739. He started out as moral philosopher, but later became professor of economics and commerce at the Universiy of Naples, being possibly the first on the European continent to hold such a chair. His writings cover a wide field. His *Lezioni di economia civile* (1765) offers a comprehensive description of utilitarian welfare economics and optimum population principles. Genovesi believed that commerce, by nature, should be free and should not demand protection.

**Friedrich von Gentz**
*German Political and Economic Writer*                                    *1764–1832*

Born in Breslau, Gentz moved to Berlin when his father was appointed director-general of the Prussian Mint. He studied law at the University of Königsberg, where he came under the influence of Kant. In 1785 he entered the Prussian civil service and worked in the war office. In Berlin he founded the *Neue Deutsche Monatschrift* (1795), which in 1798 became the *Historisches Journal*. His persistent attacks on the French Revolution and his anti-Napoleonic attitude forced him to leave the Prussian government service. He became the most trusted adviser to Fürst von Metternich, the leading Austrian statesman. Gentz had great influence on internal and foreign affairs and enjoyed the high regard of many European princes. He became a close friend of Adam Müller, together with whom he was a typical representative of German Romanticism. He shared Adam Smith's optimism and was convinced that providence guides each individual to contribute toward the common good even if self-interest alone motivates his actions; duties to others are closely interwoven with individual rights.

**Henry George**

*American Writer and Social Reformer*  *1839–1897*

George was born in Philadelphia into a lower-middle-class environment, as the son of a printer. He had little formal education, went to sea at age 14, and became a printer 3 years later. All his life he was a devoted reader. In 1858 he went to San Francisco to be a miner, and there became an inspector in government service and finally a journalist. In 1886 he attempted to enter politics in New York, but failed. He made many friends and had a great number of followers who were impressed by his logic, simplicity, and sincerity of conviction. He published *Our Land and Land Policy* (1870), *Social Problems* (1883), *Protection or Free Trade* (1886), and other books and papers. *The Science of Political Economy* was completed and published (1898) by his son. His best-known work, *Progress and Poverty* (1879), brought international fame and sold millions of copies. In it, George searched for an answer to the question why, in spite of all progress, the poor become poorer while the rich constantly become richer—an answer to the question why, in spite of increasing productivity, wages tend to the minimum of bare living. He came to the conclusion that private property in land leads to the enslavement of the labor class. He proposed a single tax upon land values, which would permit the abolishing of all other taxes. Landowners would retain titles to the land, but speculative gains in land value would cease, since through taxation unearned additions to land value would become income for the society as a whole.

**Isaac Gervaise**

*English Writer*  *died approx. 1740*

In 1720 Gervaise published *The System or Theory of the Trade of the World, Treating of the Different Kinds of Value, of the Balances of Trade, of Exchange, of Manufactures, of Companies, and Shewing the*

*Pernicious Consequences of Credit, and That it Destroys the Purpose of National Trade.* Professor Foxwell called this little tract of 30-odd pages "one of the earliest formal systems of political economy," and Professor Viner republished it in 1954. It is an excellent example of early arguments for free trade. Gervaise contributed to the growing concept of automatic mechanism in international trade by stating that an increase in credit will increase income and consumption, hence decrease exports and eventually necessitate credit restriction.

| | **Silvio Gesell** |
|---|---|
| *German Businesman* | *1862–1930* |

Gesell was born in St. Vity, Belgium. In 1887 he emigrated to Buenos Aires, Argentina, where he successfully engaged in business. However, he was always highly concerned with socioeconomic problems. In 1891 he published *Die Verstaatlichung des Geldes*, proposing a reformation of coinage. In 1914 he returned to Germany and in 1919 became finance minister in the short-lived government of Bavaria. Gesell authored *Die Natürliche Wirtschaftsordnung*, later translated into English as *The Natural Economic Order* (1936). Emphasizing the velocity of money circulation, he proposed a stamped paper currency that would lose value (0.1 percent) each week, so that it would not be withheld from the market. He also advocated the abolition of interest to prevent the hoarding of money. Clearly his ideas were a reaction against laissez-faire, but also against Marxian socialism. The book and its author would most probably be forgotten if Keynes had not given them "improportionate" space in his *General Theory*, in which he expressed his belief that the future would learn more from the spirit of Gesell than from that of Marx.

| | **Charles Gide** |
|---|---|
| *French Economist* | *1847–1932* |

Born in Uzès, Gide was educated at the Collège d'Uzès and became professor of political economy at the universities of Bordeaux, Montpellier, and Paris. In 1921 he accepted the chair of the theory and history of cooperation, endowed at the Collège de France by the consumers' cooperative of France. Gide wrote *Principes d'économie politique* (1883), *Les Sociétés cooperatives de consommation* (1904), and *Les Colonies communistes et cooperatives* (1928); but best-known is his widely used *Histoire des doctrines économiques* (with Rist; translated into English by Smart in 1913). He devoted great efforts to international understanding and, in particular, to cooperation among intellectuals of different countries. He was also a pioneer in stressing the importance of the consumer.

**Sir Robert Giffen**
*British Statistician and Writer*          1837–1910

Giffen, born in Strathaven, Scotland, studied at Glasgow University. He was editor of the *Journal of the Royal Statistical Society* (1876–91) and became assistant editor of the *Economist* (London) under Walter Bagehot. From 1876–97 he served as chief of the Statistical Department and on the Board of Trade. His numerous statistical studies include the first attempt to measure industrial progress in the United Kingdom in the last century. Giffen was also a recognized expert on financial theory and policy in his time. He wrote *The Growth of Capital* (1889) and *Stock Exchange Securities*. He directed the first national census of wages in 1886.

**Melchiorre Gioja**
*Italian Political Theorist and Economist*      1767–1829

Born at Piacenza and educated at Collegio Alberoni, Gioja has been called the first champion of Italian unification. In the economic sphere, he had an ability to anticipate developments, and foresaw the labor-saving effects of machinery. He recognized increased consumption as an important factor in civil and cultural progress, and advocated state participation in stimulation of industrial development and in measures for the protection of labor. His basic ideas were closely related to the utilitarian attitudes of Bentham. Among his numerous writings, *Nuovo prospetto delle scienze economiche* (1815) should be listed. In it, he attacked Smith and Say severely and called for large-scale enterprises.

**William Ewart Gladstone**
*English Prime Minister*          1809–1898

Born in Liverpool, Gladstone was a member of Parliament from 1832–95, and the leading force in the Liberal Party from 1868. He was twice chancellor of the exchequer (1852–55, 1859–66) and four times prime minister (1868–74, 1880–85, 1886, 1892–94). He is mentioned here as a master of finance, the man who helped the principle of laissez-faire to its greatest triumph, and who removed the last obstructions to private activity. He insisted on a balanced budget, opposed progressive taxation, and put little reliance on direct taxation of incomes, concentrating instead on indirect taxes (mainly on luxury articles).

**Jean Baptiste André Godin**
*French Industrialist*          1817–1888

Godin, the owner of an ironworks in Guise, changed the business to a "familistère," a cooperative with profit-sharing by the workers. The factory had several thousand workers and did a very large business.

After Godin's death, his widow managed the enterprise exactly as her husband had done.

**William Godwin**
*English Political Philosopher* 1756–1836

Born in Wisbeach, Godwin was educated for the Dissenting ministry but instead became a radical journalist and writer, always on the edges of poverty. His book *Enquiry concerning Political Justice and Its Influence on Morals and Happiness* (1793) created a sensation. He blamed the government for the unhappiness of man and argued against private property, but his main thesis was the perfectibility of man, of which he was firmly convinced. The book was much discussed, especially by father and son Malthus, who took different stands on it. In 1797 Godwin published *Enquirer*, a collection of essays that included "Avarice and Prodigality." In reply, the younger Malthus brought out his famous *Essay on the Principles of Population*, which Godwin answered with *On Population* (1820). Godwin has been called an anarchist and socialist, and, in fact, both movements spurred his writings.

**Samuel Gompers**
*American Labor Leader* 1850–1924

Born in the ghetto of East London, England, Gompers became a cigar-maker, as his father was, but displaying fortitude and perseverance, he attended night school. He came to the U.S. in 1863, where the family lived in a two-room tenement apartment next to a slaughterhouse in New York City's lower east side. Married at age 17, he fathered 14 children. Gompers was most sincere in his devotion to the labor movement, and he and his family experienced much misery before he became president of the Cigarmakers' International Union. Gompers was the founder and president of the American Federation of Labor and a member of the Commission on International Labor Legislation at the Paris Peace Conference. He described his life and work in *Seventy Years of Life and Labor* (2 vols., 1925).

**George J. Goschen**
*English Statesman and Financier* 1831–1907

Born in London and educated at Oriel College, Oxford, Goschen entered his father's banking house in 1853 and proved himself so effective that the Bank of England made him a director when he was only 27. He served as a member of Parliament from 1863 until 1900, when he was raised to the peerage as Viscount Goschen of Hawkhurst. He was president of the Board of Trade, president of the Poor Law Board, first lord of the admiralty, and held cabinet rank for many years. From 1886–92 he was chancellor of the exchequer; in 1888 he converted the national debt successfully, and through his effective measures a financial panic in 1890 was averted. Goschen has been described as the last minister of finance in the tradition of classic liberalism. In 1861 he wrote *Theory of Foreign Exchange*, the first systematic theoretical account of the mechanism whereby international price adjustments are made.

**Hermann Heinrich Gossen**
*German Economist*                                    *1810–1858*

Born in Düren, Gossen studied in Bonn and Berlin. He was in government service, but retired in 1847 to devote himself to his studies and his book, *Entwicklung der Gesetze des menschlichen Verkehrs und der daraus fliessenden Regeln für menschliches Handeln* (The Development of the Laws of Human Intercourse and the Resulting Rules for Human Behavior) (1854). It contained the now-famous three laws of Gossen. The first clearly states the principle of diminishing utility. The second says that to attain maximum satisfaction the individual must seek to keep the marginal utility of goods equal. The third finds that value (subjective-use value) is attached to a good only when supply is smaller than demand. The book was a total failure; disgusted, Gossen ordered the publisher to destroy the complete edition and shortly afterwards died. Professor Adamson of Manchester found a copy in 1878 and brought it to the attention of Jevons, who is responsible for this work being recognized as a milestone in the development of economic theory. Gossen's philosophy was essentially utilitarian, but he included a broader sense of happiness. He formulated the marginal utility idea of value and said that confusion in economic doctrine is rooted in different conceptions of value. He developed the concept of disutility, ordered goods into different classes, and demonstrated all this in mathematical terms, presenting new mathematical methods.

**Friedrich von Gottl-Ottlilienfeld**
*German Economist*                                    *1868–1958*

Born in Vienna, studied at Vienna, Berlin, and Heidelberg (Ph.D.) where he also taught. A man who went his own ways, stressing that economics should be studied in relation to the living being and not from a starting point of resources, matters, and commodities, Gottl was greatly admired as a teacher who formed the minds of many students. Instead of value theories he used a concept of "economic dimension," with which he described economic considerations in relation to the total human life and the social order. Gottl wrote on the value idea as a veiled dogma of political economy in *Der Wertgedanke, ein verhültes Dogma der Nationalökonomie* (1897). He also published *Wirtschaft als Leben* (1925), *Wirtschaft und Wissenschaft* (1931), and *Wesen und Grundlage der Wirtschaft* (1933).

**Sir Nathanel Gould**
*English Economic Writer*   ca. 1670–1728

A director of the Bank of England and a member of Parliament, Gould was probably the first to propose a system of "sinking funds" to facilitate the repayment of public debts. He wrote *An Essay on the Public Debts of the Kingdom* (1726).

**Jacques Claude Vincent de Gournay**
*French Businessman and Economist*   1712–1759

Born near Cadiz, trained as a merchant, Gournay became superintendent of commerce. To him, rightly or wrongly, has been attributed the phrase, "laissez faire, laissez passer." His own writings are meager and of minor importance, but he translated the works of Child and Culpeper into French. Gournay wanted the government to restore liberty of commerce and to encourage competition. But he was not completely physiocratic since he believed that not only agriculture, but trade and manufacture also, are productive.

**Gracchus**
see François Noel *Babeuf*

**Frank Dunstone Graham**
*American Economist*   1890–1949

He was born of American parents in Halifax, Nova Scotia, and studied at Dalhousie University in Halifax and at Harvard University (Ph.D.). Graham taught at Rutgers University, Dartmouth College, Hautes Etudes Internationales at Geneva, Switzerland, and Princeton University, where he was a professor from 1930. He also served as adviser to various government agencies and was a delegate to the League of Nations, Institute of Intellectual Cooperation. Notable among his many works are: *Exchange, Prices and Production in Hyper-Inflation Germany (1920–1923)* (1930), *The Abolition of Unemployment* (1932), *Protective Tariffs* (1934), *Social Goals and Economic Institutions* (1942), *Planning and Paying for Full Employment* (with Lerner and others, 1946), and *The Theory of International Values* (1948).

**Jean J. L. Graslin**
*French Economist*   1727–1790

Graslin published *Essai analytique sur la richesse et sur l'impôt* (1767), which produced new ideas on the theories of income, wealth, and taxation. Rejecting the physiocratic doctrine on the sole productivity of agriculture and on the single tax, he stated that all labor is productive.

**Dirk Graswinkel**
*Dutch Lawyer*                                              *1600–1666*

Born in Delft, educated at Leyden, Graswinkel was a lawyer and public servant who in 1631 wrote a pamphlet about grain trade and regulations concerning food. His writing is of interest because of his observations in regard to speculation and forestalling, which he felt should not be allowed. He demanded freedom of the seas.

**John Graunt**
*English Haberdasher and Statistician*                      *1620–1674*

Born in London, Graunt was a successful haberdasher until the fire of 1666 destroyed his shop. He was a friend of Petty. He published *Natural and Political Observations Mentioned in a Following Index, and Made upon the Bills of Mortality* (1662). It was his hobby to study birth and death records, compare the data, and draw conclusions. Whether he can be called the father of statistics may be argued, but his study certainly helped to stimulate a form of statistical analysis. In his studies he found that the urban death rate exceeds the rural death rate and that in spite of a greater number of male births, half of the living population is female.

**Jean Grave**
*French Anarchist*                                          *ca. 1854–1939*

Born in Breuil, Grave was, together with Reclus, the best-known late-19th-century French anarchist. He became a journalist and founded *Temps nouveaux*. He wrote *La Société future* (1895), in which he said "property and want are the great incentives to crime" and "the individual was prior to society. Destroy the individual, and there will be nothing left of society."

**Sir Alexander Gray**
*Scottish Economist*                                        *1882–1968*

Gray, professor of political economy at the universities of Edinburgh and Aberdeen, published *The Development of Economic Doctrine* (1931) and *The Socialist Tradition* (1946). He also wrote many articles and papers that contain remarkable contributions to economics, particularly in the history of economic thought.

**John Gray**
*British Socialist*                                         *ca. 1799–1850*

Gray was born and educated in Edinburgh. He came to believe that the sources of social misery were not found in private control of production but in the competitive, individualistic economic system. In his first book, *A Lecture on Human Happiness* (1825), he condemned the existing social order. He regarded labor as the sole producer of value and wealth but found that those who produce receive only a minor part of the results of their labor. They are exploited because of interest, rent, and profit, which go to the parasites. To improve the conditions of labor, he felt that the system would have to be changed. In the *Social System* (1831) he described the ideal society. He called for the establishment of a bank that would exchange commodities against certificates representing labor-time required for production (Owen made such a trial and lost his money). In *Lectures on the Nature and Use of Money* (1848) he developed a labor value theory.

**Augusto Graziani**

*Italian Economist*                                          *1865–1944*

Graziani, a pupil of Ricca-Salerno, was born at Modena and became professor of political economy at Naples. His economic writings contributed greatly to the understanding of economic history in Italy. He was the author of *Lezioni di economica politica* (1900), *Istituzioni di scienza della finanze* (1911), *Teorie e facti economici* (1912), *Economisti del cinque e seicento* (1913), and other books and articles.

**Sir Thomas Gresham**

*English Businessman and Public Servant*                          *ca. 1519–1579*

Gresham, born in London, was educated at Cambridge. He was a capable banker and merchant but also served the crown as royal agent ("factor") with the greatest zeal. In the Netherlands and Spain he negotiated loans, bought war materials, and shipped gold for his government. He was the financial expert of Queen Elizabeth I, and his reports to the crown contain a wealth of analytical economic observations. Therein he hinted at the movements of the exchange rates and referred to the specie points. He also noted that if coins of equal legal tender differ in metal content, the "cheaper" coins will be used for circulation, while the better coins will disappear and will be hoarded. This has been declared "Gresham's Law," i.e., "bad money drives out good." These observations had been made before, however, and Gresham did not add anything new to them. Noting that London merchants had no place to meet similar to the Bourse in Antwerp, he offered to build one at his own expense if the city of London would make land available; thus, the Royal Exchange in London was opened in 1571.

**George Gorham Groat**

*American Economist*                                          *1871–1951*

Born in Green Island, New Jersey, Groat studied at Syracuse University, Cornell University, and Columbia University (Ph.D.). He taught at the University of Vermont. His contributions were mainly to labor economics. Groat was the author of *Trade Unions and the Law* (1905), *Attitude of American Courts in Labor Cases* (1911), *Introduction to the Study of Organized Labor in America* (1916 and 1926), and articles in professional journals.

**Hugo Grotius**
*Dutch Jurist*                                                    *1583–1645*

Born at Delft in the Netherlands as Huig van Groot, Grotius studied law at the University of Leyden and the University of Orléans (Doctor of Laws). He became fiscal advocate and later chief magistrate of Rotterdam. He is remembered because of his *De jure belli et pacis* ("Concerning the Law of War and Peace") (1625), the first work on international law. Grotius hoped that man's desire for happiness would support the prevention of war. He stated that men are social beings and have to live under some form of social organization. If human society is to survive, then natural law must be accepted and applied. These conditions are essential: fair dealing, good faith, rewards according to individual efforts, and security of property. The philosophy of natural law was thus related to economics; under Grotius' influence, trade was increasingly considered as part of the autonomy of the individual, which was believed to imply a "natural right" to trade as one pleased.

**Yves Guyot**
*French Economist*                                                *1843–1928*

Guyot was born at Dinan. When 21 years old he moved to Paris where he became city councilor (1876–85) and minister of public works (1889–92). He strongly believed in individual freedom, accepted the doctrine of the Physiocrats, advocated free trade and opposed Socialism and extensive government regulations. Guyot wrote *La Science économique* (1881), but is best known for a small book, *La Morale de la concurrence* (ca. 1895), in which he declared that producers are constantly concerned with the well-being of their customers, and merchants always try to improve their services.

# H

### Arthur T. Hadley
*American Economist*                                    *1856–1930*

Hadley, born in New Haven, Connecticut, studied at Yale University and at the University of Berlin under Adolf Wagner. He was professor of economics at Yale, and its president from 1899–1921. He wrote *Railroad Transportation* (1885); *Economics* (1896), stressing the relations between private property and public welfare; *Freedom and Responsibility* (1903); and *Problems of Democracy* (1923).

### L. Albert Hahn
*German Banker*                                         *1899–1968*

Born in Frankfurt, Hahn studied at Freiburg, Heidelberg, Berlin, and Marburg (Dr. Jur., Ph.D.), and became a professor at the University of Frankfurt. His books include *Volkswirtschaftliche Theorie des Bankkredits* (1920), *Geld und Kredit* (1924), *Economics of Illusion* (1949), and *Wirtschaftswissenschaft des Gesunden Menscheverstandes* (1954). In his theory of bank credit, Hahn offers new approaches in regard to the relationship between savings and investments.

### Sir Matthew Hale
*English Jurist*                                        *1609–1677?*

Hale was born in Alderley, studied at Oxford and Lincoln's Inn, became a member of Parliament, lord chief baron of the exchequer, and lord chief justice of the King's Bench. He cooperated in the restoration of Charles II. In 1677 he wrote *Primitive Origination of Mankind*, which later was republished under the title *Essay of Population* (1782).

### John Hales
*English State Official*                                *?–1571*

Hales held an exchequer post under Henry VIII and Edward VI, but was forced to leave England after Warwick overthrew Somerset in 1549. It is believed that he wrote *Discourse of the Common Wealth of this Realm of England*, which was published in 1581, after his death. Though he still believed in the Scholastic doctrine of justice, Hales recognized self-interest to be natural and instinctive. He felt, however that it should be regulated by state laws and used for the common good. Rather progressive, he distrusted the general restriction on imports. He also attacked the debasement of coinage. *Discourse* is of interest as a document of a time of transition.

**Elie Halévy**

*French Historian*

*1870–1937*

Halévy, born in Etretat (Seine-Inférieure), was professor at the Ecole Libre des Sciences Politiques. Of his many historical works, in particular on English history, *The Growth of Philosophic Radicalism* (3 vols., 1901–04, trans. 1928) is of importance. Halévy suggested the substitution of political government by industrial administration.

**Bernard Francis Haley**

*American Economist*

*1898–*

Born in St. John, New Brunswick, Canada, Haley studied at Stanford and Harvard universities (Ph.D.). He taught at Stanford from 1924. He published *Value and Distribution* (1948) and *Survey of Contemporary Economics* (1952) and was editor of the *American Economic Review*. During World War II he served in the Office of Price Administration and the Department of State.

**Charles Hall**

*English Physician*

*ca. 1740–1825*

Hall was a practicing physician at Tavistock. In 1805 Hall published *The Effects of Civilization on the People in European States*. He saw in the inequality of wealth the cause of all misery and noticed the ever-widening gap between the poor and the rich. He proposed the nationalization of land and a limitation of manufacturing, hoping that this would lead to greater happiness for all and to the distribution of the product according to the labor involved in production.

**Alexander Hamilton**

*American Statesman*

*1757–1804*

Born in the West Indies, Hamilton fought in the American Revolution, signed the Constitution, became the first Secretary of the Treasury, and established the Bank of the United States. He was killed in a duel by Aaron Burr. Hamilton favored a centralized government and envisioned the U.S. as a strong, wealthy industrial country. His economic views are imbedded in his state papers, in particular in the reports on the public credit (1790 and 1795), the report on a National Bank (1790), and the report on manufactures (1791). He favored bimetallism but opposed laissez-faire ideas and asked for government intervention to encourage and protect industry.

**Walton Hale Hamilton**
*American Economist*                                                    *1881–1958*

Born in Hiwassee College, Tennessee, Hamilton studied at the University of Texas and Michigan University (Ph.D.), where he also taught. He was briefly with the faculty of the University of Chicago, professor of economics at Amherst College and the Brookings Institution, and professor of law at Yale. He served as director of the Bureau of Research and Statistics of the Social Security Board, as special assistant to the U.S. Attorney General, and as U.S. Delegate to the Geneva Conference of the International Labor Organization. He wrote *Public Control of Industry, Current Economic Problems* (1914), *The Control of Wages* (1923, with Stacy May), and *The Case of Bituminous Coal* (1925). He also analyzed the pricing policies of large enterprises. Hamilton was the first to use the term "institutional economics."

**John Lawrence Hammond**
*English Historian and Journalist*                                     *1872–1949*

Born in Drightlington, Yorkshire, Hammond studied at St. John's College, Oxford. He became a journalist with the Leeds *Mercury* and Liverpool *Post*, editor of the liberal weekly, *Speaker*, and was secretary of the Civil Service Commission. Together with his wife, Barbara Hammond (1873–1961), he made considerable contributions to economic history. Their writings include *The Village Labourer, 1760–1832* (1916), *The Town Labourer, 1760–1832* (1917), *The Skilled Labourer, 1760–1832* (1919), *The Rise of Modern Industry* (1925), and *The Age of the Chartists* (1930). With these works and others, Hammond brought the suffering of workers to public attention.

**Lewis H. Haney**
*American Economist*                                                   *1882–1969*

Haney was born in Eureka, Illinois, and educated at Dartmouth College and the University of Wisconsin (Ph.D.). He taught at the universities of Michigan and Texas, and at New York University. In 1911 he published *History of Economic Thought*, which he described as a critical account of the origin and development of the economic theories of the leading thinkers in the leading nations. The third edition in 1936 was much enlarged; a fourth edition appeared in 1949. In addition, Haney published many articles and other books.

**Alvin Harvey Hansen**
*American Economist*                                                   *1887–*

Hansen, born in Viborg, South Dakota, studied at Yankton College and the University of Wisconsin (Ph.D.). He taught at Brown University, the University of Minnesota, and Harvard University, served as economist at the State Department and for the Federal Reserve Board, and was briefly visiting professor at the University of Bombay in India. He was president of the American Economic Association in 1938. Hansen made many outstanding contributions to economic literature in explaining Keynesian economics and applying it to monetary and business-cycle studies. His publications include *Cycles of Prosperity and Depression* (1921), *Economic Stabilization in an Unbalanced World* (1932), *Full Recovery or Stagnation* (1938), *America's Role in the World Economy* (1945), *Monetary Theory and Fiscal Policy* (1949), *Business Cycles and National Income* (1951), *A Guide to Keynes* (1953), *The American Economy* (1957), and *The Dollar and the International Monetary System* (1965).

**James Harrington**
*English Political Writer*                                        *1611–1677*

Born at Upton, Harrington studied at Trinity College, Oxford, and traveled widely on the Continent. He was personally attached to Charles I and retired from public life after the king's execution. Harrington published his famous *The Commonwealth of Oceana* in 1656 and was imprisoned for it in 1661, after the Restoration. In the form of utopian fiction, this work envisions an ideal form of government with a written constitution, a bicameral legislature, secret ballots, and rotation in office —ideas which influenced the forming of the American government. Harrington revived Aristotle's idea that political power must be based in economic power; if they are separated, revolution is likely to occur.

**Abram Lincoln Harris**
*American Economist*                                        *1899–1963*

Born in Richmond, Virginia, Harris studied at Virginia Union University, the University of Pittsburgh, and Columbia University (Ph.D.). He taught at Howard University and the University of Chicago. He published *The Black Worker* (1931), *The Negro Capitalist* (1936), and *Economics and Social Reform* (1958).

**Joseph Harris**
*English Master of the Mint*                                        *1702–1764*

Born in Talgarth, Breconshire, Harris moved to London where he became a well-known writer. An advocate of silver monometalism, Harris wrote *An Essay upon Money and Coins* (1757), in which he developed ideas on the theory of money and exchange, on wage differentiations in various occupations, and on the evils of coinage debasement.

**Hawkhurst**
see George J. *Goschen*

## Frederick B. Hawley
*American Businessman*
*1843–1929*

Hawley studied at Williams College. Though he became a cotton broker in New York, he remained a lifelong student of political economy. Among his writings, the following deserve listing: *Capital and Population* (1882), "A Positive Theory of Economics" (*Ann. Amer. Acad.*, 1902), "The Orientation of Economics on Enterprise" (*American Economic Review*, 1927), and particularly *Enterprise and the Productive Process* (1907). Hawley saw in economics "the study of human activities requiring joint efforts with definite personal motives." The distribution of the purchasing power created through such activities is prearranged by the entrepeneur. This was an original way to approach economics. Hawley saw the English classical theories of economics from the viewpoint of the American business executive.

## Sir Ralph George Hawtrey
*English Economist*
*1879–*

Born in Slough, England, Hawtrey was educated at Eton and Cambridge. He served with the British treasury from 1904–45 and was professor of international economics at the Royal Institute of International Affairs from 1947–52. He was president of the Royal Economic Society. In 1956 he was knighted. His publications include *Good and Bad Trade* (1913), *Currency and Credit* (1919), *Monetary Reconstruction* (1923), *The Gold Standard in Theory and Practice* (1927), *The Art of Central Banking* (1932), *Capital and Employment* (1937), *A Century of Bank Rate* (1939), *Towards the Rescue of Sterling* (1954), and *The Pound at Home and Abroad* (1963). Hawtrey's most remarkable contribution was in business-cycle analysis. He saw cyclical fluctuations to be caused by purely monetary influences.

## William Hazlitt
*English Writer*
*1778–1830*

Born in Maidstone, Kent, he became a well-known journalist. Hazlitt is mentioned here because of his attacks on Malthus, whom he accused of harshness against the poor. In *A Reply to the Essay on Population* (1807) he stressed that there is no limit to subsistence until the earth's surface is fully occupied and intensive cultivation is applied. Most of his articles appear in *Political Essays* (1819), which show that Hazlitt assigned to government one duty only: to keep order and peace.

## William Edward Hearn
*Australian Economist*
*1826–1888*

Hearn, educated at Trinity College, Dublin, was appointed professor of history, logic, and political economy at the University of Melbourne,

Australia (1854). His writings include works on the English constitution and government. Of particular interest is *Plutology, or the Theory of the Efforts to Satisfy Human Wants* (1863). Marginal utility and marginal productivity are indicated; in the work the influences of Darwin and Spencer can be traced. Hearn maintained that two factors cooperate in satisfying human wants: labor and natural agents.

**Eli F. Heckscher**
*Swedish Economist* *1879–1952*

Heckscher, born in Stockholm, studied at Uppsala University, where he earned his doctorate in 1907. In 1909, he was appointed professor of economics and statistics at the new Stockholm School of Economics and Commerce, and in 1929 he became research professor of economic history. In 1915 he published *The Continental System, an Economic Interpretation* and in 1932 *Mercantilism*, a comprehensive work which promptly won great attention and was translated into German, English, Italian, and Spanish. A revised edition appeared in 1953. Heckscher tried to prove that, contrary to the general belief, wealth and comfort, and not power for power's sake, are the driving forces behind Mercantilism.

**Arnold Hermann Ludwig Heeren**
*German Historian* *1760–1842*

Heeren, born in Arbergen, near Bremen, was professor in Göttingen, where he had also been educated. His historical works fill many volumes. He became a pioneer in the economic interpretation of history and a leader of the German opposition to the Manchester School. He wrote *Ideen über die Politik, Verkehr und Handel der Vornehmsten Völker der alten Welt* (1821).

**Georg Wilhelm Friedrich Hegel**
*German Philosopher* *1770–1831*

Born in Stuttgart, Hegel studied theology at Tübingen. He wrote on matters of theology and philosophy and taught at Jena and Heidelberg, moving to Berlin University after the publication of his *Encyclopedia of the Philosophical Sciences* (1817). In 1830 he became Rector at Berlin. According to Hegel, the entire universe is a manifestation of God, the Absolute, and its purpose is revealed in the human mind. An idea develops a thesis which meets objections in the antithesis. Out of this clash emerges a solution, the synthesis, which is the new thesis. With every cycle, man and society move closer to perfection and freedom. True freedom is found through association within the family, the Church, and the state. The good of all is the purpose of society. Hegelian philosophy had a tremendous influence on the formation of economic thought, notably on Marx.

**Eduard Heimann**
*German Economist*                                   *1889–1967*

Born in Berlin, Heimann studied in Vienna, Berlin, and Heidelberg. He taught at the universities of Cologne, Freiburg, and Hamburg, the New School for Social Research (New York), the University of California at Berkeley, in Japan, and back in Germany at the universities of Göttingen and Bonn. He published *Das Soziale System des Kapitalismus* (1929), *Communism, Fascism or Democracy* (1938), *History of Economic Doctrines* (1944), *Freedom and Order* (1947), and *Reason and Faith in Modern Society* (1961).

**Adolf Held**
*German Economist*                                   *1844–1880*

Born in Würzburg, Held studied in Munich under Hermann. He taught at Poppelsdorf and at the University of Bonn and participated in the formation of the Verein für Sozialpolitik. Held wrote *Die Einkommensteuer* (1872), *Carey's Sozialwissenschaft und das Mercantilsystem* (1886), *Sozialismus, Sozialdemokratie und Sozialpolitik* (1877).

**Karl Helfferich**
*German Economist and Statesman*                     *1872–1924*

Helfferich was born at Neustadt. After studying under Knapp at Strassburg he was appointed professor at the University of Berlin, joined the German cabinet in 1915 as secretary of the treasury, and later became vice-chancellor. He remained a lifelong monarchist. Helfferich's studies were mainly concerned with monetary and fiscal theory and policy. He published *The Reform of the German Monetary System* (1898, in German) and *Das Geld* (1903), which was translated into English and appeared under the title *Money* in 1927 (2 vols.). Basically, *Money* is a defense of the gold standard. In 1923 he participated in the German monetary reform that brought the hyperinflation in Germany to an end. Helfferich has been credited with the introduction of the Rentenmark, a currency backed by agricultural mortgage bonds.

**Claude Adrien Helvétius**
*French Philosopher*                                 *1715–1771*

Helvétius, born in Paris, resigned his position at the Queen's court in 1750 to dedicate himself to philosophy, and in 1758 published *De l'Esprit*. The work was censored by the Sorbonne, the Pope, and the French parliament and was burned in public, but it had its influence on Mandeville, Adam Smith and the utilitarians. Helvétius gave to self-interest in the social realm the role that the law of gravity has in physical science. He also criticized the distribution of income in the society of his time.

Friedrich Wilhelm Benedikt von Hermann
*German Economist and Statistician*                              *1795–1868*

Hermann was born in Kinkelsbühl, Bavaria, and studied at Erlangen and Würzburg. He became one of the leading German professors of political economy in his time, and a leading member of the liberal revolution in the Frankfurt Parliament of 1848. He was appointed professor of political economy at the University of Munich (1827) and director of the Bavarian statistical bureau (1839). His greatest contributions to economics are found in his *Staatswirtschaftliche Untersuchungen* (1832). He opposed the wage-fund theory and found that in the final analysis wages are paid out of the income of the consumers, who earn this income through their own economic activities. Hermann pointed out that economics is not a pure science because it is much too closely related to society, constantly changing. He defined capital as "all sources of income which endure and have exchange value" and was the first to distinguish between productive and consumption capital. Recognizing capital as a production factor, he also demanded for labor the right of self-determination.

Jean Herrenschwand
*Swiss Economist*                                              *1728–1811*

Herrenschwand lived in Paris and London. He was an economist whose independent ideas did not permit him to be attached to the Physiocrats or any other school. In *Discours fondamental sur la population* (1786) he anticipated Malthus. He also published *De l'économie politique moderne* (1786) and *Du vrai principe actif de l'économie politique* (1797).

Most of Herrenschwand's works were written in France, where he held a judicial post, but for political reasons they were published in London. His evolutionary ideas gave him hope for the possible improvement of man. These improvements should be directed by political economy. He saw three stages of economic development: hunting, pastoral, and agricultural, to which he added also industrial activities. He warned that foreign trade made a country dependent on foreign supplies, and advocated moderate profits, low interest rates, and fair wages. His hopes for a better future, based on human intelligence, were expressed in *De l'économie politique et morale de l'espèce humaine* (1796).

Theodor Hertzka
*German Agrar-socialist*                                       *1845–1924*

Hertzka may be called a disciple of Henry George and Franz Oppenheimer. In his *Freiland, ein soziales Zukunftsbild* (1889) he gives a utopian picture of life in a country with community property of land.

**Bruno Hildebrand**
*German Economist*                                            *1812–1878*

Hildebrand was born in Naumburg and studied at Breslau, where he later taught. He also taught at Marburg, and then, forced by political difficulties to go to Switzerland, at the universities of Zurich and Bern. In Bern he established the first statistical bureau in Switzerland. He returned to Germany and was appointed professor at Jena. While in Jena he founded the *Jahrbücher fur Nationalökonomie und Statistik*, in which many of his articles first appeared.

Hildebrand was a member of the so-called Older Historical School in Germany. He was actively interested in social reforms, social affairs, politics, and business. He wrote numerous articles on many subjects, but his book, *Die Nationalökonomie der Gegenwart und Zukunft*, was never completed. Only the first volume was published (1848). He placed emphasis on the moral character of economics, rejected the idea of natural laws, and criticized the classics severely. His monographs on the history of some German industries show that he thought the historical method would contribute to economics more than abstract analysis could.

The speech Hildebrand delivered on becoming rector at Jena is remarkable. In dealing with the significance of statistical research, he expressed the hope that statistics would liberate economics from abstract speculation. Statistics would only be valid as a science, however, if it succeeded in uncovering the relationships, differences, and equalities that show the internal connections between past and present.

His son, Richard, wrote *Theorie des Geldes* (1883) setting forth a theory that money is not a commodity but rather just the opposite.

**Rudolf Hilferding**
*German Socialist*                                            *1877–1943*

Helferding was born in Vienna and received an M.D. from the University of Vienna, where he became interested in social problems. Intelligent and personally attractive, he was invited by the Socialist leaders to come to Berlin to lecture at the party school. Soon he became editor of *Vorwärts*, a daily party newspaper, and a leading member of the party's Reichstag delegation. He was twice finance minister in the Weimar Republic, both at the time of hyper-inflation and at the time of depression. When Hitler came to power, he sought refuge in Switzerland and France. Planning to leave for the U.S., he was arrested by the French police on board a steamer in Marseilles and was handed over by the Vichy government to the Nazis. He ended his life immediately.

Hilferding has been called the ablest of the Marxian economists. Though most of his economic writings are in journals, his ideas are well represented in the book *Das Finanzkapital* (1910), in which he stated that the concentration of industrial capital is controlled by banks, the real dominating force in late-stage capitalism. He attempted to explain monopoly pricing with the value theory of labor and to develop a business-cycle theory based on employment in heavy industries. Though he was deprived of success in most of his practical endeavors, Hilferding was a brilliant man of great vision and optimism.

**Hippolyte**

see Jean Hippolyte, Baron de *Colins*

**Franz Hitze**

*German Social Reformer*                                         *1851–1921*

Born in Hanemicke, Kreis Olpe, Hitze was ordained a Catholic priest but soon devoted himself exclusively to the welfare of the laboring classes. He became secretary general of the Arbeiterwohl association, was elected to the Reichstag, and became professor at the University of Münster.

Early in his career Hitze advocated a Christian Socialism with a guild-like structure, the right to work, the right of labor to organize, and the right to be heard in the determination of the production process. He was one of the leading social legislators at the turn of the century. His most important book was entitled *Die Arbeiterfrage und die Bestrebungen zu ihrer Lösung* (1900).

**Thomas Hobbes**

*English Philosopher*                                            *1588–1679*

Hobbes was born in Westport, studied at Magdalen Hall in Oxford, and became mathematics tutor to the earl of Devonshire. Influenced by the growing knowledge in mathematics and physics and closely connected with Francis Bacon, whom he served as a secretary, Hobbes developed a materialistic and mechanistic philosophy. Of particular interest is his *Leviathan* (1651), emphasizing individualism, the human impulse of self-preservation and referring to the value (or worth) of a man as the price given for his services and depending upon the judgment of others. Since, by nature, man is brutal and nasty and in conflict with other men, they all must submit to a sovereign who will protect people and promote the truth. Thus, the absolute state was the way of obtaining the greater good for all, in Hobbes' opinion.

The impulse to self-preservation is caused by fear of pain and desire for power. Hobbes' ideas influenced the later classical school of economics as well as Bentham. But Hobbes also felt that reason and rationality can only succeed if the main motivation of human behavior and action is based on the desire for more durable and higher gains.

**John Atkinson Hobson**
*English Economist* *1858–1940*

Hobson was born in Derby and studied at Oxford. His writings on the evils of the industrial revolution and his demand for social justice prevented him from finding a regular academic teaching position, and so he was an extension lecturer at Oxford and London. In his many articles and some 35 books he was concerned with the welfare of man more than with wealth as such. His most notable books are *The Physiology of Industry* (1889), *The Evolution of Modern Capitalism* (1894), *Economics of Distribution* (1900), *Work and Wealth* (1914), *Taxation in the New State* (1919), and *The Economics of Unemployment* (1922).

His business-cycle theory was basically an underconsumption theory. He had the idea of taxing all surpluses away, not only those from land as proposed by Henry George. He sought a solution to the problem of poverty. Hobson refused to treat ethics, politics, and economics separately; for him, they were closely interrelated, and his best works are in the fields where they intersect. Many of his social ideas were influenced by John Ruskin.

**Thomas Hodgskin**
*English Journalist* *1787–1869*

Hodgskin was a naval officer before he became a journalist. He was a friend of Francis Place and Herbert Spencer. Hodgskin wrote many articles and books, of which *Labour Defended against the Claims of Capital, or The Unproductiveness of Capital Proved with Reference to the Present Combinations among Journeymen* (1825) is of great interest. The book contains a careful study of the economic system, in particular of the function of capital and the process of production. For the author, labor alone produces wealth, but it does not get the fruit of its efforts, to which it is entitled. In his opinion, it is the capitalist who has acquired the dominant position in economic life and who absorbs all surpluses (not the landowner, as Ricardo believed). It is the capitalist who determines the rents, wages (which are merely subsistence wages), and prices, always with an eye to sufficient profit for himself. The government should maintain order and peace, he felt, but should in no way interfere with the rights of individuals. In fact, his individualism was so extreme that he has been called an anarchist, though others call him a predecessor of Marx. Hodgskin believed that natural law will ultimately bring harmony when unrestricted self-interest is allowed to prevail, when competition becomes the rule of economic activity, and inheritance or wealth is no longer protected by governments. Capital and wealth is only stored-up labor; the energy, skill, and knowledge of the workers is of much greater importance. In the natural social order, labor will be deprived neither of a full livelihood nor of the means of production. Hodgskin doubtless had a great influence on Marx, who read his *Popular Political Economy* (1827).

**Jacob Harry Hollander**
*American Economist*                                                    *1871–1940*

Hollander, born in Baltimore, Maryland, studied at Johns Hopkins University and became professor of political economy there. He served in governmental offices at home and abroad and was once treasurer in Puerto Rico. Hollander wrote *David Ricardo* (1911), *The Abolition of Poverty* (1914), *Economic Liberalism* (1925), and *Want and Plenty* (1932). He also brought out new editions of classical works and of Barbon's *Discourse of Trade* (1690).

**Paul Thomas Homan**
*American Economist*                                                    *1893–1969*

Born in Indianola, Iowa, Homan was educated at Willamette University, Oregon; Oxford University; and Brookings Institution (Ph.D.). He taught at Cornell University, the University of California at Los Angeles, and Southern Methodist University. He was managing editor of the *American Economic Review* and published *Contemporary Economic Thought* (1928), *The National Recovery Administration* (1935), *The Sugar Economy of Puerto Rico* (1938), and *Government and Economic Life* (1940).

**Francis Horner**
*Scottish Politician*                                                   *1778–1817*

Horner was born in Edinburgh, studied there, admitted to the Scotch bar in 1800, went to London in 1802 and became a member of Parliament in 1806. A man respected because of his sound knowledge and integrity, he became chairman of the Bullion Committee in 1810. The report of this committee was prepared mainly by Horner with Thornton. Together they believed that the rise in prices was not caused by foreign demand for gold, as many thought, but by the overissue of paper money. The report was hotly discussed and criticized. Horner published a great number of articles in the *Edinburgh Review*.

**Philipp Wilhelm von Hornigk**
*Austrian Cameralist*                                                  *1638–1712*

Hornigk was born in Mainz, Germany. He studied law in Ingolstadt, practiced law in Vienna until 1690, and then entered public service. Though his political writings are of little importance, his *Österreich über Alles, wann es nur will* (1684) was highly popular. In it, his completely mercantilist views are plain, though he found that while gold and silver are essential for the subsistence of the country, other things, too, are necessary to feed and clothe people and to make the country independent. He emphasized self-sufficiency and propagated 9 rules for public economy to make Austria strong and free from foreign dependence. The best use must be made of the country's soil. Material that must be refined or fabricated for use should be transformed within Austria. Population should be kept as large as the country can support, and should be guided and encouraged to productive services. The efficiency of labor should be increased through better training. Gold and silver should be kept in circulation, but not exported. Consumption should be confined to the products of the country. Imports (when necessary) should be exchanged against domestic products, and they should be restricted to raw materials for domestic production. Export, however, should be paid in gold or silver. Even cheaper foreign products may not be imported if a sufficient supply is available at home, because "to spend two units of the currency at home is better than to spend one unit abroad."

**Robert Franklin Hoxie**
*American Economist*               *1868–1916*

Hoxie was born in Emerton, New York, and was educated at Cornell University and the University of Chicago, where he also taught. His contributions were mainly in labor economics, in which he conducted extensive research. His best-known publications are *Scientific Management and Labor* (1915) and *Trade Unionism in the United States* (1917, with Fine).

**François Huet**
*French Catholic Socialist*               *1816–1869*

Huet was born in Villeau, Eure-et-Loire. He was professor at Ghent, Belgium. A social idealist and liberal Roman Catholic, Huet was opposed to individualism, which he felt is caused by materialism, and to communism, which he felt is caused by pantheism. Huet thought that land should belong to society, and recognized private property only insofar as it was earned by work. Limiting the rights of inheritance, Huet suggested that property, particularly land, should be divided among young people when the owner died. His best-known work is *Le Règne social du christianisme* (1853).

**Gottlieb Hufeland**
*German Jurist and Economist*               *1760–1817*

Born in Danzig, where he later became mayor, Hufeland studied at Leipzig, Göttingen and Jena. At Jena he was appointed professor.

Hufeland was one of the early German followers of Adam Smith, but went further than Smith in defining profit as an income for entrepreneurial functions, quite different from interest. He showed the velocity of monetary circulation during inflation and produced a kind of subjective-value theory related to the productivity theory of distribution. He published *Neue Grundlegung der Staatswirtschaftskunst* (1807) and *Die Lehre vom Gelde und Geldumlaufe* (1819).

**Thomas Hughes**
*English Lawyer*                                                    *1822–1896*

Born in Uffington, Berkshire, Hughes studied at Rugby and Oriel College, Oxford, was called to the bar, and became a county court judge and member of Parliament. He supported the cause of Social Protestantism (also called Christian Socialism). His famous story *Tom Brown's School Days* (1857) stressed the immoral character of an industrial society and envisioned an economic society guided by the Golden Rule. A defender of the working man, with Kingsley and Maurice he founded the Working Men's College (1854) and in 1872 became its principal. During a visit to the U.S. he tried unsuccessfully to establish a cooperative settlement in the manner of Owen and Fourier in Tennessee.

**David Hume**
*Scottish Philosopher*                                              *1711–1776*

Hume was born in Edinburgh, the son of a Scottish lord, and studied in Edinburgh and on the Continent. It was in France that he wrote his most important work, *A Treatise of Human Nature* (3 vols., 1739–40). He taught at Edinburgh University, joined the diplomatic service, and was secretary to Lord Hertford, the British ambassador to France. In 1765 Hume was British chargé d'affaires in Paris. In 1767 he became British under-secretary of state. In 1769 he retired to Edinburgh and remained until his death in this center of intellectual life.

Hume was for over 25 years a close friend of Adam Smith, and it has been said that without Hume, Smith never would have been what he was. Hume gave labor a chief role in economic development and held that everything is purchased by labor. Man's wants are the only causes of labor. He adopted a utilitarian position and regarded happiness as the only desirable end. All activities should help promote the happiness of the society. His hedonism is therefore less individualistic than universal. Society is indispensable for human happiness. Man always lived in some sort of community. All should have the necessities of life.

Hume was a forceful opponent of mercantilism. He developed a theory on international trade and applied the quantitative theory of money to all countries that entertain trade relations. In *Political Discourses* (1752) he included essays on money, interest, balance of trade, and commerce, and stressed the notion of an automatically regulated balance of trade and an automatic money supply. International division of labor would be beneficial to all countries, he believed; the wealth of neighbors would be reflected in the domestic economy. Some of his most important writings were *Essays Moral and Political* (1741–42) and *History of England* (1754–62).

**Francis Hutcheson**
*Scottish Philosopher and Economist*                                   *1694–1746*

Hutcheson, the son of a Presbyterian minister, was born in Ireland. Educated in Glasgow and later in Dublin, he became professor of moral philosophy at Glasgow College and lectured on philosophy, politics, jurisprudence, and political economy. An outstanding scholar and excellent teacher, he had a great influence on Adam Smith, who was his student from 1737–40.

Hutcheson was convinced that truth could be found by reason, that man has certain rights that should be respected, and that harmony will exist when liberty and justice prevail. Nature, in his opinion, is beneficent, and "the greatest happiness to the greatest number" will be assured when enlightened self-interest is exercised without interference. In economics, Hutcheson had clear concepts on value, exchange, money, and division of labor. Among his many writings, in which he used mathematical formulae for his explanations, *A System of Moral Philosophy* (1755, published by his son), remains the most characteristic and contains most of his insights on economics.

**Aldous Leonard Huxley**
*English Writer*                                                        *1894–1963*

Huxley, a prolific essayist and novelist, was born in Godalming, Surrey, and educated at Eton and Oxford. In 1932 he published *Brave New World*, a novel of a nightmarish utopia set 600 years in the future. Highly critical of the existing social order, he warned of the dangers of moral anarchy in a scientific age. In 1958 he published *Brave New World Revisited*.

# I

**Karl Theodor von Inama-Sternegg**

*Austrian Statistician and Economist*            *1843–1908*

Born in Augsburg, Inama-Sternegg studied in Munich. He taught at the universities of Munich, Innsbruck, Prague, and Vienna and was widely known as a stimulating and powerful teacher. He gained international reputation as head of the Austrian Statistical Bureau, and was appointed a life member of the Austrian Upper House in recognition of his outstanding work. His main interest, however, was in historical studies. He wrote about the markets and towns during the early Middle Ages and published *Deutsche Wirtschaftsgeschichte* (1879–1901). He was the editor of the *Zeitschrift für Volkswirtschaft, Sozialpolitik und Verwaltung.*

**John Kells Ingram**

*Irish Scholar*            *1823–1907*

Born in Donegal, Ingram studied at Trinity College in Dublin. His wide cultural background permitted him to be professor of English and Greek as well as librarian at Trinity College. He had similar high qualifications in philosophy, science, and political economy. Ingram accepted much of the positivist philosophy of Comte. His writings covered wide fields, and one volume contains sonnets and songs.

In economics, Ingram belonged to the English historical school. He published *The Present Position and Prospects of Political Economy* (1878) and *A History of Political Economy* (1888). He opposed the classics as too individualistic, unmoral, and materialistic, and demanded that new economic studies be made in the light of modern physics and biology. He protested the isolation of economics from the other social sciences, and in his writings stressed historical relativity and evolution.

**Isaak Iselin**

*Swiss Physiocrat*            *1728–1782*

Iselin, a convinced Physiocrat, propagated ideas of this school in Switzerland. As secretary of the city council of Basel, he successfully insisted that a chair for Physiocracy be established at the University of Basel.

# J

**Ludwig H. von Jakob**
*German Philosopher and Economist*      *1759–1827*

Jakob was born in Wettin, studied at Merseburg and Halle, and taught political economy at Cracow and philosophy at Halle. He attempted to combine Kant's philosophy with the the teaching of Adam Smith. In his *Grundsätze der Nationalökonomie* (1805) he followed Smith closely but recognized that national borders cause variations in economic problems so that solutions cannot be generalized.

**Thomas Jefferson**
*American Statesman*      *1743–1826*

Jefferson, born at Shadwell, Virginia, attended the College of William and Mary and studied law with George White in Williamsburg. He became the author of the Declaration of Independence in 1776, served as minister to France (1785–89), became U.S. secretary of state, vice president and the 3rd president of the United States. In Paris he had met the leading physiocrats, and he shared with them the conviction that agriculture is of greatest importance and value to the society. He was less interested in industrial developments. This resulted in serious controversies with Alexander Hamilton. Jefferson had a deep aversion to public debts and disliked all complicated financial transactions.

**Henry Charles Flemming Jenkin**
*British Engineer and Economist*      *1833–1885*

Jenkin, born in Dungeness, was a professional engineer and a professor of engineering at Edinburgh University, but he also made important contributions to economics. He published *Trade Unions* (1868), *The Graphic Representation of the Laws of Supply and Demand and Their Application to Labor* (1870), and *Essays on Political Economy* (1868–84). Especially interested in wage theory, Jenkin also showed the relationship between saving and interest rates, and demonstrated the concept of elasticity.

**Richard Jennings**
*English Economist*      *1814–1891*

Little is known about Jennings, and he might have been forgotten if Jevons had not mentioned him in his *Theory* as the man who had the clearest concept of the nature and importance of the law of utility.

Jennings published *Natural Elements of Political Economy* (1855) and *Social Delusions concerning Wealth and Want* (1856).

**Williams Stanley Jevons**

*English Economist*                                                                                                 *1835–1882*

Jevons was born in Liverpool. He started to study chemistry and mathematics at University College, London, but soon left to spend 5 years as an assayer in the Australian Mint. Returned to London, he completed his B.A. and M.A. degrees in logic and political economy. He was professor of political economy at Owens College, Manchester, from 1866, and then at University College, London, from 1876. He resigned in 1880 to devote himself to research and writing.

Jevons holds an outstanding place in the history of economic analysis. His *Theory of Political Economy* (1871) deals with the fundamental theoretical problems of consumption, exchange, and distribution, but also develops the whole concept of marginal analysis. Jevons believed that the dominating force in economic activities is the calculation of pleasure and pain, as shown by Bentham, and that the basic problems should be studied from the standpoint of psychology. Although convinced that economics could become a true science only by using mathematical methods, he created a system that was foremostly psychological in approach. Still, he became a pioneer in mathematical statistics and produced business-forecasting devices far ahead of the time. In addition, he made great contributions to capital analysis and value theory.

**John XXIII**

*Pope*                                                                                                                       *1881–1963*

Born near Bergamo, Italy, Angelo Giuseppe Roncalli became Pope John XXIII in 1958. In order to bring the Church into line with the present times, he organized the Second Vatican Council, which met from 1962–65. In 1961, on the 70th anniversary of Leo XIII's encyclical *Rerum novarum*, Pope John issued the encyclical *Mater et magister* (called *Christianity and Social Progress* in English), updating and extending the social doctrines of Leo XIII and Pius XI. In it, he noted "the immeasurable sorrowful spectacle of vast numbers of workers in many lands and entire continents who are paid wages which condemn them and their families to subhuman conditions of life." Wages should be determined according to justice and equity; taxes must also be based on these principles, and the burden must be proportioned to the capacity of the people to contribute. Pope John defended the ownership of private property as "a natural right which the state cannot suppress," but emphasized that individual freedom and welfare must be achieved in a society where community values and social justice are stressed. He urged a world-wide war against hunger and poverty and said, "The principle of solidarity between all human beings must be emphasized and exalted." His encyclical *Pacem in terris* (1962) found extraordinary attention as a plea for world peace addressed not only to Catholics, but to all men of good will.

**Richard Jones**
*British Economist*                                                            *1790–1855*

Educated at Cambridge, Jones was appointed professor of political economy at King's College, London, but soon became the successor of Malthus at Haileybury College, where he remained until retirement. He was opposed to utilitarianism and called for a new approach to economics, stressing that economists should view the world as it really is and should rely on empirical research. In this he was a forerunner of the historical school. He exposed shortcomings of Ricardo's rent theory and disagreed with Malthus on the population problem. He stressed distribution of wealth. Best known is his book *An Essay on the Distribution of Wealth and on the Sources of Taxation* (1831), but also *Lectures on the Political Economy of Nations* (1852) and *Literary Remains* (published in 1859, after his death) should be mentioned.

**Clement Juglar**
*French Physician*                                                            *1819–1905*

Born at Paris, Juglar studied medicine in Paris but practiced for 2 years only. Although he came late to economics and had no formal training in this field, he made original contributions to business cycle theory in his *Of Commercial Crises and Their Periodic Return in France, England, and the United States* (1861, in French). He distinguished 3 phases of the business cycle and came to a conclusion, which he called the "law of crisis," whereby recessions and depressions are the consequences of unbalanced situations created by preceding periods of prosperity. He described in detail the causes of such unbalances.

**Johann Heinrich Gottlob von Justi**
*German Cameralist*                                                            *1717–1771*

Justi was born at Brucken in Thuringia and studied law at several German universities. He taught at the Ritterakademie in Vienna and at the University of Göttingen. He became director of mines and superintendent of glass and steel works in Berlin. In 1765 he was appointed administrator of mines by Fredrick the Great. Later, because of irregularities in accounts, he was put in prison, where he died.

Justi has been called the leading representative of Cameralism. His numerous writings show talent for organization and sound judgment. Two works stand out: *Staatswirtschaft* (1755) and *System des Finanzwesens* (1766). He stressed the importance of population for national growth and wealth but realized the need for additional food supply. He suggested that a certain proportion between the size and number of industrial and agricultural enterprises should be established and kept. Justi accepted the social-contract theory of states and saw in the desire for self-preservation and progress the force that keeps society together.

As a theoretician, he was concerned with what the German historians called the welfare state (Wohlfahrtsstaat), in which the government, through a comprehensive planning and efficient organization of the economy, promotes a strong, self-sufficient, and prosperous state. His ideal government, however, would show flexibility in its practical regulations; his bureaucracy would not assert itself when no intervention is needed. He supported the theory of government intervention but made the effort to keep cameral science or economics (Kameralwissenschaft) separated from the study of the general administration of the state (Polizeiwissenschaft).

**Justinian**

*Roman Emperor*                                                     *483–565*

Justinian succeeded his uncle Justin I and became emperor in 527. His reign was a reign of imperial greatness and success. He was supported by his wife Theodora (died 548) who determined many of the emperor's actions and suppressed the Nika sedition in 532. Africa was recovered from the Vandals and Italy from the Goths. In Constantinople the Hagia Sophia was built. But the chief accomplishment for all time was the codification of Roman law, the *Corpus Juris Civilis,* which contains valuable information about economic institutions and behavior of that time.

# K

German Philosopher

**Immanuel Kant**
*1724–1804*

Kant was born in Königsberg and lived quietly there as a professor of logic and metaphysics at the university. His influence on philosophy was enormous and profound. His social theories arose from his belief in a conflict between man's sociability and his selfishness, resulting in the growth of man's natural capacities. In its progress toward perfection, society passes from anomy (the primitive stage, in which man's impulses are innocent and uncontrolled), through heteronomy (civilization as we know it, with its externally imposed moral laws), to autonomy (the ideal stage, in which the individual obeys laws he imposes on himself). Kant wrote "act as if the maxim from which you act were to become through your will a universal law of nature." He recommended a state that would ensure individual freedom, curbing it only when it encroached on the general welfare and the freedom of others. In international affairs he proposed a similar freedom of sovereign states within the framework of a world federation that would keep order and prevent war.

American Economist

**Abraham David Hannath Kaplan**
*1893–*

Born in New York City, Kaplan studied at New York University, the University of Denver, and Johns Hopkins University. He taught at the University of Denver, George Washington University, Rollins College, University of Delaware, Institute of World Affairs (Mondsee, Austria), and in India. He was connected with government agencies, the Committee for Economic Development, and the Brookings Institution. Kaplan published *Liquidation of War Production* (1944), *Guarantee of Annual Wages* (1947), *Small Business* (1948), *Big Enterprise in a Competitive System* (1954), and *Pricing in Big Business* (1958).

German Prince and Physiocrat

**Karl Friedrich, Margrave of Baden**
*1728–1811*

Karl Friedrich followed his grandfather to the throne when he was 10 years old. He was first margrave, then elector, and finally grand duke (1804). He accepted the physiocratic doctrine. His *Abrégé des principes de l'économie politique* (1772) was dedicated to Mirabeau and had a preface written by Dupont de Nemours. Karl Freidrich tried to apply the single-tax concept of the Physiocrats in his country, but with little success.

### Karl Kautsky
*German Socialist*        *1854–1938*

Kautsky was born in Prague and studied in Vienna. He was private secretary to Engels in London (1881), founded the socialist paper *Die Neue Zeit* in Stuttgart, and was regarded as the leading interpreter of Marxism after Marx's death. He had known Marx personally, and he edited after the deaths of Marx and Engels the fourth part of *Das Kapital, Theorien über den Mehrwert* (3 vols., 1905–10).

Unquestionably loyal to Marx, Kautsky himself was a prominent theorist, respected because of character and ability. Among his writings are *Der Einfluss der Volksvermehrung auf den Fortschritt der Gesellschaft* (1880), *Das Erfurter Program* (1891; trans. into English as *Class Struggle*), *Communism in Central Europe in the Time of the Reformation* (1897; trans. by Mulliken), *Die Agrarfrage* (1899), *Krisentheorien* (1901), *Karl Marx' ökonomische Lehren* (1912), and *Die materialistische Geschichtsauffassung* (1929).

### Edwin Walter Kemmerer
*American Economist*        *1875–1945*

Kemmerer was born in Scranton, Pennsylvania, and studied at Wesleyan and Cornell universities. He taught at Purdue, Cornell, and Princeton universities, and was one of the leading experts on monetary theory in his time. Kemmerer was internationally recognized for his work in restoring and stabilizing the currencies and banking systems of 14 nations, including Egypt, Mexico, Guatemala, and the Philippines (about which he published papers and reports). Outstanding among his publications are: *Money and Credit Instruments in Their Relation to General Prices* (1907), *Modern Currency Reform* (1916), *Six Lectures on the Federal Reserve System* (1920), *High Prices and Deflation* (1920), *Kemmerer on Money* (1934), and *The ABC of Inflation* (1940). Excellent, too, are his papers on gold-exchange questions.

### Wilhelm Emmanuel, Baron von Ketteler
*German Social Reformer*        *1811–1877*

Born in Münster, Ketteler studied at Göttingen, Berlin, Munich, and Heidelberg and was ordained a priest. He became a member of the Frankfurt Parliament (1848), Bishop of Mainz, and one of the most outstanding social reformers in Germany during the time of the Kulturkampf.

**John Maynard Keynes**
*English Economist* *1883–1946*

Keynes was born in Cambridge and studied mathematics, philosophy, and economics at King's College, Cambridge. In 1906 he entered the civil service in the India Office but returned to Cambridge as a lecturer (1908–15). At age 28 he became editor of the *Economic Journal.* He served on the Indian Currency Commission and at the British Treasury (1915–19), which he represented at the Versailles peace conference. He held advisory positions in British finance, industry, and government, and was appointed director of the Bank of England. He also managed his own business interests, including insurance companies, and was a patron of the theater and arts. In 1944 he led the British delegation at the monetary conference at Bretton Woods, New Hampshire, taking an active part in the establishment of the International Monetary Fund and the International Bank for Reconstruction and Development. His international reputation brought him repeatedly into contact with the president of the U.S. In 1942 he was made Lord Keynes of Tilton.

His most important publications are *Indian Currency and Finance* (1913), *The Economic Consequences of the Peace* (1919), and *The General Theory of Employment, Interest, and Money* (1936).

Keynes revolutionized economic concepts and studies. He himself became the best proof of his thesis that the "ideas of economists and political philosophers are more powerful than it is commonly understood. Indeed, the world is ruled by little else." His influence has extended all over the world, and his era has been called the "Age of Keynes." His friend Austin Robinson describes Keynes' "three independent claims to greatness": Keynes' relinking of the analytical studies of academic economics to administrative problems, his integration of the analytical and statistical approaches, and his insistence on searching out the assumptions that underlie arguments. Keynes' macroeconomics stressed the interdependence of all within an economy and the interdependence of all economies in a shrinking world. He took a human problem, the employment question, as a starting point in his work not for humanitarian reasons but in recognition that this is a basic problem for the well-functioning economy in a modern society.

**John Neville Keynes**
*English Logician and Economist* *1852–1949*

Born in Salisbury, Keynes was educated at University College, London, and Pembroke College, Cambridge. In both of these institutions he became a Fellow. Later he was lecturer in moral science at Cambridge (1884–1911), register, and administrator. From 1908–20 he was chairman of the Special Board for Economics and Politics at Cambridge University. He wrote *Studies and Exercises in Formal Logic* (1884) and *The Scope and Method of Political Economy* (1891), which became a standard work.

Keynes' wife, Florence Brown, one of the first female graduates of Cambridge, became mayor of Cambridge. Their three children distinguished themselves: Geoffrey as a physician and writer; Margaret as a pioneering social worker; and John Maynard as a leading economist.

**Gregory King**
*English Administrator*                                    *1648–1712*

King was registrar of the English College of Arms when he became interested in economic statistics, in particular in population statistics. His book *Natural and Political Observations and Conclusions upon the State and Conditions of England* was written in 1696 but not published until 1801. However, Davenant and Chalmers knew about the manuscript and incorporated some of King's ideas in their books. King clearly implies the elasticity concept in his observations. His main contribution, known as "King's Law," attempts to explain the effect on the price of wheat of a deviation of wheat supply from a normal harvest.

**Wilford Isbell King**
*American Mathematical Economist*                          *1880–1950*

King was born in Douglaston, New York, and studied at the universities of Nebraska and Wisconsin (Ph.D.). Of his many publications, of particular interest are *The Elements of Statistical Methods* (1911), *Exercises in Statistical Methods* (1913), *Employment, Prices and Earnings in Prosperity and Depression* (1923), *Index Numbers Elucidated* (1930), *Causes of Economic Fluctuations* (1938), *Keys to Prosperity* (1948), and *Wealth and Income of the People of the United States* (1915). King was associated with the National Bureau of Economic Research.

**Charles Kingsley**
*English Christian Socialist*                              *1819–1875*

Born in Devonshire, Kingsley became a minister of the Church of England and for a brief time professor of history at Cambridge. He was a successful writer, and his novel *Alton Locke* (1850) has been described as the first socialist fiction written. It revealed the horrors of a journeyman tailor suffering under the sweating system.

In 1850 Kingsley played a leading role in forming a society for promoting workingmen's associations, and this society issued the paper *The Christian Socialist*. In the same year Kingsley published *Cheap Clothes and Nasty*. All these works drew much attention, but a sensation was created in 1851 when in London he preached a sermon saying that it is contrary to the spirit and revelations of Christ to have a social system that enables the few to come into the possession of capital and land that the ancestors of the masses once cultivated; these capitalists now have workers who live in the condition of serfdom. The sermon was later published as *The Church's Message to the Workers*. Kingsley's aim was to awaken the people of his time to a sense of responsibility and duty toward all men.

### Kasper Klock
*German Cameralist*                                    *1584–1655*

Klock studied law at Marburg and Cologne and became an administrator in Bremen and Minden. Later he was in the service of the counts of Stolberg. In 1651 he wrote *Tractus juridico-politico-polemico-historicus de aerario*, which is listed here because it has been called the classic of mercantilism and has been discussed by many authorities. It contains interesting observations on tax policies and public finance. Klock felt that taxes should be leveled according to ability to pay; that is, they should be based on income and wealth.

### Georg Friedrich Knapp
*German Economist*                                    *1842–1926*

Knapp was born in Giessen, educated at Munich, Berlin, and Göttingen, became director of the Statistical Bureau of Leipzig, and was professor at the universities of Leipzig and Strasbourg. As a distinguished member of the younger historical school in Germany, he specialized in agricultural and monetary studies. He wrote *Die Bauernbefreiung und der Ursprung der Landarbeiter* (2 vols., 1887) and *Staatliche Theorie des Geldes* (1905), which was translated into English and appeared in 1924 as *State Theory of Money*. These works have been recognized as first-rank contributions to systematic theoretical studies.

### Karl Knies
*German Economist*                                    *1821–1898*

Born at Marburg, Knies prepared for a teaching profession. He became a member of the so-called older historical school in Germany. He taught with great success at Marburg, Freiburg, and, for 31 years, Heidelberg, where he established a study and research center. He wrote *Geld und Kredit* (3 vols., 1873–79), and *Politische Ökonomie vom geschichtlichen Standpunkte* (1883). He believed that all economic decisions and judgments should take historical changes, social relationships, and institutional developments into account.

### Frank Hyneman Knight
*American Economist*                                    *1885–1972*

Knight was born in Atlanta, Georgia, and studied at Milligan College, the University of Tennessee, and Cornell University (Ph.D.). He taught at Cornell, the State University of Iowa, and the University of Chicago, and in 1950 was president of the American Economic Association. Knight wrote *Risk, Uncertainty, and Profit* (1921), translated Max Weber's *Economic History: The Ethics of Competition and Other Essays* (1935), wrote *Economic Order and Religion* (1945, with Merriam), *Freedom and Reform* (1947), *The Economic Organization* (1951), and *Essays on the History and Method of Economics* (1951).

*German Economist*

**Christian Jacob Kraus**
*1753–1807*

Kraus was born in Osterode, East Prussia. He studied at the University of Königsberg under Kant and became professor of practical philosophy there in 1781. He had an unusually wide and intensive education not only in philosophy but also in the classical languages, history, political science, and mathematics. Not until 1790 did his main interest turn to political economy. Kraus was one of the first in Germany to acclaim Smith's *Wealth of Nations*. He advocated free trade, freedom in industry, elimination of state monopolies, and restriction of government interference. To support such concepts in Prussia at this time was more difficult than in England. His most important book was *Staatswirtschaft* (1807). His lectures, which had inspired a great many students, were published posthumously.

*Russian Anarchist*

**Prince Peter Alexeivich Kropotkin**
*1842–1921*

Kropotkin was born in Moscow, joined the imperial army, and made himself a name as the author of remarkable works in geography and natural history which showed that he was a disciple of Darwin. He abandoned his military career to study at the University of St. Petersburg, but science did not satisfy him. People and politics caught his attention, and he renounced his title and went out of his way to meet, live with, and educate workingmen. Charged with political conspiracy, he was imprisoned. He managed to escape, but a few years later was arrested in France and confined for 3 years for his supposed complicity in an anarchist outbreak in Lyons in 1884. Thereafter, he lived in England, though he visited Russia after the Revolution, despite his opposition to Bolshevism.

Kropotkin's ideas are best expressed in his book *Mutual Aid, a Factor in Evolution* (1902). In his opinion, the state is the root of all evil, and society does not need a government. Government, he felt, should be replaced by cooperative organizations.

# L

### Barthelemy de Laffemas
*French Mercantilist Writer*                                     *1545–1612*

Laffemas was in the service of King Henry IV and became his general controller of trade. He wrote pamphlets in which he proposed developing industries and employing the unemployed in government-sponsored workshops. With the help of additional exports he hoped to increase the country's wealth through the inflow of precious metal, which in his opinion was essential to wealth and power. He also suggested that the export of raw material be prohibited.

### Robert M. La Follette
*American Politician*                                            *1855–1925*

Born in Primrose, Wisconsin, La Follette studied at the State University. As governor of Wisconsin, he introduced reform legislation known as the Wisconsin Idea, putting into effect many of Commons' recommendations. He was later a U.S. senator and in 1924 ran for President on the Progressive Party ticket. One of his sons, Robert M. La Follette, Jr., became a U.S. senator, and another, Philip La Follette, was governor of Wisconsin.

### Harry Wellington Laidler
*American Socialist*                                             *1884–1970*

Laidler was born in Brooklyn, New York, studied at Wesleyan University and Columbia University (Ph.D.), and received a law degree from the Brooklyn Law School. He founded the Intercollegiate Socialist Society (1905) and was the editor of the *Intercollegiate Socialist* (1913–19). Later he became director of the National Bureau of Economic Research and ran unsuccessfully for political office. His many pamphlets and books have had a wide circulation, notably his longer works, *A History of Socialist Thought* (1927) and *Social-Economic Movements* (1945). He also wrote about and propagated the cooperative movements, particularly consumer cooperatives.

### Robert de Lamennais
*French Christian Socialist*                                     *1782–1854*

Born in Saint-Malo, Lamennais was ordained a Catholic priest in 1817, but later became a bitter critic of the Church and a member of an extreme leftist group. Some of his extensive writings were condemned by the Church. He was sentenced to prison, where he died. Lamennais hoped to improve the position of labor through the democratic process, bargaining power, and educational opportunities.

In 1848 he published his ideas on economics in *La question du travail*.

**Carl Landauer**
*American Economist*                                                        *1891–*

Born in Munich, Germany, Landauer studied at Munich, Berlin, and Heidelberg (Ph.D.) and taught at Kiel, Berlin, and the University of California at Berkeley. His book *Theory of National Economic Planning* (1947) is one of the first on national planning theory, a subject he also discusses in his *Comparative Economic Systems* (1964). Another notable work of his is *European Socialism: A History of Ideas and Movements* (1956).

**Oskar Lange**
*Polish Economist and Politician*                                         *1904–1965*

Born in Tomaszow, Poland, Lange studied at Krakow and in the U.S. at the University of California and Stanford University. He taught at Krakow, Michican, California, Stanford, and Chicago universities. At the University of Warsaw he was Rector of the School of Planning and Statistics (1952–55) and in 1955 was appointed professor of economics there. He was Polish ambassador to the U.S. (1945–46), delegate to the U.N. Security Council (1946–47), and, after holding various positions in the party and government, became chairman of the Polish Economic Council (1957–62). He believed that consumers in a socialist country can, after a period of trial and error, obtain what they want and have a free choice if the instruments of production are in public hands. He wrote *On the Economic Theory of Socialism* (1938), *The Coexistence of Two Economic and Social Systems* (1951), *Theory of Statistics* (1952), *Price Flexibility and Employment* (1952) *Introduction to Econometrics* (1958), and *Essays on Economic Learning* (1959).

**Pierre Simon, Marquis de Laplace**
*French Mathematician*                                                     *1749–1827*

Laplace was born in Beaumont-en-Auge, and educated at the military school there. He became professor at the Royal Military School, minister of the interior, and senator. Laplace was Cournot's teacher and made great contributions to probability theory, especially in his works *Théorie analytique des probabilités* (1812) and *Essai philosophique sur les probabilités* (1814). He also did important work in astronomy.

**Harold Joseph Laski**
*English Economist*                                    *1893–1950*

Born in Manchester, England, Laski studied at New College, Oxford, and taught at the London School of Economics and the University of London. He also lectured extensively in America during 1914–20, at Harvard University and McGill University in Montreal. He was chairman of the British Labour Party (1945–46) and a member of the executive committee of the Fabian Society. During the course of his career he changed from a rather pluralistic attitude to purely Marxian socialism. His numerous political writings include *Authority in the Modern State* (1919), *Political Thought from Locke to Bentham* (1930), *Reflections on the Revolution of Our Time* (1943), and *The American Democracy* (1948).

**Ferdinand Lassalle**
*German Socialist*                                    *1825–1864*

Lassalle was born in Breslau and studied at the universities of Breslau and Berlin. He was a brilliant man, strongly influenced by Hegel's philosophy, and an idealist who hoped to establish a socialist industrial system. He founded the German Workers' Association and was the first to speak about "The iron law of wages," defining it as the minimum subsistence pay permitting survival and the raising of children under given conditions. In profit he saw a payment to the capital-owner for abstaining from immediate consumption of his assets. His speeches to the workers have been published. He broke with Marx over the role of government in the solution of social problems. Lassalle was mortally wounded in a duel fought over a lady he intended to marry.

**Theodor Ludwig Lau**
*German Cameralist*                                    *1670–1740*

Lau, of Königsberg, developed and improved the cameralistic ideas of the Austrians. A man with vigor and vision, he recommended the rapid increase of population, going so far as to suggest polygamy. Lau also made new propositions on money and credit.

**James Maitland, 8th Earl of Lauderdale**
*Scottish Statesman*                                    *1759–1839*

Maitland was educated at Oxford and Glasgow. He became a Scottish barrister. He was a member of the House of Commons until he succeeded to the earldom and entered the House of Lords. He began as a Whig, but became a reactionary in later life, voting against the Reform Bill of 1832. He was sent by the British government on various missions to foreign countries.

Lauderdale disagreed with Adam Smith, believing that private and public interest are not necessarily always in harmony, that national wealth is not only the sum of individual wealth, and that the values a country has to offer go far beyond those that Smith seemed to admit. He stressed invention as the most important factor for capital formation and stated that savings do not automatically improve a nation's wealth. His most important book is *An Inquiry into the Nature and Origin of Public Wealth* (1804). He also wrote *The Depreciation of the Paper Currency of Great Britain Proved* (1812) and *Letter on the Corn Law* (1814.). Lauderdale overemphasized national viewpoints in reaction to Adam Smith, and is often called a founder of the Nationalist School. He felt that money must be spent to be useful and offered a sound theory on profit.

James Laurence Laughlin
*American Economist*                                                      *1850–1933*

Born in Deerfield, Ohio, Laughlin studied at Harvard (Ph.D.) and taught there until he became president of the Manufacturers' Mutual Insurance Company of Philadelphia (1888). He was appointed professor of political economy at Cornell (1890) and chairman of the department of political economy at the University of Chicago (1892). His extensive writings include *A History of Bimetallism in the United States* (1886), *Money and Prices* (2 vols., 1919), and *Exposition of Money, Credit, and Prices* (1931). He was editor of the *Journal of Political Economy* from 1892–1933.

Laughlin did important work in 1897 in the commission report on banking and monetary reform for the city of Indianapolis. He was also influential in the National Citizen's League, which helped prepare the way for the adoption of the Federal Reserve System in 1913. It was Laughlin who arranged a scholarship for Thorstein Veblen when Veblen arrived penniless at Cornell, and who helped Veblen obtain a teaching fellowship at Chicago.

Wilhelm Launhardt
*German Mathematical Economist*                              *1832–1918*

Launhardt, born in Hanover, was professor at the Technological Institute of Hanover where he had studied. He taught the economics of Jevons and Walras, to which he added some original contributions. In 1885 he wrote *Mathematische Begründung der Volkswirtschaftslehre,* in which he offered a mathematical interpretation of the ideas of the Austrian School. Launhardt was a prominent exponent of the mathematical method in economics during his time. In a study of railroad costs he came to the conclusion that in the interest of the public, maximum charges should be equal to marginal cost, and he used this same argument in pleading for government ownership of railroads.

**Emile de Laveleye**
*Belgian Economist*
*1822–1892*

Born in Bruges, Laveleye became a professor at Liège. He wrote *De la Propriété et de ses formes primitives* (1873), *Le Socialisme contemporain* (1881), and *Eléments d'économie politique* (1882), which was later translated into English with an introduction by Taussig. In his teaching, Lavaleye belonged to the so-called academic socialists. He believed that all property was originally community property and that government intervention in the interest of the common good is necessary. He also advocated international bimetallism.

**John Law**
*Scottish Financier*
*1671–1729*

Law, the son of a goldsmith and banker, was born and educated in Edinburgh. He was widely traveled and well acquainted with financial institutions. In consequence of a love affair he shot his opponent in a duel and was sentenced to life imprisonment but managed to escape to Amsterdam. Returned to Scotland 10 years later, he proposed starting a land bank in which notes would be backed by the value of the state's land property, but the idea was rejected by the Scottish Parliament. Law then had the fortune to meet the Duke of Orléans, then regent of France. With his permission, Law founded the Banque Générale, which after 2 years became the Banque Royale. The bank had a monopoly on note circulation. The notes were backed by royal revenue and landed securities. At first they were redeemable in silver; later this was discontinued. For a while the plan was a complete success and could have been expected to remain so had the spirit of this brilliant promoter not wandered off into new ideas. Law established the Mississippi Company for the development of Louisiana (1717), inviting frantic speculation which was intensified when Law was made director general of French finances (1720). The Mississippi bubble burst, more for psychological than economic reasons. Law was forced to resign and barely managed to escape from France. He went to Belgium but in 1725 moved to Italy where he died, occupied to the end with original schemes.

Law's contributions to monetary theory are contained in his tract *Money and Trade Considered, with a Proposal for Supplying the Nation with Money* (1st ed. 1705, 2nd ed. 1720). Although he is considered a dreamer, he possessed more insight into economic matters than most of his predecessors. A mercantilist, he believed that a nation's wealth depends on commerce, and "commerce depends on specie," or gold and silver. Both metals were scarce in the expanding economies of his time. His idea of substituting paper money for specie, secured by the value of the nation's land, would have resulted in an increase in money and stimulation of the economy without price increase, given a proper management of the paper currency. Despite the failure of his scheme, he became the ancestor of the idea of managed currency.

*German Socialist*

**Emil Lederer**
*1882–1939*

Lederer was born in Pilsen. In spite of his saying that the propositions of economics are unverifiable and irrefutable, Lederer made considerable contributions in detailed studies concerning technical progress and employment. In the 1920's he was the leading academic socialist in Germany. He was a professor at Heidelberg, Mannheim, and Berlin, and during the last few years of his life at the New School for Social Research in New York. His attitude in regard to business cycles is clearly demonstrated in his *Grundzüge der ökonomischen Theorie* (1922), *Konjunktur und Krisen* (1925), and *Technischer Fortschritt und Arbeitslosigkeit* (1938). Lederer offered a modified underconsumption theory of business cycles.

*Russian Communist*

**Vladimir Ilyich Lenin**
*1870–1924*

Lenin, whose original name was Ulyanov, was born in Simbirsk (now Ulyanovsk) as the son of a school inspector. He studied law and foreign languages at the universities of Kazan and St. Petersburg. He gave up legal practice to devote his life to fighting autocracy, landowners, the bourgeoisie, and all "exploiters" of the working classes. When he was 17 his brother Alexander was executed, charged with plotting the murder of the tsar. This left a great imprint on the mind of Vladimir. Twice he was exiled to Siberia but each time managed to leave Russia. He was a disciple of Marx, and in his own words only wanted to put Marx's ideas into reality in Russia. All his studies and work were directed toward achieving this purpose. He realized that Marx wrote for the proletariat of developed industrial countries, whereas he had to apply these ideas in a principally agrarian country with conditions like those in most underdeveloped areas of the world. He became the founder of Bolshevik Russia, established under the "dictatorship of the proletariat," and created the Union of Soviet Socialist Republics. His books were exclusively political. He condemned non-Marxist economists as unable to understand the basic problems of economics and opposed any revision of the Marxian doctrine. His writings include *The Development of Capitalism in Russia* (1899) and *Imperialism, the Highest Stage of Capitalism* (1917).

*Pope*

**Leo XIII**
*1810–1903*

Gioacchino Vincenzo Pecci was born in Carpinetto (near Anagni), studied at the Jesuit College at Viterbo and at Collegio Romano for the priesthood. Elected pope in 1878, he became the leading Christian social reformer in his time. During his long reign he issued 8 encyclicals dealing with questions of social justice, the most outstanding being *Rerum Novarum* (The Condition of the Working Classes, 1891). Leo defended private property but warned against abusing it. Although he opposed socialism, particularly the concept of class struggle, he condemned the exploitation of the working man and demanded Christian justice from employers. He also called on governments to help and protect the poor and weak and to promote social justice. To him, in the proper form of society the interest of the community comes before that of individuals, and the sense of brotherhood guides economic relationships. He criticized unrestricted individualism and profit in the market economy, believing that economic life should be governed by a consideration for human value and dignity.

**Le Pesant**
see Pierre le Pesant, Sieur de *Boisguillebert*

**P. G. Frédéric Le Play**
*French Social Reformer*                     *1806–1882*

Born at Le Havre, Le Play was by profession a mathematician and mining engineer who became a professor of metallurgy at the L'Ecole des Mines and a counselor of the state. His ideas on social reform were largely related to wage earners' family budgets. He recommended that the role of the family as a social unit be enforced and increased, that there be greater freedom of bequest, and that the role of the employer be extended beyond the mere cash nexus. Le Play denounced what he called the "false dogmas of '89," i.e., the error, promulgated during the French Revolution, that man would enjoy peace and happiness as an automatic result of the conditions of the "free society" without any personal effort. No society could hope to survive by being content with the rules of natural law, which would mean, in Le Play's opinion, to be ruled by the instincts of the brute. In 1856 Le Play founded La Société d'Economie Sociale, which published a fortnightly review, *Réforme sociale*. His book *Les Ouvriers européens* (1855) was based on case studies of the lives of 300 families over 12 years, and his *La Réforme sociale* (1864) has been described as the most original, useful, and courageous book of the century.

**Le Prestre**
see Sébastien Le Prestre, Seigneur de *Vauban*

**Pierre Leroux**
*French Social Philosopher*                     *1797–1871*

Leroux was born in Paris. He became chief editor of the *Revue encyclopédique* (62 vols., 1819–33). He founded the magazine *Le Globe*, which served the Saint-Simonian movement from 1831 on. Later he and Bazard broke with this movement, disagreeing with Enfantin's ideas on marriage. In 1848 he was a member of the Constituent Assembly and in 1849 a member of the Legislative Assembly. For political reasons he was exiled, but returned at the collapse of the Empire. Leroux had a great influence upon his countrymen, and was honored by a state funeral. He lived simply and modestly throughout his life. Sincere in all that he did or wrote, in his private life he set an excellent example. He stood steadfastly for equality, saw in individualism an evil and in property a sin, and believed that only collectivism could promote the welfare of all. In spite of his socialistic ideas, for him the existence of God was an absolute fact. Among his numerous articles, the most memorable is "Malthus et les économistes, ou y aura-t-il toujours des pauvres?" (1849). It was he who introduced the term "socialism."

**Paul Leroy-Beaulieu**
*French Economic Journalist*                                      *1843–1916*

Born in Saumur, Leroy-Beaulieu studied in Paris, Bonn, and Berlin and spent many of his early years in England. At age 24 he won first prize in a contest with his essay, "Morality and Its Influence on Wage Rates." He was a landowner and practicing farmer as well as professor of public finance at the Ecole Libre des Sciences Politique and of political economy at the Collège de France. He edited journals and in 1873 founded the *Economiste Français*, a weekly paper to which he also contributed. His books *Essai sur la répartition des richesses* (1881) and *Traité d' Économie politique* (1895) drew considerable attention. A supporter of economic liberalism, Leroy-Beaulieu has been recognized as a brilliant man. In his contention that the mathematical method is "pure delusion and a hollow mockery" and that it "has no scientific foundation and is of no practical use," however, he went counter to the trend in modern writings on economics.

**Thomas E. Cliffe Leslie**
*Irish Economist*                                      *1827–1882*

Born in Wexford and educated at William's College in Dublin, the University of Dublin, and Trinity College, Dublin, Leslie was one of the first to use the historical method in economics. He rejected the deductive approach of British economists. His comparative study, *Land Systems and Industrial Economy of Ireland, England, and Continental Countries* (1870), and his *Essay in Political and Moral Philosophy* (1879) are excellent. Leslie criticized the classics as narrow-minded and one-sided in accepting the profit motive as the only factor leading to economic activity. He also attacked the cost-of-production theory, which in his opinion does not apply to the national economy as such.

## Guillaume Francis Le Trosne
*French Jurist and Physiocrat*      *1728–1780*

Born in Orléans, Le Trosne was a member of the group that called itself "les économistes" under the leadership of Quesnay, presently known as the Physiocrats. He was mainly interested in the natural-law aspects of the physiocratic system. In the field of economics he embraced the school's orthodoxy with some reservations. His *Liberté du commerce des grains* (1765) is of some importance.

## Emile Levasseur
*French Historical Economist*      *1828–1911*

Levasseur was born in Paris. He made an outstanding contribution to economic and social history with his description of the conditions of the French laboring classes in *Histoire des classes ouvrières en France* (1859).

## Hermann Levy
*German Economist*      *1881–1935*

Levy was professor of economics at Jena. He wrote *Die Grundlagen des ökonomischen Liberalismus in der Geschichte der englischen Volkswirtschaft* (1912) and *Industrial Germany* (1935), dealing with cartels, trusts, and monopoly problems.

## Leone Levy
*English Economist and Businessman*      *1821–1888*

Levy was born in Ancona, Italy, but at an early date went to Liverpool and became an English citizen. An active businessman, in 1849 he wrote a pamphlet, *Chambers and Tribunals of Commerce*, which helped in the foundation of a Liverpool chamber of commerce. Other cities, including London, followed suit. Levy became professor of commercial law at King's College in London after he had published a very successful book, *Commercial Law: Its Principles and Administration* (1852). He was free-trader and documented his ideas with much statistical material.

## Wilhelm Lexis
*German Statistician*      *1837–1914*

Born in Eschweiler, Lexis was professor of political economy at the universities of Strassburg, Freiburg, Breslau, and Göttingen. He was in the front line of the critics when the third volume of Marx's *Das Kapital* was published. He also wrote about monetary policy, foreign trade, and Gossen's second law. But his interests were predominantly with the theory of statistics. He published interesting statistical material in *Einleitung in die Theorie der Bevölkerungspolitik* (1875).

### Richard Lieben
*Austrian Banker*                          *1842–1919*

Born in Vienna, Lieben was educated at the polytechnic schools of Vienna and Karlsruhe and became a banker and vice-president of the Academy of Commerce. Together with Rudolf Auspitz he wrote *Untersuchungen über die Theorie des Preises* (1887, 1889), acclaimed as one of the greatest theoretical contributions of the time. Lieben saw price theory as the central problem of political economy and mathematical economics. He was also in favor of the gold standard.

### Wilhelm Liebknecht
*German Socialist*                          *1826–1900*

Wilhelm Liebknecht was born in Giessen, studied at the universities of Giessen, Bonn, and Marburg, and founded, together with Bebel, the Marxist German Social Democratic Party. Under the anti-socialist laws of Bismarck, Liebknecht was imprisoned for 2 years. He became chief editor of the socialist newspaper *Vorwärts* and a member of the Reichstag from 1874–1919. In 1892 he published *Robert Owen*.

### Karl Liebknecht
*German Socialist*                          *1871–1919*

The son of Wilhelm Liebknecht, Karl Liebknecht was born in Leipzig. From 1912–16 he served in the Reichstag as a radical-wing member of the Social Democratic Party. During World War I he refused to support the government, and with Rosa Luxemburg he founded the Spartacus Party, the forerunner of the German Communist Party. After the unsuccessful Spartacist revolt in 1919 he was arrested and murdered along with Luxemburg before reaching prison. Karl Liebknecht did not accept the theory of labor value but established his own concept on the basis of modern value theory.

### Robert Liefmann
*German Economist*                          *1874–1941*

Liefmann, born in Hanover, was professor of economics at the University of Freiburg. His pioneering studies on capitalistic organization forms, *Die Unternehmerverbände* (1897), *Die Unternehmungsformen* (1912), and especially *Kartelle, Konzerne und Trusts* (1919), brought him fame. His book *Grundsätze der Volkswirtschaftslehre* (1920) attempts to offer a value-free economic system based on psychological considerations.

**Erik Lindahl**
*Swedish Economist*                                    *1891–1960*

Lindahl was a student of Wicksell and made considerable contributions to monetary theory and equilibrium analysis. Of his numerous writings, *The Means of Monetary Policy* (1930) and *Studies in the Theory of Money and Capital* (1939) are significant.

**Simon N. H. Linguet**
*French Journalist*                                    *1736–1794*

Linguet was born in Reims. A prolific writer, he covered many fields, was a barrister and an opponent of the Physiocrats. He took part in many controversies. Of interest is his *Théories des loix civiles* (1767), a challenging book dealing with the enslavement of the masses. It was considered to be an attack on Montesquieu. Linguet was executed during the French Revolution.

**Friedrich List**
*German Economist*                                    *1789–1846*

Born in Reutlingen, List was at an early age employed in public service. He used his time for study and reading, had an opportunity to attend lectures, and was finally appointed professor of administration and politics at the University of Tübingen. His part in publishing a liberal newspaper made him unpopular with a highly conservative administration, and he lost his professorship, was excluded from the Württemberg parliament, and was arrested. After serving a 9–month prison term, he went to America. There he joined Lafayette, befriended the Careys, and became one of the central figures in favor of protectivism and nationalism. His lectures appeared under the title *Outline of American Political Economy* (1827). Discovering coal on his property, he became a mine owner and the builder of a railroad, accumulating a fortune. But his mind was still with his home country, and in 1832 he returned to Germany as American consul at Leipzig. List advocated the formation of a customs union to strengthen the German states economically, but he was ahead of his time and failed in his efforts. In despair, he committed suicide. His masterwork is *Das nationale System der politischen Ökonomie* (1841). List included in the concept of productivity certain efforts of the national economy that do not become evident in the market, like administration, education, communication, and legal order. He also developed a system of economic evolution in stages.

**Rev. William Foster Lloyd**
*English Economist*                                    *1795–1852*

Lloyd was born in Gloucestershire. He studied at Westminster and at Christ Church, Oxford, where he became a reader in Greek, lecturer in mathematics, and later professor of political economy. He was elected to the Royal Society. He saw the value problem from the viewpoints of utility and exchange. Lloyd's lectures (on population, value, rent, and the Poor Laws) were published in 1837 as *Lectures on the Notion of Value*.

**John Locke**
*English Philosopher and Political Theorist*          *1632–1704*

Born in Somersetshire, Locke was educated at Christ Church, Oxford, where he was also a tutor. He entered the civil service and became a member of the Board of Trade. He had to leave England because he supported the opposition to James II, but returned after William III became king.

Locke broke with the scholastic tradition and advocated tolerance, liberty, and extended education. In his *Essay concerning Human Understanding* (1690) and *Two Treatises on Government* (1689) he stressed the idea of natural rights. His writings exercised great influence upon the founders of the U.S.

Locke's hedonistic philosophy furnished the psychological basis for the classical economics of Adam Smith. Human happiness Locke supposed to consist of the satisfaction of wants; and men, as rational beings, he believed to be able to determine which goods are sources of happiness for them. To propose that consumers be made kings, i.e. the determining factors, and producers be free to produce goods wanted by consumers was a logical conclusion from Locke's philosophy.

Locke had a deep understanding of economic concepts, as evidenced in his *Some Considerations of the Consequences of Lowering the Interest and Raising the Value of Money* (1691). His specific economic contribution was in monetary theory. He denied the intrinsic value of money, introducing the idea of its subjective value. Also, economic theory owes to him the first, albeit hesitant, enunciation of an improved quantity theory of money. Not only did he introduce the idea that the velocity of circulation affects the price level, he also proposed the volume-of-trade idea: that an increase in the supply of goods when there iș an unchanged demand for them in money makes for a fall in prices. Though his successors formulated the theory more precisely, there was substantially little that remained to be added.

**Francis Davy Longe**
*English Lawyer*          *1831–1910*

Longe, an Oxford graduate and a lawyer, was in the service of the government. He was interested in the labor movement and labor organizations. He opposed the wage-fund theory and published *A Refutation of the Wage Fund Theory of Modern Political Economy as Enunciated by Mr. Mill, M.P.* (1866).

**Samuel Mountifort Longfield**
*Irish Economist and Jurist*                    *1802–1884*

Longfield was born in Dublin and became the first professor of political economy at Trinity College, Dublin. His writings include *Lectures on Political Economy* (1834). He dealt with the entire known economic theory and produced his own system of exposition. He rejected the labor theory of value, the wage-fund theory, and the idea that an increase of population automatically means lower wages. He also contributed to the theory of distribution and the theory of international trade. His views on interest and capital are unusually valuable, anticipating later doctrinal developments.

**Achille Loria**
*Italian Economist*                    *1857–1943*

Loria was born in Mantua and studied at Bologna, Rome, Berlin, and London. He was appointed to the faculties of the universities of Siena and later of Padua, and from 1902–32 he was professor of economics at the University of Turin. Outstanding among his publications is *Annalisi della proprietà capitalista* (1889), which was translated into many languages, including English (as *The Economic Foundations of Society*, 1914). Loria was basically a historical economist. He attached great importance to the idea of free land, in which he saw an essential influence on economic development and capital formation; in fact, this concept became the keynote of all his writings on economics. He felt that land became the property of the powerful by means of force and that ownership of land by the wealthy robbed the workers of their independence. Many of Loria's ideas are similar to those of Franz Oppenheimer. Loria's book *La sintesi economica* (1909) gives his philosophy of life.

**August Lösch**
*German Economist*                    *1906–1945*

Lösch, born in Öhringen, Württemberg, studied at Tübingen, Kiel, Freiburg, and Bonn. Lösch made himself a name with *Die räumliche Ordnung der Wirtschaft* (1940), an equilibrium approach and a model of space-economy under imperfect competition. Thus, Lösch made a remarkable contribution to the location theory and "Raumwirtschaft."

**Adolph Lowe**
*American Economist*                    *1893–*

Lowe, born in Stuttgart, Germany, studied in Munich, Berlin (LL.D.), and Tübingen. After several years in the civil service of the Weimar Republic he taught at the universities of Kiel and Frankfurt. Dismissed from his professorship by the Nazi government, Lowe became a special lecturer at the University of Manchester. He has been professor at the New School for Social Research since 1941. Lowe wrote *Economics and Sociology* (1935) and *On Economic Knowledge* (1965). He also wrote *The Price of Liberty* (London, 1937). Lowe made the circular-flow principle the center of his thought, stressed the dynamic force of technical progress, and described fluctuations and cycles in connection with economic transformation.

**Loyd**
see Samuel Jones Loyd, Lord *Overstone*

**Juan de Lugo**
*Spanish Cardinal*                                                       *1583–1660*

Lugo was a late scholastic who interpreted Aquinas' "prudent economic reason" as condoning every lawful way of gaining by economic activities or transactions. He clearly stated that business profit is justified as a payment for rendered social services. He also noticed that goods in themselves have no utility.

**Erik Lundberg**
*Swedish Economist*                                                            *1895–*

Lundberg was born in Stockholm and went to the university there. His main works, *Studies in the Theory of Economic Expansion* (1937) and *Business Cycles and Economic Policy* (1957), are among the best contributions of the Stockholm School. Lundberg saw in monetary policy a much better instrument for stabilizing the economy than fiscal policy, especially in a free market system. He stressed the delay in the adjustment of consumer-goods production when demand changes. This has been called "Lundberg-Lag."

**Martin Luther**
*German Church Reformer*                                                 *1483–1546*

Born at Eisleben as son of a miner, Luther studied at Erfurt, became an Augustinian friar, and ultimately was the founder of German Protestantism. He upheld the economic teaching of the Scholastics in regard to usury, just price, and interest. Stressing the authority of princes and governments to rule over economic matters, he felt that everybody has the duty to work and to be obedient.

**Rosa Luxemburg**
*German Socialist*                                                       *1870–1919*

Rosa Luxemburg was born in Russian Poland. A brilliant speaker and writer, she became a leader in the German Social Democratic Party. During World War I she and Karl Liebknecht founded the radical

Spartacus Party, and she was placed in protective custody by the government. On her release in 1918 she helped transform the Spartacus Party into the German Communist Party. She and Liebknecht were arrested after an uprising in 1919 and on the way to jail became the victims of political murder.

Most of her works were published posthumously in 1925, but her most important book, *Die Akkumulation des Kapitals*, appeared in 1913. Here she stated that capitalism could survive only as long as the capitalist market could be expanded. As soon as the pre-capitalist markets of the world were absorbed into the capitalist orbit, the system would fail and automatically come to an end. She believed that the downfall of capitalism was imminent. In 1917 a second book appeared under the same title but with the subtitle *Was die Epigonen aus der Marxschen Theorie gemacht haben.*

# M

**Gabriel Bonnot de Mably**
*French Socialist*                                            *1709–1785*

Born in Grenoble to aristocratic parents, Mably entered a seminary but left after receiving the subdiaconate and joined the staff of Cardinal de Tencin, who was foreign minister. Mably severely attacked the Physiocrats, whom he called greedy and foolish. He also disapproved of landed property and finally declared all private property as evil and the source of all ills. Science, arts, and industry were for him elements of corruption and decadence. Mably had clearly communistic inclinations and was a forerunner of the French Revolution. Of his many books, one must be noted here: *Doutes proposés aux philosophes économistes sur l'ordre naturel et essentiel de sociétés politiques* (1768).

**Niccolò Machiavelli**
*Italian Statesman and Political Writer*                        *1469–1527*

Born in Florence, Machiavelli was for 20 years a leading statesman in the Florentine republic. His ideas, best expressed in his book *The Prince* (1512), have had a tremendous influence on political and economic thought. He was convinced that politics should be formulated free from ethical or theological influences. Morality should be the guide for private conduct, but the strong ruler is justified in using all means necessary to keep the state in sound condition. A state must expand or perish.

**Henry Dunning MacLeod**
*Scottish Banker*                                               *1821–1902*

MacLeod was born in Edinburgh and studied mathematics at Trinity College, Cambridge. Later, he became a lawyer and established the first poor-law union in Scotland. He was appointed director of the Royal British Bank in 1854 and immediately turned his interest toward economics, remedying his lack of formal training in this field by an extensive study of theoretical economics and economic history. In 1855 he published *Theory and Practice of Banking*, which was widely read and went through 5 editions. Dissatisfied with the economic literature, in particular the classics, in 1857 MacLeod published *Elements of Political Economy*, declaring that economics should be a science of exchange, dealing exclusively with exchange value. He stated that the general laws of exchange or principles of commerce remain the same over time and space and will remain so in the future; he concluded that economics should be both a moral and a physical science, since it can be conducted with the exactitude of the physical sciences. Value, in his opinion, is not a quality of an object, but a product of the mind, relating something external with the individual; and the decision to obtain the external creates the demand. Only when demand is created does economics become involved; it has no business going into the psychological explanation of demand. Nevertheless, he took immaterial items into account when speaking about exchangeability and wealth, and clearly declared that it is an error to limit the concept of wealth to material goods. He favored free trade. In 1862, vol. 1 of his *Dictionary of Political Economy* appeared (a contemplated vol. 2 never followed). He also published *Lectures on Credit and Banking* (1882), *The Theory of Credit* (1894), *History of Economics* (1896), and *Indian Currency* (1898). He was the first to describe in detail how bank credit is created.

The academic profession remained cool to MacLeod, and his dream of becoming a university professor was never realized. His work found greater acceptance on the Continent than at home.

**Magnus**
see *Albertus Magnus*

**Sir Henry James Sumner Maine**
*English Jurist*                                              *1822–1888*

Maine was born in Hancepassed, Jersey. Educated at Pembroke College, Cambridge, Maine was a professor of civil law at Cambridge from 1847–54, and also lectured on law at the Inns of Court in London. During 1863–69 he helped codify Indian law and was vice-chancellor of Calcutta University. In 1869 he was made the first professor of historical and comparative jurisprudence at Oxford, and from 1887 he taught international law at Cambridge. He is known for his book *Ancient Law* (1861), a pioneering study of comparative law that showed how ancient ideas, as reflected in the laws of the time, have influenced the basic concepts of modern thought. His work had an impact on both political theory and anthropology, and inspired Leslie and Bagehot in the same way Savigny inspired the German historical economists. Also interesting are Maine's *Early History of Institutions* (1875) and *Dissertations on Early Law and Custom* (1883).

**Maitland**
see James Maitland, 8th Earl of *Lauderdale*

**Nicolas de Malebranche**
*French Philosopher*                                          *1638–1715*

Born in Paris, Malebranche became a priest and a follower of Descartes. He believed that God is the cause of all, matter and mind. His influence as the leading philosopher of his time brought a dash of idealism into Physiocracy and counteracted the influence of Helvétius.

**Malines**
see Gerard de *Malynes*

*English Economist*                                   **Thomas Robert Malthus**
                                                           *1766–1834*

Born in Surrey, Thomas Robert Malthus was the son of Daniel Malthus, a highly respected country gentleman and lawyer. He studied at Cambridge and became a curate in the Church of England. He married when nearly 40 and the following year, in 1805, became a professor at the College of Haileybury, newly founded by the East India Company. He was much admired by his students, who affectionately called him "Pop."

His famous *Essay on the Principle of Population as It Affects the Future Improvement of Society* arose from a friendly disagreement and many discussions with his father. It was published anonymously in 1798 and created a sensation. Malthus vigorously denied the notion that there is no limit to the progress of mankind in wealth and happiness. He claimed indirectly that the irrational actions of man are obstacles in the way of progress and that neither self-interest nor sexual instinct can be managed sufficiently to clear the way. Population will outgrow food supply. He did not mean his pamphlet to be a scientific work, but public reaction to it prompted him to try to prove his case more scientifically. He traveled through France, Switzerland, Russia, and Scandinavia to collect historical and statistical material and in 1803 published an enlarged edition of the *Essay*, this time under his name. The work attracted wide attention and has had great influence ever since.

Malthus' other economic works have only recently achieved the prominence they deserve. His *Principles of Political Economy* (1820) deals with price, profit, rent, supply and demand, use and exchange values, diminishing return, labor, labor value, cost of production, business cycles, return, and wealth. Despite its high quality, it was overshadowed by Ricardo's *Principles*. Malthus also wrote *The Measure of Value* (1823) and *Definitions in Political Economy* (1827).

Malthus and Ricardo had many disagreements but respected each other highly. Eleven days before his death Ricardo wrote to Malthus "these discussions however never influence our friendship; I should not like you more than I do if you agreed in opinion with me."

*English Mercantilist*                          **Gerard de Malynes (or Malines)**
                                                           *1586–1641*

Malynes was born in Antwerp of English parents. The family moved back to England. As master of the Mint he was often invited to advise the government in foreign trade matters. In *A Treatise on the Canker of England's Commonwealth* (1601) he explained the automatic mechanism of foreign exchange: how, if a country's currency falls below its mint par value, causing an outflow of coins, prices will fall in that country and rise abroad. He also wrote *The Maintenance of Free Trade* (1622), *The Center of the Circle of Commerce* (1623), and other pamphlets. He favored the prohibition of bullion export. He urged the government to control the exchange dealings of private financiers, whose transactions he believed not only caused gold to flow out of the country, but also raised the interest rate, leading to a contraction of the country's economic activity. It has been said that he was the first English writer to use the concept of natural law.

### Bernard de Mandeville
*Dutch Physician*     *1670–1733*

The son of a physician in Rotterdam, Mandeville studied medicine at Leiden. He spent much of his life in England, where he married. In 1705 he published a satire, *The Grumbling Hive, or Knaves Turned Honest*, which was expanded and republished as the *Fable of the Bees; or, Private Vices, Publick Benefits* (1714). The expanded 1723 edition was branded a public nuisance by the grand jury of Middlesex; yet the *Fable of the Bees* survived and has been read widely ever since. Mandeville saw private vices like avarice, selfishness, and spending (instead of saving) as contributions to public welfare since expenditure generates income. Human greed, tempered not by altruism but by justice, he saw as beneficial to society and progress. He advocated laissez-faire and the division of labor. In a satiric way he was expressing what Adam Smith later advanced in his *Wealth of Nations*.

### Hans Karl Emil von Mangoldt
*German Economist*     *1824–1868*

Mangoldt was born in Dresden. He studied at Leipzig, Geneva, and Tübingen. He became professor at Göttingen and Freiburg. Two of his works deserve notice: *Die Lehre vom Unternehmergewinn* (1855), explaining profit as rent of differential ability, and *Grundriss der Volkswirtschaftslehre* (1863). In the latter he contributed to the evolution of economics as a science and gave the method of partial analysis a stronger application. He was a theorist of considerable merit.

### Thomas Manley
*English Mercantilist Writer*     *1628–1690*

From 1672 until his death Manley was a member of the bar and the King's council. He took an active part in public affairs (advocated preventive war against France), wrote about religious subjects, and favored the use of English instead of Latin in legal literature. His work *Usury at Six Per Cent Examined* (1669) is of interest to economists. In it, he argued with Culpeper and Child, which may remind one of the modern debates among economists. He made a good point when he said in defense of high interest rates, "it is the scarcity of money that makes the high interest rate."

**Paul J. Mantoux**
*French Historian*                                                                1877–1956

Mantoux, who was born in Paris and attended L'Ecole Normale Supérieure, is mentioned here because of his *The Industrial Revolution in the Eighteenth Century* which appeared in French in 1905 and was translated into English in 1927. Well versed in economic literature, particularly that of the 18th century, Mantoux came to the conclusion that the industrial revolution was mainly the consequence of greater division of labor, newer production devices, and the widening of markets. Mantoux found that it was foremostly the American Revolution and not the writings of Smith that demonstrated the decay of the traditional political economy. The war proved that prosperous colonies could revolt and proved the uselessness of a protective tariff. He supported his call for free trade also by citing the urgent need of British merchants and manufacturers for new markets, and the high price of grain, which had been caused by protectionism.

**Mao Tse-Tung**
*Chinese Communist Leader*                                                    1893–

Mao, born in the province of Hunan, joined the revolutionary forces and is credited with new contributions to the socialist theory. His revisions are more radical than those of the Russians. He demanded self-sacrifice for the public cause and called for continuing the class struggle after the takeover by the socialists to avoid corruption and selfishness. He published *Selected Works* (4 vols., 1961).

**Mar**
see Alexander *Del Mar*

**Jane Marcet**
*English Writer*                                                                  1769–1858

Mrs. Marcet wrote about political economy in the form of tales easily understood by housewives. *Conversations on Political Economy* (1816) was a great success and went through 7 editions. She claimed that it is the workers' "industry" that makes the profits. For Mrs. Marcet, the truth about economics and economic policy was already well established and fully comprehended. She also published *Johns Hopkins'*

*Notions on Political Economy* (1833); *Rich and Poor* (1851), in which she said that the rich are friends, not enemies, of the poor; and books on chemistry and philosophy.

**Marlo**
see Karl Georg *Winkelblech*

**Alfred Marshall**
*English Economist*                                                1842–1924

Marshall was born in Clapham, near London, and studied mathematics at St. John's College, Cambridge. He developed an interest in philosophy and social disciplines, and to study Kant in the original language, he visited Germany, where he also met German economists of the historical school. Thus Marshall came to speak 5 languages and be well acquainted with philosophy, mathematics, anthropology, psychology, and history as well as economics, finance, and politics. He taught moral science briefly at St. John's, visited the U.S. and in 1877 married Mary Paley. He became principal of the University College, Bristol. He taught a year at Oxford and then became professor of political economy at Cambridge (1885–1908), succeeding Fawcett.

In 1879 in collaboration with his wife he published *Economics of Industry*. His *Principles of Economics* (1891) established his reputation. His other masterpieces, *Industry and Trade* (1919) and *Money, Credit, and Commerce* (1923), appeared late although they were actually written much earlier, for Marshall subjected his manuscripts to much revision. His pupil J. M. Keynes collected other writings by him in *Official Papers by Alfred Marshall* (1926).

Marshall founded the Neo-Classical School of economics and introduced the term "economics" to replace "political economy." In his *Principles*, which was the leading textbook for many decades, the classical notions of cost of production were integrated with the marginal utility principle. Marshall introduced the time factor as an element of analysis, elasticity of demand, consumer surplus, quasi-rent, and many other concepts now common in economic science. He also helped establish the application of quantitative analysis and used money as the measurement standard of utility.

Marshall was drawn to economics by his interest in social ethics and his fundamentally religious nature, and all his studies were motivated by the desire to improve social relations. His personality impressed itself on many students, such as Pigou, Robertson, and Keynes.

John Maynard Keynes wrote a biography of Mary Paley Marshall (1850–1944) praising her understanding and support for her husband's work, her activity at Newnham College as first woman lecturer of economics at Cambridge, and her part in the development of the Marshall Library of Economics at Cambridge during the last 20 years of her life, during which she also wrote *What I Remember* (1942).

**Cognetti de Martiis**
*Italian Economist*                                           *1844–1891*

Martiis was a representative of the younger historical school of economists, and has been called a sociological economist. He wrote *Le Forme primitive dell'evoluzione economica* (1881).

**Harriet Martineau**
*English Writer*                                              *1802–1876*

Born in Norwich, Miss Martineau was deafened in early childhood and was an invalid for much of her life. But she wrote voluminously, promulgating religious liberalism and the abolition of slavery, and popularizing the work of classical economists like Malthus and Ricardo. Her *Illustrations of Political Economy* (25 vols., 1832–34) was a tremendous success, selling tens of thousands of copies in an era when the new economic science had conquered the public imagination. Also notable are her *Poor Laws and Paupers Illustrated* (10 vols., 1833–34) and *Illustrations of Taxation* (5 vols., 1834). Later in life she espoused a more utopian view of society, and popularized the positivist philosophy of Comte.

**Karl Heinrich Marx**
*German Socialist*                                            *1818–1883*

Born in Trier, Marx was the son of a well-established lawyer. It was intended that he pursue law, and for a year he did so at the University of Bonn. Then he studied philosophy and history at Berlin and received the Ph.D. at Jena. Unable to find a teaching position because of his radical opinions, he became editor of the *Rheinische Zeitung* in Cologne. The paper was suppressed by the government, and in 1843 Marx fled with his wife, Jenny von Westphalen, to Paris, where he became editor of the *Franco-German Yearbook*. Here he met Engels, who became his close friend and supporter. Marx's contact with the French socialists, including Proudhon, was to lead to the publication of his *Misère de la philosophie* (1847), in which he criticized Proudhon severely. Prussian government protests about his periodicals forced him to leave Paris for Brussels in 1845. A worker association, the League of the Just, with numerous branches on the Continent and also in London, requested Marx and Engels to write a program, which appeared in January, 1848, as the *Communist Manifesto*. Marx was expelled from Belgium and returned to Cologne, starting the *Neue Rheinische Zeitung*, which was soon suppressed. Again, Marx had to leave Germany, went to Paris, from which he was banished, and finally settled in London, where he spent the rest of his life. He and his family survived a life of misery and near-starvation only with the financial support of Engels and a meager, irregular income from articles in newspapers (including the New York *Tribune*). But it was also a life of constant and painstaking research, study, and writing, which produced *Grundriss der Kritik der politischen Ökonomie* (1859), and his masterwork, *Das Kapital* (1867), the book that became the bible of socialism and communism. Marx did not make many friends, and when he died it was Engels who delivered the funeral oration; only 8 persons attended his burial.

Marx was not satisfied with economic theories alone, nor with the introduction of a new philosophical concept; he intended to create an entirely new social system and was convinced that capitalism was doomed to failure. His "mode of production," "theory of surplus value," "theory of wages," and "theory of value and distribution" are contributions that still are much discussed. He was obsessed by the idea of remedying evil. *Das Kapital* was written to reveal shortcomings in modern economics and to show the self-destructive tendencies of "capitalism," as Marx called it. Volumes 2 and 3 of *Das Kapital* were edited by Engels and published in 1885–94.

**Joseph Massie**
*English Mercantilist Writer*                                               *died 1784*

Massie compiled a collection of over 1,500 treatises and pamphlets written from 1557–1763. The catalogue of this collection is now in the British Museum. He himself wrote several essays on the rate of interest, calculation of taxes to be imposed on various imports, public finance, war supplies, and problems in selected industries. He also wrote about foundling hospitals, charity houses for deserted women and girls, and education as a national concern. The success of his writings was not encouraging and it seems that he stopped writing circa 1764. Perhaps his best essay was *Essay on the Governing Causes of the Natural Rate of Interest* (1750).

**Frederick Denison Maurice**
*English Christian Socialist*                                               *1805–1872*

Maurice was born in Normanston, Suffolk. He was ordained in the Church of England and became professor of moral philosophy at Cambridge. He openly declared that every Christian must be a socialist and actively supported the paper *The Christian Socialist* in cooperation with Kingsley. As Maurice understood it, socialists favor cooperation whereas anti-socialists support competition. Maurice was befriended by John Stuart Mill and founded a Working Men's College at which he taught for a short time.

**Richmond Mayo-Smith**
*American Economist*                                          *1854–1901*

Born in Troy, Ohio, Mayo-Smith studied at Amherst College and in Germany at Berlin and Heidelberg. He became a professor of political economy and social science at Columbia College. His principal contribution, however, was to statistics, and he was the first to offer a statistics course for undergraduates. Among his many articles and books, *Statistics and Economics* (1899) should be noted. At the time of his death he was considered the most eminent academic statistican in America. His friendly personality made him an excellent teacher. He was also much interested in public affairs and was one of the founders of the American Economic Historical Association.

**Ugo Mazzola**
*Italian Economist*                                          *1863–1899*

Mazzola studied law at Naples. For the Italian government he prepared a report about social insurance in Germany which was published in 1885. He became professor at the University of Camerio and later the successor of Cossa at Pavia (1896). Mazzola was interested mainly in welfare economics and public finance. He cooperated in the reestablishment of the *Giornale degli economisti* in 1886. In 1890 he made the interesting statement that the consumption of public goods is necessarily a joint procedure; this characteristic distinguishes public goods from other goods. He wrote about workmen's insurance and progressive taxation and was a convinced free-trader.

**Harlan Linneus McCracken**
*American Economist*                                          *1889–1961*

He studied at Haverford College and the universities of Pennsylvania and Wisconsin (Ph.D.). Among his writings, the following are important: *Monopolistic Competition and Business Fluctuations* (1938), *Economic Contradiction* (1947), and *Keynesian Economics in the Stream of Economic Thought* (1961). McCracken taught at Louisiana State University at Baton Rouge for a number of years.

**John Ramsey McCulloch**
*Scottish Economist*                                          *1789–1864*

Born in Withorn, McCulloch studied at the University of Edinburgh. During this time he wrote the economic articles in *The Scotsman* and later, for many years, in the *Edinburgh Review*. He organized a lecture series in economics and from 1828–32 was professor of political economy at the newly established University of London. He spent the remainder of his life as a controller.

His main work, *Principles of Political Economy* (1825), saw many editions and was translated into French, German, and Italian. In it, he essentially follows Ricardo. His major contribution to economic theory is an expansion of the wage-fund theory, which he relates directly and proportionally to the amount of investments; this theory was abandoned by the next generation. Longer-lasting were his contributions to statistics: he did outstanding work as a collector of statistical material and was a pioneer in the use of such material in theoretical studies. He was in favor of free trade and accepted and adopted Say's utility concept. His edition of Smith's *Wealth of Nations* was reprinted 4 times during his life. His publications include a biography of Ricardo, numerous essays, monographs, statistical dictionaries, also *The Literature of Political Economy* (1845), a classified catalogue, and *A Treatise on the Circumstances which Determine the Rate of Wages* (1851). All are noteworthy.

**John McVickar**
*American Economist*                                              *1787–1868*

McVickar, born in New York City, was the first professor of political economy at Columbia College. It has been said that he wrote *First Lessons in Political Economy for the Use of Elementary Schools* (1830) because he was convinced that the economic science was already complete. McVickar favored free trade and opposed protectionism.

**August Meitzen**
*German Economist and Statistician*                              *1822–1910*

Meitzen, born at Breslau, is mentioned here for his outstanding contribution to the historical studies of organizational developments in agriculture. His *Siedlung und Agrarwesen* (1895) should be noted, and also his *Geschichte, Theorie, und Technik der Statistik* (1896).

**Jean François Melon**
*French Public Servant*                                         *1675–1738*

Born in Tulle, Melon was secretary to John Law while Law was in France. He wrote *Essai politique sur le commerce* (1734), which saw 4 editions and was widely read in France and abroad, and in 1738 translated into English. He favored a type of mercantilist system and slavery in the colonies.

**Anton Menger**
*Austrian Writer*                                               *1841–1905*

Menger was born in New-Sandec and educated at Vienna and Prague. He was the brother of Karl Menger. He wrote *Recht auf den vollen Arbeitsertrag* (1886), which was translated into English as *Right to the*

*Whole Produce of Labour* (1899). He also pioneered for state socialism and wrote a number of political monographs.

**Karl Menger**
*Austrian Economist*                                          *1840–1921*

Menger was born in Galicia, studied economics and law at the universities of Vienna, Prague, and Cracow, joined the civil service in Austria, and in 1871 published *Grundsätze der Volkswirtschaftslehre*. He was appointed extraordinary professor at Vienna and later became the tutor of Crown Prince Rudolf, whom he accompanied on his travels. From 1879–1903 he was professor of political economy at Vienna. He then retired to his immense private library in economics (now located in the Tokyo University of Commerce) to devote himself to research. In recognition for his work he was made a member of the Austrian House of Peers in 1900, but he did not care for politics. Few books had as much influence as his *Grundsätze*, as students from all parts of the world studied under him. He wrote other books on the methods of social sciences, on the errors of the historical school, on German political economy, on the theory of capital, and many articles which appeared in the *Jahrbücher für Nationalökonomie*. He became the founder and leader of the so-called Austrian school, and wrote on the nature of value, on exchange, determinants of value, subjective value, utility, and the theory of money, among other topics. "All things are subject to the law of cause and effect," he said, and he showed the interrelation of economic activities. His contributions were not only extremely valuable for economic theory but are still also of greatest interest in the methodological sense. The *Collected Works of Karl Menger* (4 vols.) were published in London in 1933.

**Pierre François Mercier de la Rivière**
*French Physiocrat*                                          *1720–1793*

Mercier, born in Saumur (Indre et Loire) as son of a "président tresorier" of France, studied law and became one of the most important followers of the physiocrat doctrine. Mercier was at one time controller of the French colony of Martinique. His book *L'Ordre naturel et essentiel des sociétés politiques* (1767) attempts to outline a philosophy based on a natural order under which the state should function, and it demonstrates the principles of physiocracy. Mercier visited a number of foreign dignitaries, including Catherine of Russia, to explain physiocracy. His demonstrations before Catherine were very successful.

**Angelo Messedaglia**
*Italian Economist and Statistician*                                          *1820–1901*

Born near Verona and educated at Pavia, Messedaglia was a trained physician and mathematician; however, in Padua he became professor of administrative law and later in Rome, professor of political economy and statistics. His *Della Teoria della populazione* (1858) evoked much interest. Against Malthus, he argued that population increase cannot be described in terms of a geometric ratio, as a shorter food supply would cause the growth rate to decrease to an arithmetic progression. Messedaglia warmly propagated the introduction of more scientific methods in economics. He contended that use should be made of statistical, mathematical, and historical tools. However, he warned not to expect that these alone could explain the complexity of economic phenomena. He published a great many books on statistics. All his writings distinguished themselves by their clarity, precision, and thoroughness.

**Robert Meyer**
*German Economist and Statistician*                          *1855–1914*

Meyer is remembered for his books *Wesen des Einkommens* (1887) and *Principien der gerechten Besteuerung* (1884). A student of Menger, he was a follower of the Austrian School throughout his life.

**Leonhard Miksch**
*German Economist*                          *1901–1950*

Born at Teplitz-Schönau, Miksch studied at Tübingen and became a professor at Freiburg. His most important works are *Wettbewerb als Aufgabe* (1947) and the article in the journal *Weltwirtschaftsarchiv* "Zur Theorie des räumlichen Gleichgewichts" (published posthumously in 1951). Here he combined the location theory with the equilibrium theory and opened new ways by constructing four models for various competitive systems of the market.

**James Mill**
*British Historian, Philosopher, and Economist*                          *1773–1836*

Mill was born in Scotland as the son of a shoemaker, studied at the University of Edinburgh, and was licensed to preach. Failing to be appointed to the ministry, he became editor of the *Literary Journal* and the *St. James Chronicle* in London. Here he began work on his major book, *History of India* (1818), the success of which prompted the East India Company to offer him a position in its London office.

In 1808 Mill met Bentham. This was an important event both to him and to Bentham, who, shy and retiring, needed somebody with the ability and courage to publicize his utilitarian philosophy and social reform ideas. Mill became the leader of the Philosophical Radicals, a group that included his close friend David Ricardo, whom he persuaded to put his economic thoughts in the form of a book. Together they founded the Political Economy Club, which met at Ricardo's house. In 1821 Mill published *Elements of Political Economy*, in which he stressed the need to limit the population to a certain relation to capital in order to assure income and employment. The value of a good, he explained, depends upon the number of labor hours needed for production, and he stated that the proper income for tax purposes would be the unearned increment derived from land. Mill, possibly as an outcome of discussions in the Club, set up some essential rules for the scope of economic science. These were: 1) to study the laws that regulate the production of commodities; 2) to study the laws by which distribution takes place and commodities are exchanged; and 3) to set up laws to regulate consumption. All other considerations, he felt, should be left out. Mill also published *Commerce Defended* (1808) and *Analysis of the Phenomena of the Human Mind* (1829).

More of a catalyst than an innovator, Mill discharged every duty with greatest care and was forceful, impressive, animated, and effective. His influence on the British reform movement was strong. He was a strict but devoted father who directed the education of his eldest son, John Stuart Mill.

**John Stuart Mill**

*English Philosopher and Economist*                                    *1806–1873*

John Stuart Mill was born in London as the son of James Mill, under whose guidance he started to study Greek at age 3. At age 8 he began Latin and at 12 he added algebra and geometry and proceeded to calculus. He was introduced early in life to the literature of economics, and had the advantage of being in close contact with Bentham, Ricardo, and others in the Philosophical Radicals group. He also visited Say in France. In 1822 he entered his father's office in the East India Company, became assistant examiner in 1828, and took his father's position as head of the office when James Mill died. He served in the House of Commons in 1865–68. His friendship with the invalid Mrs. Harriet Taylor became marriage when Mr. Taylor died. Her influence on Mill's intellectual and moral development was extraordinary. She collaborated with him on the book *Liberty*, and he said of her that her excellence of mind and heart were "unparalleled in any human being" he had "known or read of."

For Mill, economics was a science, and he carefully followed the growing literature in this field. To economic theory he added only little. His greatest contributions were in his book *Principles of Political Economy with Some of Their Applications to Social Philosophy* (1848), which in succeeding decades was the most widely read book on economics. It is an outstanding synthesis of classical teachings, particularly those of Ricardo, and some ideas of the later supporters of the classical economists. In *Utilitarianism* (1863) Mill showed himself one of the leaders of this school. He distinguished different grades of utility, assigning to the highest order utilities that benefit the mind. Happiness, in his opinion, includes physical, spiritual, and moral welfare as well as the greatest possible amount of material wealth. In his later years he grew to be more of an idealist, highly interested in social problems and even in socialist notions.

Among his other works, *System of Logic* (1843) and *Auguste Comte and Positivism* (1865) should be noted. Also important are his contributions to the *Westminster Review* and the *London Review*, and his celebrated *Autobiography* (1873).

**Victor Riquetti, Marquis de Mirabeau**
*French Physiocrat*                                     *1715–1789*

Mirabeau, born in Pertuis, gave up a military career to devote himself to writing. In 1756 he published *L'Ami des hommes, ou traité de la population*, a book which demonstrated the close connection between population and agriculture. This highly popular book attracted the attention of Quesnay, who invited him to the meetings of his circle. This friendly relation helped to create the first school in economics. Now called the physiocrats, the members of this school called themselves merely "The Economists." Mirabeau wrote *La Théorie de l'impôt* (1760), an attack on the finance administration of the government, which brought him a brief prison term and exile from Paris to Bignon, his country home. In 1763 his *La Philosophie rurale* appeared, representing a complete description of the physiocratic doctrine. It was accepted as the first textbook of physiocratic orthodoxy. Mirabeau wrote numerous other tracts and books and did much to bring the ideas of physiocracy to the attention of large groups in France and abroad. Like all the other members of this group, he admired Quesnay, calling his *Tableau économique* the greatest discovery after the introduction of writing and of money. He described the state as a tree with roots in agriculture, branches in industry, and leaves in commerce and the arts.

**Ludwig von Mises**
*Austrian Economist*                                     *1881–1973*

Born in Lemberg, Mises studied and taught at the University of Vienna. He also taught at the Graduate Institute of International Studies in Geneva, Switzerland. He came to the U.S. in 1940 and remained as a visiting professor at New York University. His numerous books, written in German, were mostly translated into English and some should be listed here: *Economic Calculation in the Socialist Commonwealth* (1920), *Socialism* (1936), *Contemporary Economic Theory* (1932), and *The Anti-Capitalist Mentality* (1956). Von Mises was a leading exponent of the Austrian School of traditional economic thought. All his works stress free markets and regard laissez-faire as the system of equilibrium, blaming shortcomings on outside interferences with the highly delicate market mechanism.

**Edward Misselden**
*English Mercantilist Writer*                              *ca. 1608–1654*

Misselden was deputy governor of the Merchant Adventurers for 10 years. In defense of this company's policy, in 1622 he wrote *Free Trade, or, The Means to Make Trade Flourish*. A reply by Malynes was the cause for another book entitled *The Circle of Commerce, or, The Balance of Trade in Defense of Free Trade* (1623). This did not end the controversy, but it has to be noted that Misselden changed his arguments. In fact, a significant feature of Misselden's *Circle of Commerce* was its author's change of mind regarding the East India Company's trade. While in *Free Trade* he held the company responsible for the decline of British trade through its export of silver, in the *Circle of Commerce* he accepted such export as desirable on the grounds that the foreign goods, paid for by silver exports, might be re-exported in order to bring in more silver. This was the position taken by later mercantilists. In *Circle of Commerce* he also advocated an increase of the money supply to stimulate trade by depreciating the silver content of coins. He admitted that such a step would lead to an increase in prices but believed that the result would be beneficial, not harmful. Although he was a convinced mercantilist, Misselden distinguished himself with a free and outspoken discussion of the problem of trade. He felt that only if the general welfare makes it necessary should the state intervene.

**Wesley Clair Mitchell**
*American Economist*                                      *1874–1948*

Born in Rushville, Illinois, Mitchell studied at the newly established University of Chicago (Ph.D.) and obtained a fellowship to go to Germany. He taught at the University of Chicago, University of California, Harvard University, Columbia University, and the New School for Social Research before returning to Chicago, where he was professor from 1922–40. He helped organize the National Bureau of Economic Research, serving as research director until 1945, and did consultation work in Washington for such groups as President Hoover's Committee on Social Trends and the National Resources Board. For the Labor Department he wrote *The Making and Use of Index Numbers* (1915). Of his many articles and books, the following should be mentioned: *A History of the Greenbacks* (1903), *Gold Prices and Wages under the Greenback Standard* (1908), and the book that made him internationally famous, *Business Cycles* (1913; 2nd ed., 1927, entitled *Business Cycles: The Problem and Its Setting*). Mitchell became one of the leading American economists and a leader of the Institutional School. For him, economics was a science of human behavior, and the future lay in the success of understanding changing economic life and institutions. The dynamic quality of economic activities was for him a characteristic that required the study of economics in motion. His last interesting publications were *The Backward Art of Spending Money* (1937) and *Measuring Business Cycles* (1946).

**Louis de Molina**
*Italian Scholastic*                                              *1535–1600*

Father Molina, who had remarkable concepts about demand and supply, spoke about the "natural price" in the market. But he warned against private monopolies and pointed out that every merchant or businessman has to see his work as a service to all of the community in which everyone has the right to take his proper place.

**Molinaeus**
see Charles *Dumoulin*

**Gustave de Molinari**
*French Journalist and Economist*                                 *1819–1911*

Molinari, born in Liège, was professor in Brussels (Belgium) and Antwerp (Belgium). He returned to France and edited the *Journal des debats* and later the *Journal des économistes* (1881–1909). In his many books and articles he dealt mainly with the application of natural law in economics, and with economic policy. Here should be noted *Théorie de l'évolution* (1908). Molinari was highly individualistic and reduced all activities to self-interest, competition, and value. He was for the unrestricted play of the "natural forces," and assigned to the state only the role of protecting and preserving the liberty of individual initiative. In the corporation he saw the business-organization form of the future. He was for an international labor exchange to grant labor greater mobility and a better bargaining position. He opposed tariffs and trade restrictions and was in favor of a customs union of all major European states. While he saw in war an expression of the competitive principles, he also declared that modern wars are in fact an economic illusion and are harmful to both victors and losers.

**Arthur Eli Monroe**
*American Economist*                                              *1874–1956*

Born in Cambridge, Massachusetts, Monroe studied at Harvard University (Ph.D.). His dissertation, *Monetary Theory before Adam Smith*, was published in 1923. He also wrote, in addition to many articles, *Early Economic Thought* (1924) and *Value and Income* (1931). His works have been widely quoted.

**Geminiano Montanari**
*Italian Mathematician, Astronomer, and Economist*               *1633–1687*

Montanari was born in Modena. He became a professor of mathematics at Bologna. Later he moved to Padua and taught meteorology and astronomy. He also wrote two books on money, which were published in the collection of Graziani in 1751. Montanari gave a clear description of the quantity theory of money and stated that the most important factor in determining value is scarcity. He has been considered by some as one of the first psychologically oriented economists.

### Antoine de Montchrétien
*French Writer and Mercantilist*    *ca. 1575–1621*

Born in Falaise, Montchrétien, a writer of poems and dramas, in 1615 published *Traité de l'économie politique*, making him one of the first mercantilist writers in France. For him, however, it was the labor of the citizens that makes the state wealthy, not gold and silver supplies. Therefore, he insisted that the state encourage industry and artisans. The import of manufactured articles should, he believed, be prohibited, and the export of French raw materials be restricted through high export duties. Gold and silver export should be forbidden. His program was designed to strengthen the position of France. Although he promoted nationalism, it is reported that he revolted against the king and was killed in 1621. In his tract Montchrétien introduced the term "political economy."

### Charles de Secondat, Baron de la Brède et de Montesquieu
*French Political Theorist*    *1689–1755*

Montesquieu was born at Château de la Brède, France. He studied law at Bordeaux University but never practiced it since his financial circumstances permitted him to devote himself to studying, writing, and traveling. On a trip to Italy he met John Law. Of his works, only *De l'Esprit des lois* (1748) should be noted here. An excellent treatment of political theory, this long work deals with the interdependence of the nations of Europe, and with commerce, peace, and the separation of powers. He proposed a direct tax on the surplus wealth of individuals. Montesquieu regarded society as a unity, some of whose activities are concerned with economics.

### Henry Ludwell Moore
*American Statistician and Economist*    *1869–1958*

Moore, born in Maryland, studied at Randolph Macon College, abroad at the University of Vienna, and at Johns Hopkins University (Ph.D.). He was professor at Columbia University. His interests concentrated on business cycles and forecasting. He developed the 8-year cycle theory and proposed a sunspot theory of business cycles. He published *Economic Cycles: Their Law and Cause* (1914), *Forecasting the Yield and the Price of Cotton* (1917), *Generating Economic Cycles* (1923), and, systematizing the work of a lifetime, *Synthetic Economics* (1929). In the latter, he pioneered in mathematical economics in America.

**Sir Thomas More**
*English Statesman*                                  *1478–1535*

Born in London, More pursued humanistic studies at Oxford and law at New Inn. He became a member of Parliament, master of bequests, treasurer of the exchequer, speaker of the House of Commons, and lord chancellor (1529). Disagreeing with Henry VIII on the question of divorce, he resigned, and when he refused to recognize the king as head of the English church, Henry had him imprisoned and beheaded. He was a brilliant writer, much liked by his contemporaries for his shrewd wit and gentle humor. He was canonized by the Catholic church in 1935.

Among his many writings, of particular interest here is *Utopia* (written in Latin in 1516, translated into English in 1551 and later into French, German, and Italian). It describes the evil conditions in different countries at that time and depicts an ideal commonwealth where social life is regulated by natural reason, where toleration is dominant, and where people live together in a sort of communistic cooperation.

**Andre Morellet**
*French Writer and Economist*                        *1727–1819*

Born in Lyons, Morellet studied at the Sorbonne and then took holy orders. But the title "Abbé" was all that was clerical about him. At the Sorbonne he had met Turgot, who became his lifelong friend. Morellet also was one of the most loyal disciples of Gournay, and he collaborated with the Encyclopedists. In his economic writings he took a strong stand for liberation of commerce and industry. He published *Réflexions sur les avantages de la libre fabrication et de l'usage des toiles peintes en France* (1758), *Dialogues sur les commerces des blés* (1770), and many books and papers on history and other subjects.

**Morelly**
*French Land Reformer*                               *ca. 1700–1780*

Little is known concerning his personality but Morelly expressed his ideas on landed property in prose and verse, especially in his utopian *Naufrage des îles flottantes* (1753) and *Code de la nature* (1755).

**William Morris**
*English Writer*                                      *1834–1896*

Morris, born in Essex, a graduate of Oxford, wrote a utopian story named *News from Nowhere* (1891), which clearly shows a socialist leaning. He deals rather more emotionally than scientifically with the ills of the industrial system and with poverty. He also wrote *A Dream of John Ball* (1888) and *Socialism: Its Growth and Outcome* (1893).

**Adam Heinrich Müller**
*German Economist*                                    *1779–1829*

Müller was born in Berlin and studied law at the University of Göttingen. He belonged to the circle of Schelling, Schleiermacher, Novalis, and von Kleist—i.e., the so-called Romantic movement, which embraced literature, art, aesthetics, and philosophy, as well as social thought. His friend Friedrich von Gentz introduced him to Metternich, the conservative Austrian statesman, who appointed Müller to various important political positions and used him in his diplomatic maneuvers. Müller wrote extensively. Of special interest are his *Die Elemente der Staatskunst* (3 vols., 1810), *Die Theorie der Staatshaushaltung* (1812), and *Versuch einer neuen Theorie des Geldes* (1816). The feudal society was for Müller the ideal social system. He saw the society as a community organized within the state, to which the individual must be subordinated; outside the framework of the state the individual cannot exist. These ideas had great consequence much later in Germany, and helped to develop a totalitarian system. Müller was opposed to practically everything for which Adam Smith stood.

**Alfred Müller-Armack**
*German Economist*                                    *1901–*

Müller-Armack was born in Essen, studied at the University of Cologne, and taught at the universities of Münster and Cologne. A close associate of Ludwig Erhard, he was chairman of the committee on business fluctuation of the European Common Market and director of the Institute for Economic Social Policy. He coined the term *Soziale Markt-Wirtschaft* (Social Market Economy) for the economic style adopted in 1948 by the West German government—a free-enterprise economy based on free competition and minimum government interference but directed toward social welfare as the final goal of all economic activities. Many of his numerous writings are collected in *Wirtschaftsordnung und Wirtschaftspolitik* (1966). They show that Müller-Armack based his economic ideas on cultural and even religious attitudes. This is also shown in his *Das Jahrhundert ohne Gott* (1948), and *Religion und Wirtschaft* (1959).

**Sir Thomas Mun**
*English Mercantilist*                                *1571–1641*

Born in London, Mun became a successful businessman and a director of the East India Company. His great experience and outstanding personality made him preeminent among the English mercantilist writers. In 1621 he published *A Discourse of Trade from England into the East Indies.*

Mun wrote his most important tract before 1628; however, it was published only in 1664 posthumously under the title *England's Treasure by Foraign Trade, or the Balance of our Foraign Trade is the Rule of Our Treasure.* Here he defined the doctrine of the balance of trade and laid down what became the accepted commercial policy. He argued that foreign trade is the only means of making England wealthy and of obtaining the supply of gold and silver needed. "To sell more to strangers than we consume in their value" he said, must become the rule. He pointed out that the only way a nation without mines can increase its supply of gold and silver is by exporting more goods than are imported, receiving the difference in precious metals. In order to accomplish this, he set forth a number of practical propositions: England's wastelands should be cultivated to avoid the importation of food from foreign countries; goods should be exported on the country's own ships to secure the freight charges; the English should do their own fishing instead of leaving it to the Dutch; sumptuary laws should be applied to restrain the consumption of foreign luxury goods; money itself should be exported if the result is that a greater quantity of money is received in return. He defended the export of bullion because too much money kept at home would only boost prices and thus affect exports adversely; for in order to attract foreign buyers, domestic products must be cheap.

**Gunnar Myrdal**

*Swedish Economist, Sociologist, and Statesman*          *1898–*

Myrdal was born in Gustafs, studied at the University of Stockholm, and became a professor of political economy. Active in public affairs, he was elected to the Swedish parliament and was minister of trade and commerce (1945–47). Invited to the U.S. to study the Negro problem, he published his findings in *The American Dilemma* (1944). He served as executive secretary of the U.N. Economic Commission for Europe (1947–57) and studied problems of underdeveloped countries, especially in Southeast Asia. He was appointed to the new chair of international economics at the University of Stockholm. Besides many articles of eminent value he published *The Political Element in the Development of Economic Theory* (Swedish ed., 1929; German ed., 1932), *Monetary Equilibrium* (1939), *Population: A Problem for Democracy* (1940), *An International Economy: Problems and Prospects* (1956), *Value in Social Theory* (1958), and *Beyond the Welfare State* (1960).

# N

**Erwin Nasse**

*German Economist*                                                      *1829–1890*

Born in Bonn, Nasse studied at Bonn University, where he obtained his doctorate with a very significant dissertation in the field of Roman economic history, published in 1851. He taught at the universities of Basel, Rostock, and Bonn. His main field of interest was money and banking, wherein he enjoyed an extraordinary reputation. He was co-founder of the Verein Für Sozialpolitik, which published most of his writings. He was elected to the Prussian legislature as a Free Conservative but refused to be reelected, not wanting to support the protective tariff policy of Bismarck. He stressed the need to apply moral ideas to the national economy by action of the state.

**Martinus de Azpilcueta Navarrus**

*Scholastic Philosopher*                                                *died 1586*

Born in Spain, Navarrus taught at Toulouse, Cahors, and Salamanca. He deserves mention here for his progressive attitude toward interest, as expressed in many of his writings. The development of the quantity theory of money took place at Salamanca.

**Emilio Nazzani**

*Italian Economist*                                                     *1832–1904*

Nazzani is listed here since he has been named the most eminent Italian exponent in the classical theory. His essays, republished in one volume in 1881, show his close association with the theories of the English Classics and expand their ideas on rent, profit, and wages.

Nazzani was president of the Technical Institute of Forlì. He refused to accept an invitation to the chair of political economy at the University of Pisa.

**Karl Friedrich Nebenius**

*German Statesman*                                                      *1785–1857*

Born in Landau, Nebenius studied law at Tübingen. He entered the Baden ministry of finance and remained with the administration of the Grand Duchy nearly all his life, serving as privy councilor of state, minister of the interior, and president of the cabinet council. He applied his liberal policy effectively to many reforms, especially in the field of taxation. He cooperated actively in the establishment of the German

Customs Union (Zollverein). Nebenius was also curator of the University of Heidelberg. Well known are his books *Der öffentliche Kredit* (1820), on public credit; and *Der deutsche Zollverein* (1835), on the customs union.

**Jacques Necker**
*Swiss-French Banker and Statesman*                                    *1732–1804*

Born in Geneva, Switzerland, Necker became a much-respected banker in Paris. He criticized the free-trade policy of Turgot, became director of the Treasury of France and later, after Turgot's fall, director-general of finances. His efforts to introduce stringent economy in the administration and at court made him many enemies. He resigned after 5 years, making the financial situation public with his *Compte rendu* (1781). Louis XVI recalled him when France was on the verge of bankruptcy in 1788 and made him minister of state. Necker's recommendation to call the States-General made him very popular, but not with the court party, which demanded his dismissal. The populace stormed the Bastille and insisted on his reinstatement (July 14, 1789), but Necker resigned in 1790 and returned to his estate in Coppet, Switzerland.

In his *Éloge de Colbert* (1773) Necker praised Colbert as the wisest and most prudent statesman of all time. In this swan-song of mercantilism Necker warned that economic liberalism would lead to a stronger power position of capital and thereby reduce the status and influence of the individual. His anti-physiocratic convictions were recorded in his book *Sur la législation et le commerce des grains* (1775). The physiocrats always considered him as a formidable adversary.

**Oswald von Nell-Breuning, S. J.**
*German Writer and Educator*                                         *1890–*

Nell-Breuning was born in Trier, studied at the universities of Kiel, Munich, Strasbourg, Berlin, Innsbruck, and Münster, and became professor of philosophy at the College of St. George and at the University of Frankfurt. He was on the advisory board of the German ministry of economics after World War II and was highly influential in socioeconomic developments. His extensive writings include *Börsenmoral* (1928), *Reform und Moral* (1930), *Wirtschaft und Gesellschaft heute* (3 vols., 1955), and *Reorganisation der Sozialen Ökonomie* (1935).

**Nemours**
see Pierre Samuel *Dupont de Nemours*

**John von Neumann**
*American Mathematician and Physicist*                                *1903–1957*

Born in Budapest, Neumann studied in Berlin, Zurich, and Budapest (where he received a doctorate in mathematics), and taught at the universities of Berlin and Hamburg. In 1930 he settled in the U.S., where he taught mathematical physics at Princeton University, was prominent in the development of atomic energy, and became a member of the Atomic Energy Commission. His monumental *Mathematical Foundations of Quantum Mechanics* (1932) is a major contribution to physics.

Of great interest to the social sciences is his *Theory of Games and Economic Behavior* (1944, with Oskar Morgenstern), which opened the door to entirely new approaches in the study of economic behavior. Game theory is a branch of applied mathematics analyzing situations in which conflicts of interest and control are involved, and it has become useful in setting up theoretical models in economics.

**Simon Newcomb**

*American Astronomer and Mathematician*      *1835–1909*

Newcomb was born in Nova Scotia, studied at Harvard University, and became professor of mathematics at the U.S. Naval Observatory. His contributions to astronomy were so great that he received honorary degrees from 7 American and 10 European universities. Yet even early in his life he also showed interest in economics. On the basis of his writings and lectures he became known as "the sound-money man" and a courageous defender of laissez-faire. In 1877 he published *The ABC of Finance* and in 1886 *Principles of Political Economy*. Closely following the Classical School, he argued against flooding the economy with paper currency and against social policies, socialism, labor unions, and automation in business enterprises, which he felt would hurt the workers. Newcomb developed the exchange equation $MV=PT$ where $M$ stands for money, $V$ for velocity of circulation, $P$ for the general price level, and $T$ for the total product transaction.

**Sir Isaac Newton**

*English Physicist and Philosopher*      *1642–1727*

Newton, giant in the natural sciences, was born on the day Galileo died. He studied at Trinity College, Cambridge, where he spent 40 years and was professor of mathematics. His discovery of the calculus, formulation of the laws of gravitation and motion, and writings *Mathematical Principles of Natural Philosophy* and *Principia* greatly influenced all sciences and opened the way to what has been called the "New Economics," the scientific approach to economic problems. In 1699 he was appointed Master of the Mint and efficiently reestablished the financial system of Britain by recoining all coins and enforcing standards in their weight and fineness.

**Alfred Neymarck**

*French Statesman and Statistician*                    *1848–1921*

Neymarck was born at Châlons, became a banker, served on governmental research commissions and wrote many articles. He was president of the Statistical Society and vice president of the Society of Political Economy. Neymarck was an individualist who opposed any state intervention and protectionism. He was also hostile to socialism. He is mentioned because of his outstanding book, *Turgot* (1885).

**Joseph Shield Nicholson**

*British Economist*                    *1850–1923*

Nicholson was born in Lincolnshire and educated at Edinburgh and Cambridge, where he won the Cobden Prize. He also studied at the University of Heidelberg and London University, and later became lector at Cambridge and professor of political economy at Edinburgh. He was a devoted disciple of the Classical school but added historical and statistical observations in his 20 books. His main contribution was in the monetary field: *The Silver Question* (1886), *Money and Monetary Problems* (1888), and *Rates and Taxes* (1905). He was less successful, being overshadowed by Marshall, with his *Principles of Political Economy* (3 vols., 1893–1911) and *Elements of Political Economy* (1903). Also noted should be his *Historical Progress and Ideal Socialism* (1894).

**Hezekiah Niles**

*American Journalist and Economist*                    *1777–1839*

Born in Chester County, Pennsylvania, he became eminent as editor of *Niles' Weekly Register*, in which he pleaded for protection of industry. He was closely associated with Matthew Carey and Henry Carey and was influential in the nationalist economic school. He was an active force at the protectionist conventions at Harrisburg (1827) and New York (1831).

**Sir Dudley North**

*English Merchant and Nobleman*                    *1641–1691*

Born in London as the son of Dudley, 4th Lord North, Sir Dudley North engaged in large-scale trade with the Near East and was appointed royal treasurer and commissioner of customs. A conservative in politics, but a liberal in economics, he saw the whole world as an economic unit and was convinced that free trade would be to the advantage of all, since trade is only consummated when both parties are certain to gain. Peace, industry, and freedom he believed to be prerequisites of wealth and trade. Wealth can exist independently from gold and silver; it is the ability to satisfy wants. No one would be rich if he had money only. A too great supply of money would cause a decline in its value. The lending of capital (which he called "stock") is similar to the lending of land: land brings rent and capital brings interest. When there are more lenders than borrowers the interest rate will be low. Legal restriction on the interest rate will only produce hoarding or evasion. North objected to state regulations and interference since, in his opinion, supply and demand would be a better regulator. He attacked the Mercantilist doctrine and felt that a nation can acquire the money it needs without regulating bullion transactions; if there is an oversupply of bullion, he argued, it will depreciate in value for monetary uses, be melted, and exported as a commodity in spite of legal restrictions. He expressed his opinions in *Discourses upon Trade* (1691), which appeared anonymously and was recovered in 1822, after having been lost for a long time.

**Roger North**
*English Jurist* **1653–1734**

Roger North, brother of Dudley North, is known for his *A Discourse of the Poor, Showing the Pernicious Tendency for the Law Now in Force for Their Maintenance and Settlement* (8 vols., 1753). Herein he claimed that the laws of his day would lead to depopulation and have unfavorable influences on trade, labor, and land. He proposed replacing punitive laws with measures encouraging betterment.

**Ragnar Nurske**
*American Economist* **1907–1959**

Nurske was born in Estonia and studied at Edinburgh University and the University of Vienna. He was connected with the League of Nations and after World War II became a professor at Columbia University. In his *Problems of Capital Formation in Underdeveloped Countries* (1954) he drew attention to external economics and the need for a broad front of progress in underdeveloped countries. He said that the "vicious circle of poverty" is the reason some countries remain poor.

# O

### Georg von Obrecht
*German Law Professor*                                        *1547–1612*

Born in Strasbourg, son of the mayor, Obrecht studied at the University of Tübingen and in Besançon, France, and became a celebrated professor in Strasbourg, his birthplace. He proposed that parents make deposits in the public treasury for children at the time of birth. Bearing 6% interest, the deposits would be paid to girls at age 17 and to boys at age 21. If the children did not reach these ages, most of the money would stay in the public treasury. Obrecht admired Bodin but was mainly interested in economic institutions and additional revenues for the prince. Obrecht suggested inheritance taxes, duties on luxury goods, and new forms of fees and fines, mostly on property. After his death, *Funff underschiedliche Secreta Politica* (1617) was published by his son.

### Bronterre O'Brien
*English Reformer*                                           *1805–1864*

O'Brien was born in Granard County, Longford. He was a disciple of Owen, became the leader of the Chartist movement, which started ca. 1838. Basically it was a socialist movement which hoped to obtain general economic welfare and well-being through universal manhood suffrage. Some of the Chartists intended to secure these rights through peaceful means; others called for force. The failure of the general strike in England (1848) brought the movement to an end.

### George August Thomas O'Brien
*Irish Social Reformer*                                      *1892–*

O'Brien was born in Dublin, where he studied economics. He wrote *An Essay on the Economic Effect of the Reformation* (1923) and *An Essay on Medieval Economic Teaching* (1920). O'Brien has been called an Agrarian-socialist since he argued in favor of limitation of land property or socialization of land. He predicted that capitalism would evolve inevitably into a form of natural socialism. In 1943 he published in *Economica* letters and correspondence between John Stuart Mill and J. E. Cairnes.

### William Ogilvie
*English Land Reformer*                                      *1736–1819*

Ogilvie was one of the first to add socioeconomic considerations to the study of land-property rights. He published *Essay on the Right of Prop-*

erty in Land (1782) and distinguished between 1) original land-value, 2) land-value as consequence of expected value increases, and 3) added value because of human work. Only the first two kinds of values should be included in land-reform projects.

**Bertil Ohlin**
*Swedish Economist*                                                 *1899–*

Ohlin studied under Cassel at the University of Stockholm, and became a leading member of the Swedish School. He took an active part in national affairs and served as a cabinet member. He was also on several international commissions and directed a study on world economic depressions (1931) for the League of Nations. He published *Theory of Trade* (1924), *Interregional and International Trade* (1933), *International Economic Reconstruction* (1936), *The Capital Market and Interest Rate Policy* (1941), and numerous other works on economic theory. Ohlin recommended international capital movements through shifts in international bank balances instead of through gold shipments.

**August Oncken**
*German Economist*                                              *1844–1911*

Born in Heidelberg, Oncken studied at Heidelberg, Karlsruhe, Munich, and Berlin (Ph.D.). He taught at the Agricultural College in Vienna, the Polytechnikum in Aachen, and the University of Bern. Notable among his works are *Die Maxime "Laissez faire et laissez passer", ihr Ursprung, ihr Werden* (1886), *Geschichte der National-ökonomie* (1902), *Die Entwicklung der deutschen Volkswirtschaftslehre im neunzehnten Jahrhundert* (2 vols. 1908).

**Franz Oppenheimer**
*German Economist*                                              *1864–1943*

Born near Berlin, Oppenheimer studied medicine at Freiburg and Berlin (M.D., 1885), but later he decided to study economics at the University of Kiel (Ph.D., 1908) and lectured at Berlin (1909–19). In 1919 he accepted a professorship of economics and sociology at Frankfurt-Main. He left Germany in 1933 and taught as visiting professor in France, Palestine, and the United States, where he died.

A powerful teacher, Oppenheimer exercised great influence on his students. One of them was Ludwig Erhard. He advocated social liberalism and the elimination of unearned income, but was opposed to dogmatic Marxism. Some of his works are: *Grossgrundeigentum und die soziale Frage* (1898), *Das Grundgesetz der marxischen Gesellschaftslehre* (1903), *Der Staat* (1907), *Die soziale Frage und der Sozialismus* (1912), *Theorie der reinen und politischen Ökonomie* (1919), *Erlebtes, Erstrebtes, Erreichtes* (1931).

**Nicole Oresme**
*French Scholastic Writer* *1325–1382*

Born in Caen, Oresme studied in Paris. He became grand-master of the College of Navarre, dean of Rouen, and bishop of Lisieux. A highly educated and scholarly man, he was interested in many fields: theology, philosophy, mathematics, astrology, and economics. His *Tractus de Origine, Natura, Jure et Mutationibus Monetarum* (1360) has been called the first theoretical monograph in economics. He went beyond the traditional teaching of the scholastics and had some very advanced ideas about economic matters. He denounced debasement of coins and called it "worse than usury."

**Giammaria Ortes**
*Italian Economist and Mathematician* *1713–1790*

Born in Venice, Ortes was given to a monastery as a young boy but left it when he was 30 years old and traveled around the European continent and probably also in England. He was a scholar in many fields, including economics, mathematics, physics, and philosophy, and in addition he was a poet. His economic ideas were conservative in some matters and extremely liberal in others; in fact socialist leanings resulted in the banning of his writings in Tuscany, the Papal States, and even in Venice. He attacked the "mercantilist confusion" of money and wealth and advocated free trade. He believed that charging interest was wrong and economically disadvantageous. In *Riflessioni sulla populazione* (1790) he anticipated Malthus' population theory, asserting that the increase of population tends to proceed geometrically so as to exceed the available food supply, making it necessary to resort to celibacy in order to avoid extreme misery and vice. In *Economia nazionale* (1774) he stressed consumption as a limiting factor for total output. The welfare of the entire state (not that of the prince) was for him the guideline for a national economy.

**Ottlilienfeld**
see Friedrich von *Gottl-Ottlilienfeld*

**Samuel Jones Loyd, Lord Overstone**
*English Financier and Banker* *1796–1883*

Born in London, educated at Eton and Cambridge, Overstone entered his father's bank where he later became his father's successor. He was a member of Parliament and a leading member of the so-called Currency School, a brilliant and wealthy man who was influential in politics and whose ideas helped shape the English Bank Act of 1844. He never wrote a systematic work, but his contributions appeared in *Tracts and*

*Other Publications on Metallic and Paper Currency* (1857) and are professed in his *Evidence before the House of Commons Select Committee of 1857* (1858). Both were edited by McCulloch.

**Robert Owen**
*English Social Reformer*                                    *1771–1858*

Born in Newton, North Wales, Owen became co-owner of a successful textile mill. His business prospered, and he and his partners decided to buy control of textile mills at New Lanark, Scotland. Here Owen made himself a name by introducing technical improvements in production, establishing model dwellings for workers, and offering free education. Children under age 10 were not employed but educated free. Recreation facilities were made available; a company store offered goods at low prices. Wages were raised and working hours shortened; sickness and old-age insurance was introduced. The moral standards of the workers were high; cleanliness, sobriety, thrift, and order were obvious consequences. Lanark drew visitors, who came to learn how to imitate what was so successfully done. Even foreigners wanted to inspect this new system of enterprising. During the depression of 1806 the plant was closed for 4 months but the wages were paid. The difficulties started when Owen proposed that his partners be satisfied with a 5% return on their investments. The partnership was dissolved but new partners were found, one of them being Bentham. In a pamphlet called *New View of Society* (1816) Owen described his principles. He argued that environment can change and improve individuals and was convinced that men could not be held responsible for evil-doing when living under conditions that were based on false concepts.

In 1820 he went to America to establish a model communal system. He bought New Harmony, a village in Indiana, and assembled 900 people there. The experiment failed, as did Orviston in Scotland. Owen's financial losses were substantial, but he was not discouraged. In 1830 he returned to England and in 1832 founded the National Equitable Labor Exchange for cooperative marketing. Instead of money, "labor notes" were used, based on the labor hours needed for making the product. With the notes, commodities, available at the Exchange, could be bought. Too many unsalable goods were left over, however, and this experiment also failed.

Owen actively supported labor union movements. By 1833 most of the unions had consolidated under his leadership into the Grand National Consolidated Trades Union. But a year later the organization disintegrated, mainly because of government interference.

Owen's hopes and opinions were expressed in his *The New Moral World* (1834) and *What is Socialism?* (1841). He saw the natural standard of value in human labor, advocated cooperation instead of competition, and community life of small groups (300 to 3000 persons) around community buildings. A change of institutions and beliefs, he felt, would create new social conditions. In spite of all failures it is evident that Owen initiated the cooperative movement in England and introduced socialistic ideas. He also helped draft the first Factory Bill (1819).

# P

**Thomas Paine**
*International Social Reformer*                              *1737–1809*

Paine was born in England, where he worked for the government tax office. He lost his job and had to leave for America after he had tried to organize his fellow workers to obtain better working conditions. His political tracts helped the American Revolution. He returned to England in 1787 but had to leave again because of his publications and speeches. Paine went to France, where he became a citizen in 1792 and was elected to the revolutionary National Convention. For a while he was imprisoned, suspected by friends of Robespierre. In 1802 he went back to America, where he died. Of interest here is his *Rights of Man* (1792), advocating a complete social security system under the administration and regulation of the government. In *Agrarian Justice* (1796) he made a strong case that every owner of cultivated land should pay a rent to the community. He believed that the possession of land should not automatically be permanent. Paine was also a pioneer in the movement for the abolition of Negro slavery.


**Sir Robert H. Inglis Palgrave**
*English Economist and Banker*                              *1827–1919*

Palgrave, born in Westminster, made himself a name in economics with his excellent statistical material on central banks. He published *The Bank Rate and the Money Market* (1903), and a statistical study, *Local Taxation in Great Britain and Ireland* (1871), and edited *The Economist* (1877–83) and *Dictionary of Political Economy* (1894–99). He was knighted in 1909.


**Maffeo Pantaleoni**
*Italian Economist*                                         *1857–1924*

Pantaleoni was born in Frascati and studied in Germany and at the University of Rome. He became professor of economics at the University of Pavia and later at the University of Rome. His main contributions are found in numerous articles and reports. He wrote a book on the incidence of taxation, *Teoria della translazione dei tributi* (1882) and his *Manuale di economia pura* (1889) was translated into English in 1898. Pantaleoni had a greatly stimulating effect on the study of economics in Italy. He was perhaps the first fully to understand the importance of Léon Walras' works, and he brought together Walras and Pareto, who became Walras' successor and star pupil. Pantaleoni has been called a member of the Lausanne School founded by Walras.

**Vilfredo Pareto**
*Italian Economist and Sociologist*                    *1848–1923*

Pareto was born in Paris, the son of an Italian nobleman who for political reasons had to leave Italy temporarily. Pareto studied mathematics and physics at the polytechnic school of the University of Turin and became an engineer. In 1893 he went to Lausanne, Switzerland, to succeed Léon Walras as professor at the university. Here he taught pure and applied economics and also sociology, on which he concentrated after a long illness in 1900. His great sociological study appeared in 1916 and was translated into English as *Mind and Society* (1935). In 1906 Pareto fell ill again and in 1909 he retired to his villa on Lake Geneva where he devoted himself to research until his death.

Of his many economic writings, the most important are *Cours d'économie politique* (1896) and *Manuale di economia politica* (1906). After mathematically analyzing income data from many countries, he came to the conclusion known as "Pareto's Law": regardless of social or political institutions, income distribution trends are the same. This law is hotly discussed and not generally accepted. Pareto also expanded the theory of general equilibrium, and he developed the indifference curve, through which he tried to determine consumer demand. Although he found the use of mathematical formulae in economic science indispensable and used quantitative methods widely to prove his cases, he always saw in mathematics only a matter of convenience, a mere instrument to express economic analyses effectively. The Italian fascists adopted some of his ideas.

**Frédéric Passy**
*French Economist and Statesman*                    *1822–1912*

Born in Paris, Passy became a lawyer. He co-founded the International Peace League (1867), being in favor of free international trade and convinced that this would help secure international peace, for which he worked throughout his life. In 1901, he received the Nobel Prize. He was a member of the Chamber of Deputies (1881–88) and president of the Société d'Economie Politique. Among his many publications are *Mélanges économiques* (1857), *Leçons d'économie politique* (1860), *Le Principe de la population* (1868), *L'histoire du travail* (1873), *La Solidarité du travail et du capital* (1875), and *La Vie économique* (1910). He was convinced that the existing natural resources suffice to enable men to live in peace and prosperity if they do not interfere with the free play of natural laws.

**William Paterson**
*British Banker*                                                    *1658–1719*

Paterson, a Scottish merchant, became a founder of the Bank of England. His writings were published by Saxe Bannister (ca. 1859). Paterson had the idea of establishing a note-issuing bank and was one of the early free-trade supporters in England.

**Simon Nelson Patten**
*American Economist*                                                *1852–1922*

Patten, born at Sandwich, Illinois, studied at Northwestern University but completed studies at the University of Halle, Germany (Ph.D.). He became a professor at the University of Pennsylvania in 1888, where he remained until retirement. Of his extensive writings the following should be listed: *Premises of Political Economy* (1885), *Consumption of Wealth* (1889), *Economic Basis of Protection* (1890), *Development of English Thought* (1899), *Theory of Prosperity* (1902), and *Reconstruction of Economic Theory* (1912). He was specially interested in consumer economics, favored protective tariffs, and had an optimistic and nationalist approach to economics. Patten emphasized human welfare and believed that consumption would decrease the inequality among men.

**Paul VI**
*Pope*                                                             *1897–*

Born at Concesio, Italy, Giovanni Battista Montini was elected pope in 1963 and took the name Paul VI. Educated at the Pontifical Ecclesiastical Academy, he had been representative of the Roman church in Warsaw, deputy secretary of state for ordinary affairs of the Vatican, and archbishop of Milan. As pope, he continued the Second Vatican Council called by John XXIII. Arising from the Council, his *Gaudium et spes (Pastoral Constitution on the Church in the Modern World,* 1965) refers repeatedly to the Christian solution of various contemporary economic problems and conflicts. His encyclical *Populorum progressio (On the Development of Peoples,* 1967) extended the social doctrine outlined in John XXIII's *Pacem in terris* and outlined the application of the Church's reorganization to the nations of the Third World.

**Sir Robert Peel**
*English Statesman and Financier*                                  *1788–1850*

Peel, born at Bury, Lancashire, was educated at Christ Church, Oxford, and was a member of the House of Commons. He held many high offices including the office of home secretary, first lord of the treasury, and chancellor of the exchequer. He introduced many reforms, abandoned customs duties, and repealed the corn laws. His Bank Charter Act of 1844 remained the monetary and banking basis of England until 1914.

**Selig Perlman**
*American Economist*                                         *1888–1959*

Perlman was born in Poland, studied in Italy and at the University of Wisconsin (Ph.D.), and taught at Wisconsin. He published *History of Trade Unionism in the U.S.* (1922), *A Theory of the Labor Movement* (1928), and *American Labor Movements, 1896–1932* (1935).

**Arthur Latham Perry**
*American Economist*                                         *1830–1905*

Perry was born at Lyme, N.H., and studied at Williams College, where he taught 1853–1905. He published, besides many articles, *Elements of Political Economy* (1866) and *Principles of Political Economy* (1891), which went through 22 editions and was translated into many languages, including Japanese. For Perry, economics is the science of exchange or value, and value is determined by demand. He was a close friend of Amasa Walker, whose influence is clearly shown in Perry's works. His works also show the optimistic attitude of H. C. Carey and Bastiat. Basically he was for laissez-faire and was a convinced free-trader.

**Pesant**
see Pierre le Pesant, Sieur de *Boisguillebert*

**Heinrich Pesch**
*German Economist*                                          *1854–1926*

Born in Cologne, Pesch studied at the University of Bonn and entered the Society of Jesus. During this period of formation, he spent 4 years in England, where he had the opportunity to observe labor conditions in Lancashire. This experience left a great imprint on him. He wrote a 2-volume work, *Liberalismus, Sozialismus und christliche Gesellschaftsordnung* (1896–99). In 1901 he renewed his study of economics in Berlin under Wagner and Schmoller. Here he began his 4,000-page *Lehrbuch der Nationalökonomie* (5 vols., 1905–1923). In 1918 his *Ethik und Volkswirtschaft* appeared, stressing ethical standards in economic life. Pesch named his economic system "Solidarismus."

**Sir William Petty**
*English Mercantilist Writer*                               *1623–1687*

Born in Hampshire, Petty studied at the Jesuit College at Caen (France) and pursued the study of medicine at Leyden, Utrecht, Amsterdam, Oxford, and London. He earned the degrees of Doctor of

Physics and Doctor of Medicine and was appointed professor of anatomy at Oxford. He was also a sailor, professor of music, surveyor, landlord, and man of affairs. Petty was knighted in 1662 on the occasion of the formation of the Royal Society of London for Improving Natural Knowledge. Petty wrote extensively in various fields.

His contributions to economics, *Treatise of Taxes and Contributions* (1662) and *Political Arithmetic* (1678), are remarkable. In the latter, he proposed that instead of relying on "intellectual argument," the rulers of the country should look to "Number, Weight, and Measure" for sound advice on all matters of economic policy and taxation. He thus became one of the founders of economic statistics. In his *Treatise* he explored the principles of scientific taxation, supporting the benefits-received principle and seeing in such a tax policy a means of enriching the state. Following his mercantilist leanings, he advocated that taxes be used to stimulate trade, industry, and public works, thus giving employment to the idle. Petty had a searching mind and made the first attempt to explore the value of the contributions of the "factors of production" to the value of the product, or to the wealth of the nation. Correspondingly, he also explored the theory of functional income distribution. After stating that "Labour is the Father and active principle of Wealth, as Lands are the Mother," he discussed the respective shares of labor and land. Labor's wage should equal to the cost of food necessary to sustain the worker; the remainder of the value of the product he attributed to land as rent. Petty then made this food-determined wage a general standard of value by equating it with the value of the amount of gold whose production takes as much labor time as the production of the worker's food. In other words, in the view of Petty, equal amounts of labor time "embodied," as it were, in different commodities impart equal values to them, so that they will virtually exchange for each other. For Petty, as later for Ricardo and Marx, labor time thus became the common denominator of all values. Petty, not recognizing capital as an independent factor of production, lumped together all revenue from property under the name of "rent." Petty anticipated Ricardo's concept of differential rent—the additional income accruing to lands on account of their proximity to the market. Since his suggestion that value is the determinant of price became the cornerstone of classical economics, it is possible to consider Petty, as Marx did, the founder of modern economic theory.

**Eugen von Philippovich**
*Austrian Economist*                                             *1858–1917*

Philippovich was born in Vienna and studied at Graz, Vienna, and Berlin. One of the greatest teachers of his day, he was a professor at the University of Vienna. A former student of Karl Menger, he brought together what the Austrian and German Historical schools had to offer.

He published *Grundriss der Volkswirtschaftslehre* (2 vols., 1893–99), which for many years was the leading text for German-speaking students, and had many editions. He was the first to speak about income formation through distribution, and was highly interested in social policy. Concerned over the growing concentration of business, he proposed forms of controls to assure a balance between private and public interests.

**Willard Phillips**
*American Economist* 1784–1873

Phillips, born in Bridgewater, Massachusetts, studied law at Harvard, became a lawyer and in 1828 wrote *Manual of Political Economy*. He concerned himself with the problem of national production, and was inclined to accept a protective system. He contributed to the *North American Review* and published *Propositions concerning Protection and Free Trade* (1850).

**Nicolas Gerard Pierson**
*Dutch Economist and Statesman* 1839–1909

Born in Amsterdam, Pierson had little formal education. He had a brilliant mind, however, and gained success in the cotton trade and in banking, became president of the Dutch Central Bank, and subsequently was minister of finance, prime minister and, for a brief time, professor of economics at the University of Amsterdam. A prolific writer, he published over 100 books and papers, including *Principles of Economics*, which appeared in Dutch in 1884 and was translated into English in 1902. His collected economic writings were published in 6 volumes in 1910–11. Pierson introduced important reforms in taxation but objected to Marxian Socialism.

**Arthur Cecil Pigou**
*English Economist* 1877–1959

Pigou, born on the Isle of Wight, was a student of Alfred Marshall at Cambridge and later succeeded Marshall as leader of the "Cambridge School." His special interest was in welfare economics, and he said, "The main motive of economic study is to help social improvement." Under "social welfare" he placed all and everything connected with human satisfaction, while he restricted "economic welfare" to things measurable in monetary terms. According to him, welfare depends not merely on the size of the national income but also on equality of distribution. He published *Wealth and Welfare* (1912), which reappeared in expanded form as *The Economics of Welfare* (1920). Of his numerous other books and papers the following should be listed: *Essays in Applied Economics* (1923), *Industrial Fluctuations* (1927), *A Study of*

*Public Finance* (1928), *The Theory of Unemployment* (1933), and *Keynes' General Theory: A Retrospect* (1950). Pigou had taught Keynes and encouraged him to proceed with the study of economics. Keynes nevertheless later expressed some disagreements with the ideas of his teacher and in a form that was not generally appreciated.

**Gaetan Pirou**
*French Economist*
*1886–1946*

Pirou was born at Le Mans. He became a professor at L'Ecole des Hautes Études and editor of *Revue d'économie politique*. He made remarkable contributions to the study of the development of economic analysis in his *Les Doctrines économiques* (1925) and propagated Pareto's ideas in France. He wrote many articles on economic theory.

**William Pitt**
*English Statesman*
*1759–1806*

William Pitt was the second son of the First Earl of Chatham (1708–78), the "Great Commoner" insisting on constitutional rights. Pitt became prime minister under George III. As a liberal Tory he tried to apply many of Adam Smith's ideas in practice. He introduced reforms in India and Canada and tried to reduce national debts through new taxes. The Napoleonic wars interfered with some of his plans and policies and financial support of allies produced a financial crisis at home. Pitt resigned in 1801 after the king had vetoed his Catholic Emancipation policy. Recalled in 1804, he resigned again after the defeat at Austerlitz.

**Pius XI**
*Pope*
*1857–1939*

Born at Desio, Italy, Achille Ratti became Pope Pius XI in 1922. In 1931, on the 40th anniversary of Leo XIII's encyclical *Rerum novarum*, Pope Pius issued the encyclical *Quadragesimo anno* (*Reconstructing the Social Order*) favoring governmental intervention in behalf of the laboring classes. He emphasized the principle of subsidiarity. This was the first time the Church asked for help from the state. Facing worldwide depression and political ferment, he stressed human welfare and humanitarian considerations and rejected the philosophy of unrestricted laissez-faire. In later encyclicals he condemned Communism and objected to Fascism.

**Francis Place**
*English Politician*
*1771–1854*

Born in poverty in London, Place had no formal education. Still, self-made, he was widely recognized, even by Ricardo. Place was a disciple of Bentham and member of the Philosophical Radicals. He actively promoted many of the parliamentary projects of this group, including the repeal of the Combination Acts, which had limited the activities of the unions. Place published *Illustrations and Proofs of the Principle of Population: Including an Examination of the Proposed Remedies of Mr. Malthus and a Reply to the Objections of Mr. Godwin and Others* (1822). In it, he tried to substantiate Malthus' conclusions by making a study of the consequences of immigration to America. Place publicly advocated birth control, emphasizing education as a remedy. His attitude was motivated by his concern in regard to the misery, poverty, and crime he observed.

**Plato**
*Greek Philosopher*                                                427?–347? B.C.

Plato's name was actually Aristocles (Plato was a nickname, and meant broad-shouldered). He was born in Athens, and was a student of Socrates. Bitter about the poisoning of his teacher by the democratic leaders, he left Greece and traveled to Italy, Egypt, Judaea, and India. He returned in 387 B.C. and opened the Academy, which soon became the center of education. In his *Republic* Plato outlined his ideal state. He developed ideas on economic activities, like division of labor, trade, money, and private property, that are still widely quoted. In his *The Laws* and *Republic* he described the actual economic structure and activities as he observed them, including market organization, money transactions, commerce, and the city-state administration.

**Play**
see P. G. Frédéric *Le Play*

**Georgi V. Plekhanov**
*Russian Socialist*                                                1856–1918

Born in the Tambov Province as the son of a rich landowner, Plekhanov opposed the harsh treatment of the peasants by his father, developed a sympathy for them, and joined the revolutionary movement during his student days in St. Petersburg. He went to Switzerland, became a Marxist, and propagated the idea of an evolution from the feudal system through capitalism to socialism. He wrote commentaries on Marxist theory which filled 26 volumes and *Fundamental Problems of Marxism* (published in London, 1923). Plekhanov collaborated with Lenin until 1903. The Mensheviks adopted his theory of gradual evolution.

**Pliny the Elder**
*Roman Writer and Statesman*                                        A.D. 23–79

Pliny was born at Comum but studied in Rome. He succeeded in his official career and was governor of Spain. Retaining an intense interest in history and science, he gathered information wherever he went, setting it down in his encyclopedic, 37-book *Natural History*, his only extant work. Noting a decline of industry and a rise in moral laxity, he blamed gold as the reason for the ruin of man. He preferred barter trade, though he recognized the usefulness of gold as a medium of exchange. He opposed the charging of interest and called for simpler living. He died in an eruption of Vesuvius while helping people flee from the city of Pompeii.

**Ludwig Pohle**
*German Economist*                                                *1869–1926*

Pohle was born in Eisenberg, Thuringia. He developed a new business-cycle theory. In his *Bevölkerungsbewegung, Kapitalbildung und periodische Wirtschaftskrisen* (1902) Pohle developed the idea that the cause of business cycles can be found in the relationship between population increase and the expansion of production. Lack of investments, he believed, would result in insufficient quantities of the capital goods needed to produce consumer goods. Underproduction would lead to a crisis.

**Karl Polanyi**
*Austrian Economist*                                              *1886–1964*

Polanyi was born in Vienna, studied at the universities of Budapest and Vienna (Ph.D., LL.D.), and became a lawyer in Budapest. He later moved to Vienna, where he cooperated with the leading Austrian journal *Der Österreichische Volkswirt* and published papers on economic theory and policy. For political reasons he left Austria and went to England, where he lectured in the extension division of Oxford University and at the University of London. Polanyi was in the U.S. from 1940–43 and taught at Bennington College. Among his extensive writings, *The Great Transformation* (1944) should be given special consideration.

**John Pollexfen**
*English Civil Servant*                                               *1638–?*

Pollexfen was born in Sherford, Devonshire, and lived in London. He was a merchant and member of Parliament, and also served on the commission of trade and plantation in 1675 and the Board of Trade from 1697–1705. Of his writings, *A Discourse on Trade, Coin, and Paper Credit* (1697) has been described as one of the best analytical works of that time. He pointed out that the nation's trade depends on the work of those who are willing to produce. He favored paper money as an aid to, but not as a substitute for, coin. He was for free trade and treated labor as the source of wealth. Pollexfen found justification for state legislation concerning industry and commerce.

**Malachy Postlethwayt**
*English Economic Writer*                    *1707–1767*

Postlethwayt was born in London. He published *The Universal Dictionary of Trade and Commerce* (1751–55), which included source material on theoretical and policy aspects. In 1757 his 2-volume *Britain's Commercial Interest Explained and Improved* appeared. He compared English and Dutch colonial policies and suggested improvements in the British system.

**William Potter**
*English Land Administrator*                    *ca. 1650*

Of Potter the only thing known is that he held a government position in what today would be called the Land Office. In 1652 he published anonymously *The Key of Wealth, or, a New Way for Improving Trade*. This and two other tracts proposed that a new corporation composed mainly of tradesmen be formed, which would issue bills drawn on the security of land, buildings, and similar property. These bills were to be circulated in the same way as legal-tender money.

**Richard Price**
*English Writer and Minister*                    *1723–1791*

Price was born in Tynton. In 1786 the Pitt government resumed making larger payments annually into a Sinking Fund, in order to retire the national debt. This had been related to Price's *An Appeal to the Public on the Subject of the National Debt* (1772) and *The State of The Public Debt and Finances* (1783). Price also published an *Essay on the Population in England* (1779), in which he declared that since the revolution of 1668 and in consequence of urban agglomeration, the English population had decreased by one-fourth.

**John Prince-Smith**
*German Writer and Economist*                    *1809–1874*

Prince-Smith was born in England, but lived in Germany after 1830 and became a member of the Prussian Diet and later of the Reichstag. He was perhaps the most outstanding representative of the Manchester School in Germany in his time, and stood for unrestricted freedom of enterprise and foreign trade. The only duty of a government he recognized was to guarantee security. He was opposed to any form of social legislation and stated that the economic community is built upon the market. The access to and participation in the free market are the only things which can be expected from the society; no other help or support from government should be requested. He accepted Henry Carey's optimistic attitude and Bastiat's harmony between individual and social interests. With Schulze-Delitzsch he founded the free-trade Kongress

Deutscher Volkswirte and was co-editor of the *Vierteljahrsschrift für Volkswirtschaft, Politik und Kulturgeschichte.* His writings were published as *Gesammelte Schriften* (3 vols., 1877–80).

**Pierre Joseph Proudhon**
*French Anarchist*                                                *1809–1865*

Born in Besançon, Proudhon was the child of a poor family who could not afford to pay for his education. He obtained a scholarship at the university there, where he won the class prize every year. To make a living, he became a printer and proofreader. In 1832 he started writing against religion and left the Church. A printing house he bought soon declared bankruptcy and his partner committed suicide. He went to Paris, hoping to make a living by writing articles, but this only produced the withdrawal of an award which had helped support his family. Of his writings, two stand out. The first is the famous pamphlet, *What Is Property?* (1840). His answer was "Property is theft." His book *Philosophie de la misère* met an angry answer from Marx, who wrote *Misère de la philosophie.* Proudhon was elected to the Constituent Assembly in 1848. His bill for an exchange bank was badly defeated, but in 1849 he founded a people's bank, which was to operate as a credit institution for workers. Before the bank could actually start to function, Proudhon was imprisoned because of articles attacking the president of France. Released, he soon had to serve a second term as the consequence of insults to the archbishop in one of his articles. Afterwards he went to Belgium, returning to Paris only after amnesty was granted in 1860. Proudhon hoped to eliminate private enterprise through the establishment of a bank that would grant loans to cooperatives of workers. This, in his opinion, would bring justice, which was for him equality. Such cooperatives would make any form of government unnecessary and the ideal conditions of anarchy would reign. In this belief he was so firm and so intolerant that he bitterly opposed communism as represented by Marx, Engels, and others.

**Samuel Pufendorf**
*German Jurist and Political Philosopher*                        *1632–1694*

Pufendorf, born at Chemnitz, Saxony, became a jurist, was professor at the universities of Heidelberg, Lund (Sweden), and Berlin. He was not much more than a follower of Grotius, but he wrote a treatise that became the textbook in international relations, *Elementa Jurisprudentiae Universalis* (1660). In economics he did not add much to the stock of knowledge concerning value, interest, and monopoly, but he presented the material in a systematic form. Even more important, however, is the fact that his political philosophy reconciled the benevolent absolutism of the German states of his time with the spirit of individual freedom by allowing supremacy to the sovereignty of the state but at the same time denying to it absolute control over the lives of its citizens.

# Q

**François Quesnay**
*French Physiocrat*
*1694–1774*

Quesnay was born in Mêré, near Paris. He studied surgery, obtained the degree of Doctor of Medicine in 1744, and in time became physician to Louis XV and Madame de Pompadour. The then-recent discovery of the circulation of the blood inspired Quesnay to design his famous *Tableau économique* (1758), with which he intended to explain to the king the circulation of goods and money in a free and competitive economy. His contributions to medicine brought him early recognition by learned societies; those to political economy brought him everlasting fame.

With his *Tableau* Quesnay became the leader of a small, closely knit group of French social philosophers, reformers, and political economists. Calling themselves at first simply "the economists," they came to be known as the physiocrats. Physiocracy was an ideology based on belief in a universe grounded in a natural order—a system of natural laws preordained by a wise and benevolent God, the designer of all human nature, to ensure a harmonious, orderly functioning of both the natural universe and all human societies. When these natural laws are obeyed, they produce a social system, Quesnay said, "as favorable as possible" to the common welfare. From this conception followed the maxim, first proclaimed by the physiocrats, of "laissez faire, laissez passer": let all men do the work that their interests make it "natural" for them to do and let every sequence of economic events take its "natural" course. As reformers they urged the government to carry out an enlightened and public action to create conditions under which every individual can discover for himself the true principles of the "natural laws" and "natural justice." Once the rules of justice and prudent individual conduct are observed, they felt, the quasi-mechanical laws of society will bring about the maximum happiness of all. Physiocratic ideology and economics was a reaction against the state-regulated and industry- and trade-oriented mercantilism.

Agriculture held the central position in Quesnay's program of economic policy as well as in his analytic scheme. In the physiocratic view, agriculture alone is capable of yielding a net product, the other branches (manufacturing, trade) of the economy being "sterile" in the sense that they only transform the goods created by agriculture and labor. Since agriculture is the only sector of the economy that produces a net surplus, they felt that all taxes should be levied on this net product, namely on the rents of the landowners. The principle that all products emerge from agricultural production was central to Quesnay's *Tableau*, in which he analyzed the annual circular flow of newly produced wealth. Despite the one-sided emphasis on agriculture as the only productive branch of the economy, his work is a pioneering step toward modern income analysis and input-output analysis.

**Jacques Adolphe Quételet**
*Belgian Astronomer and Statistician*                                        *1796–1874*

Quételet was born in Ghent. He was appointed professor of mathematics at the Brussels Athenaeum in 1820. In 1841 he became president of the Commission Centrale Statistique of the Belgian government, a position he held until his death. His contributions were in the field of the theory of probability, and in his promotion of international cooperation in regard to uniformity and comparability of statistical data. Of special interest is the fact that he developed rules for census work that are still the basis for modern census-taking. Quételet has been called "father of statistics." He hoped that statistics would become a tool for making an exact science out of the social sciences.

**Quincey**
see Thomas *De Quincey*

# R

**John Rae**
*American Economist* | *1796–1872*

Born in Aberdeen, Scotland, Rae studied medicine at the University of Edinburgh, but did not complete his degree. He traveled to Norway and to Canada, where he taught children of the Hudson Bay Company, came to the U.S., where he was headmaster of a grammar school, sailed to California as a ship's physician, and proceeded to the Sandwich Islands (Hawaii). Here he held the position of medical agent and district judge of the island of Maui. Finally in 1871 he traveled to New York to retire, but there he soon died.

In 1834 his *Some New Principles on the Subject of Political Economy* was published in Boston. The purpose of this book is shown in its subtitle: *Exposing the Fallacies of the System of Free Trade and of Some Other Doctrines Maintained in the Wealth of Nations.* Invention was the keystone of his message; the creation of wealth depends upon it. By his talents and capacities, the individual gains his fortune, which may result in capital formation. An individual may acquire a part of his wealth from the total wealth existing, but this is only a shift and the total wealth in a nation does not increase by it. Only by invention can wealth be increased. National interests and individual interests are not identical. Rae also put forward a notion which was called the "time preference theory of interest" when it was later developed by Böhm-Bawerk.

**Friedrich Wilhelm Raiffeisen**
*German Leader of the Cooperative Movement* | *1818–1888*

Raiffeisen was born at Hamm-an-der-Sieg. For health reasons he resigned early from civil service. The plight of the poor peasant during the disastrous years of 1846–47, together with a deep understanding of the needs of the small farmers in Germany, led him to the formation of agricultural cooperatives, loan banks, and agricultural credit cooperatives, to which he devoted his life. He was convinced that this movement would not only bring material help and assistance but would also have great moral effects. In fact, the movement grew rapidly. In 1872 Raiffeisen formed the first Regional Central Cooperative and in 1876 the National Central Cooperative. "Raiffeisenvereine" could be found in many places and continue to carry the name of the founder. Raiffeisen's most important work, *Die Darlehnskassen-Vereine als Mittel zur Abhilfe der Noth der Ländischen Bevölkerung* (1866, 1867), describes the system of agricultural cooperative banks that he advocated.

**Sir George Ramsay**
*English Economist*                                               *1800–1871*

Ramsay was the author of *Essay on the Distribution of Wealth* (1836), which added little to economic science as such but has historical value as a demonstration of contemporary attitudes and thought. Among his other books, *An Enquiry into the Principles of Human Happiness and Human Duty* (1843) is noteworthy.

**Karl Heinrich Rau**
*German Economist*                                               *1792–1870*

Rau was born in Erlangen, studied at the university there, and became professor there. In 1822 the chair of political economy at the University of Heidelberg was offered to him, and he taught there for nearly 50 years. He was an outstanding, stimulating, and highly respected teacher. Rau published *Lehrbuch der politischen Ökonomie* (3 vols., 1826–37), which became the standard German textbook and enjoyed wide acceptance. Intended as a practical guide for future administrators, it admirably succeeded in its purpose. Rau introduced a division of the material which has been used by many of his successors: volume 1 deals with theory; volume 2 with policy; and volume 3 with problems of public finance. Rau also published books on economic history and thought.

**Piercy Ravenstone**
*English Writer*                                               *?–1830*

Very little is known of Ravenstone's personality and life. In 1821 he published *A Few Doubts as to the Correctness of Some Opinions Generally Entertained on the Subjects of Population and Political Economy.* In this, he analyzed population growth by age groups and classes and came to the conclusions that it is not as large as Malthus expected and also that it is nearly equal at all times and in all places. No restrictive measures, therefore, are needed.

**Daniel Raymond**
*American Lawyer and Economist*                                               *1786–1849*

Raymond, rightly or wrongly, has been called the first American economist. He was born in Connecticut, studied law in Baltimore, and practiced law during his entire life. But he was keenly interested in economic problems and wrote what is probably the first comprehensive treatise written in the U.S., *Thoughts on Political Economy* (1820). The second edition appeared in 1823 under the title *Elements of Political Economy.* Raymond opposed Adam Smith's definition of productive labor and was a strong supporter of protectionist theories. He was a nationalist who defined political economy as a "science which teaches the nature of public or national wealth." Labor and land are the sources of all wealth, and economic affairs can best be managed under a strong central government, he believed.

**Samuel Read**
*English Economist*                                                                *ca. 1780–?*

Read wrote *On Money and the Bank Restriction Law* (1816) and two years later an essay on a safe, steady, and secure government paper currency. In 1821 he published *General Statement of an Argument on the Subject of Population in Answer to Mr. Malthus's Theory* and in 1829 *Political Economy: An Inquiry into the Natural Grounds of Right to Vendible Property of Wealth.* Here he stated that employers have not only rights but also obligations toward society. This book had an influence on discussions of profit and interest in the following decade.

**Jean Jacques Elisée Reclus**
*French Geographer and Anarchist*                                      *1830–1905*

Reclus, born in Sainte-Foy la Grande, near Bordeaux, was both a well-respected geographer and the best-known French anarchist. He studied in Montauban and Berlin (under Karl Ritter), and served as professor of comparative geography at the Université Nouvelle in Brussels. He became a member of Bakunin's secret brotherhood in France. In 1892 he received the gold medal of the Paris Geographical Society for his *La Nouvelle géographie universelle.*

   In 1898 Reclus published *L'Evolution, la révolution, et de l'idéal anarchique.* The following quotations have been culled from his book to show its general tone and character: "Every tree in nature bears its own peculiar fruit; any government, whatever the form it takes, always results in tyranny, misery, villainy, murder, and evil." "The anarchists want to see free unions established, resting upon mutual affection and based upon respect for one's self and for the dignity of others. And in that sense, in their desire to show respect and affection for all the members of the association, they are inimical to the family." "Life, which is always improving and renewing itself, can never submit to regulations which have been drawn up in some period now past." "In the great human family hunger simply is the result of a collective crime, and it becomes an absurdity when we remember that the products are more than double enough for all the needs of consumers."

**David Ricardo**
*English Political Economist*                                             *1772–1823*

Born in London of Dutch-Jewish parents, at age 14 Ricardo entered his father's stockbrokerage firm after a brief commercial education in Holland. At age 21 he married a Quaker against the will of his family, and accepted the Christian faith. His extraordinary professional abilities won him the support of some members of the stock exchange and he entered the floor trading of the Exchange on his own account. He was successful from the beginning, and it has been estimated that after 10 years he had made a fortune of £2,000,000. In his spare time he studied mathematics and science privately and also, stimulated by Adam Smith's *Wealth of Nations*, political economy. Partly retiring from business, in 1814 he bought a country estate, Gatcomb Park, where he lived for the rest of his life. In 1819 he became a member of Parliament, where he took an active part in discussions of bank reform, tax proposals, resumption of specie payment, and national debt reduction. He was also interested in public education. His friendship with James Mill proved to be most stimulating and helpful. Through him, Ricardo became a founder of the Political Economy Club in London and a member of the philosophical radicals.

Important among Ricardo's articles and pamphlets are *The High Price of Bullion, a Proof of the Depreciation of Bank Notes* (1810), originally written in letters to a newspaper; *Reply to Mr. Bosanquet's Practical Observations on the Report of the Bullion Committee* (1811); *Proposals for an Economical and Secure Currency, with Observations on the Profit of the Bank of England* (1816); *The Influence of a Low Price of Corn on the Profits of Stock* (1815); *In Protection of Agriculture* (1822); and *Plans for the Establishment of a National Bank*, published posthumously in 1824. His main work, however, is *On the Principles of Political Economy and Taxation* (1817), a highly abstract and theoretical work intended as a comprehensive demonstration of the entire field of economics. The book contains numerous original views, stressing the theory of value and distribution, wages, rent, profit, prices, money, and the comparative-costs principle in foreign-trade theory. A large part is devoted to taxation. Ricardo's work became source material for many generations and is still constantly referred to.

The author's early death was a great loss for economic science. Although Ricardo had no college education, he gained the respect and admiration of professional economists because of his courageous judgments, his logic, and his sincerity in the search for truth. He made many outstanding friends, who learned to know him as a modest, stimulating, highly talented man who stood for the liberty of all and for the common good and proved this by his generous gifts to the poor.

**Guiseppe Ricca-Salerno**
*Italian Economist*                                                                 *1849–1912*

Ricca-Salerno, born in Salerno, was professor of finance at the University of Pavia and later professor of economics at the universities of

Modena and Palermo. His greatest contributions were in the fields of value theory and fiscal theory. Of special interest are his works *Sulla teoria del capitale* (1877), *La teoria del salario* (1900), *Storia delle dottrine finanziarie in Italia* (1881) and *Scienza delle finanze* (1888).

**Umberto Ricci**
*Italian Economist*                                                    *1879–1946*

Ricci, born in Chisti, did not have an academic degree. From a small administrative position he was called by Ghino Valenti, an agricultural economist, to register agricultural property. Ricci's rise was rapid. By 1910 he was head of the statistical bureau of the International Institute of Agriculture. His work in this bureau added to his reputation, which was supported by his publications on agricultural statistics. He became professor of statistics at Macerata, Parma, Pisa, Bolgona, and finally Rome. When Fascism forced him to leave Italy he taught at Cairo until 1940, and then at Istanbul. On the way back to Italy he died in Cairo. His articles and books cover a wide field of economics. They are on the theory of capital, on savings, taxation, and the psychological foundations of the law of demand. They also venture into practical fields like public finance and international problems.

**William Zebian Ripley**
*American Economist*                                                    *1867–1944*

Born in Medford, Massachusetts, Ripley studied at the Massachusetts Institute of Technology and Columbia University (Ph.D.) He taught at Columbia until in 1901 he moved to Harvard University as professor of political economy. He was especially interested in transportation problems, becoming a member of commissions like the U.S. Shipping Board, a special examiner on consolidation of railways for the Interstate Commerce Commission, and director of the Chicago, Rock Island and Pacific Railroad. Among his writings, particularly noteworthy are *Railway Problems* (1907), *Railroads, Rates and Regulation* (1912), *Railroads, Finance and Organization* (1915), and *Main Street and Wall Street* (1927). In 1933 Ripley was president of the American Economic Association.

**Riquetti**
see Victor Riquetti, Marquis de *Mirabeau*

**Charles Rist**
*Swiss Economist*                                                    *1873–1955*

Rist was born in Lausanne and was professor of political economy at the University of Montpellier. He wrote *Histoire des doctrines économiques* (1929), *Histoire des doctrines relatives au crédit et à la monnaie depuis John Law jusqu'à nos jours* (1938). Bank notes and bank deposits were for him nothing but "material embodiments of the velocity of circulation." Rist was subgovernor of the Bank of France and financial adviser to the national banks of Rumania and Austria.

**Rivière**

see Pierre François *Mercier de la Rivière*

**Lionel Charles Robbins**

*English Economist*                         *1898–*

Robbins, born in London, was educated at University College, London, and the London School of Economics where he became a professor after being a lecturer at New College, Oxford. He was director of the economic section of the cabinet (1941–45). Important among his many publications are: *An Essay on the Nature and Significance of Economic Science* (1932), *The Great Depression* (1934), *Economic Planning and International Order* (1937), *The Economist in the Twentieth Century* (1954), *Politics and Economics* (1963), and *The Evolution of Modern Economic Theory* (1970). He believed that the satisfaction of individuals can be achieved through the general welfare of the whole society, and followed Bentham in regard to the quantitative conception of utility. For him, economics should discuss means only and should remain neutral as to ends. In 1959 Robbins received a life peerage.

**Sir Dennis Holme Robertson**

*English Economist*                         *1890–1963*

Born at Lowestoft, England, Robertson entered Trinity College, Cambridge. He returned to Cambridge after World War I until 1938 when he became professor at the London School of Economics. In 1944 he became Pigou's successor at Cambridge. His works, which offer some refinements of Marshall's concepts but also include original findings, include: *Study of Industrial Fluctuation* (1915); *Banking Policy and Price Level* (1926); *Essays in Monetary Theory* (1940), in which his theory on forced savings is specially notable; and *Utility and All That* (1952), a volume of critical essays.

**E. Austin G. Robinson**

*English Economist*                         *1897–*

Robinson was a close friend of Lord Keynes and co-editor of the *Economic Journal* in which appeared his widely praised obituary on Keynes entitled "John Maynard Keynes, 1883–1946"; it contains many intimate details. In 1932 Robinson published *The Structure of Competitive Industry*, which introduced the idea of the optimum firm. In 1940 his *Monopoly* appeared.

**Mrs. Joan Violet Robinson**
*English Economist*       1903–

Born in Cambridge, the daughter of Major General Sir Frederick Maurice, she graduated from Girton College, Cambridge, married E. Austin G. Robinson, and became one of the leading faculty members in economics at Cambridge. Her first book, *Economics of Imperfect Competition* (1933), elicited prompt and wide attention. In *Essays on the Theory of Employment* (1937) she applied Keynesian concepts to specific conditions and situations. In 1942 she published *Essays on Marxian Economics*; in 1952, *The Rate of Interest and Other Essays*; in 1956, *Accumulation of Capital*; in 1959, *Exercises in Economic Analysis*; and in 1962, *Economic Philosophy*, which merited wide attention. Many of her articles appeared in the *Journal of Political Economy* and other leading professional magazines.

**Johann Karl Rodbertus**
*German State Socialist*       1805–1875

Born in Greifswald, Rodbertus was the grandson of August Schlettwein, a leading German physiocrat, and the son of a professor of Roman law. He studied law in Göttingen and Berlin and joined the Prussian civil service. In 1848 Rodbertus was a liberal member of the Prussian National Assembly and for a short time was minister of education. He bought an estate in East Prussia near Jagetzow and named himself Rodbertus von Jagetzow. He spent nearly all his life in study, writing, and research, and became one of the best-educated men of his time. He wrote books on the conditions of the working classes, the normal working day, and the credit problems of farmers and landowners. His social letters with von Kirchmann and Lassalle are famous: *Soziale Briefe an von Kirchman* (3 vols. 1850–1852) and *Nachlass, Briefe von Lassalle* (published by Wagner, 1878).

Basically he followed Ricardo, but he was also influenced by the ideas of Sismondi, Saint-Simon, and Proudhon. Positive social reform was in his opinion the responsibility of the state, and he demanded a better share of the national income for the laboring classes. He proposed socialization of property over time, in a form of evolutionary process, and hoped for a Christian social solution eliminating poverty. Contrary to Marx, he opposed revolution in every form. His goal was distributive justice, a change of the institutional pattern carried through with the support of the majority of the people.

**Rodriguez**
see Pedro Rodriguez, Count *Campomanes*

**James Edwin Thorold Rogers**
*English Economist*                                     *1823–1890*

Rogers, born in West Meon, Hampshire, was ordained as a minister but subsequently became professor at King's College, London (1859–90). He distinguished himself by his careful historical and statistical demonstrations. Rogers belonged to the earlier historical school of economics in England. Outstanding were his contributions in *History of Agriculture and Prices in England 1259–1793* (7 vols., 1866–82) and *The Economic Interpretation of History* (1888), in which he took a strong stand against Ricardo and his followers. He also published *Manual of Political Economy* (1868), *Six Centuries of Work and Wages* (1884), *The First Nine Years of the Bank of England* (1887), and other books, but his fame rests on his studies of agricultural prices and on his contributions to the economic history of England.

**John Rooke**
*English Farmer and Politician*                          *1780–1856*

Rooke, born in Cumberland, remained a farmer until age 30. He was entirely self-taught. He founded *Farmer's Journal* (1814), to which he contributed many articles. He developed a doctrine of rent and the marginal-cost concept as a universal principle, and strongly supported free trade. He wrote *Remarks on the Nature and Operations of Money* (1819), *An Essay on the National Debt* (1822), and *An Enquiry into the Principles of National Wealth* (1824).

**Raymond Adrian de Roover**
*American Economist*                                     *1904–1972*

De Roover was born in Antwerp, Belgium, studied at the Institut Supérieur du Commerce, Antwerp; at Harvard University; and at the University of Chicago (Ph.D.). He taught at Wells College, Boston College, and Brooklyn College. His greatest contributions were in history of economic thought. Notable is his *The Medici Bank* (1948); for *The Rise and Decline of the Medici Bank, 1397–1494* (1963) he was awarded the Paine Prize.

**Wilhelm Röpke**
*German Economist*                                       *1899–1966*

Born in Schwarmstedt, Röpke studied in Göttingen and Tübingen. He taught at the universities of Marburg, Jena, and Graz (Austria). Forced to leave when the Nazis took over, he then taught at the University of Istanbul. After 1937 he was at the University of Geneva Institute for International Studies. He published *Die Lehre von der Wirtschaft* (1936), *Die Gesellschaftskrise der Gegenwart* (1942), *Internationale Ordnung-heute* (1945), *Jenseits von Angebot und Nachfrage* (1958), which was translated into English as *A Humane Economy* (1960), and many other books and articles. Röpke may be called a neo-liberal. He strongly believed in competition and the market economy, but with an attitude that contributed to the social-market-economy notion applied after 1950 in the reconstruction of Germany and other European countries, in which he was influential.

**Wilhelm Georg Friedrich Roscher**
*German Economist*     *1817–1894*

Roscher, born in Hanover, studied jurisprudence and political economy at the universities of Göttingen and Berlin. He also studied philology and history. He taught at Göttingen and for 46 years at Leipzig. He was a founder of the Historical School, which grew in importance during his lifetime and later. His gentle and highly cultivated attitude was matched by honesty and scholarship based on common sense. He established his reputation with *Grundriss zu Vorlesungen über die Staatswirtschaft, nach geschichtlicher Methode* (1843). His other works include *System der Volkswirtschaft* (5 vols., 1854–94) and *Geschichte der National-ökonomie in Deutschland* (1874). Roscher was one of the first writers on the subject of the location of industry.

**Count Pellegrino Luigi Eduardo Rossi**
*Italian-French Economist*     *1787–1848*

Born in Carrara, Rossi was educated at the universities of Pavia and Bologna and earned the Doctor of Law degree. He taught at the Collège de France as the successor of Say, whom he followed faithfully. In 1834 he became a French citizen and later he entered the diplomatic service and was ambassador to the Vatican. After the fall of Louis Philippe (1848) he resumed his status as an Italian citizen and Pope Pius IX named him minister of the interior. He attempted an Italian confederation under the leadership of the Papal States but was assassinated in Rome. His most notable work in economics was *Cours d'économie politique* (2 vols., 1838). In 1857 *Mélanges d'économie politique d'histoire et de philosophie* was published posthumously (2 vols.).

**Jean-Jacques Rousseau**
*French Philosopher*     *1712–1778*

Rousseau was born in Geneva, Switzerland. His mother died at his birth, his father abandoned him at age 10, and he was given to an engraver as an apprentice. He ran away and led a restless, wandering life. In 1741 he came to Paris, where he composed and taught music and, meeting Diderot, began to travel in high intellectual circles. He had never written, but in 1749 an essay prize offered by the Dijon Academy inspired in him a flood of ideas about the contradictions of the social system—ideas that found an immediate response among his contemporaries. He won the prize and became famous. He returned to Geneva in 1754 and published another widely popular essay, *Discours sur l'origine et les fondements de l'inégalité parmi les hommes* (1755). He quarreled with Diderot and in 1757 retired to a cottage near the forest of Montmorency, where he wrote *Emile* (1762) and *Le Contrat social* (1762). When these books were condemned in Paris, he fled first to Switzerland and then to England, where he began his *Confessions* (1781). He soon quarreled with Hume, who had taken him in, and returned to France, spending his last days in retirement at Ermenonville.

Rousseau had perhaps more influence on the development of economic and social thought in the 18th century than any other single man. He believed that man is by nature good and is only corrupted by civilization; and that laws are instituted to preserve the inequality of those opposed to the privileges of the oppressors. Equality had disappeared with the establishment of property and all that is connected with it. Only a return to nature offers a solution to the dilemma; what the established society has done is evil and should be eliminated. Like Locke, Rousseau based his property theory on the idea of natural rights, but where Locke had employed natural rights to justify property, Rousseau used the doctrine to condemn it.

**Rouvroy**
see Claude Henri de Rouvroy, Comte de *Saint-Simon*

**John Ruskin**
*English Author and Art Critic*                                  *1819–1900*

Ruskin, born in London of well-to-do parents, studied painting and graduated from Christ Church, Oxford. He began lecturing at the Workingmen's College in 1854, and in 1870 became the first professor of fine arts at Oxford. He was also involved in a cooperative enterprise, the St. George's Company, "to slay the dragon of Industrialism," and himself wielded a broom in a project to clean London streets. His earlier works like *Modern Painters* (5 vols., 1843–60) and *The Seven Lamps of Architecture* (1849) state that art reflects the moral tone of individuals and society, and condemn the materialism and exploitation of the Victorian era. Seeking a social order that would produce worthy art, with *Unto This Last* in 1860–62 he began a series of books suggesting reforms, many of which were later adopted in England. Written for the common man in a simple style, these books included *Sesame and Lilies* (1865), *The Crown of Wild Olive* (1866), *Time and Tide* (1867), and *Fors Clavigera: Letters to the Workmen and Labourers of Great Britain* (1871–74). *Munera Pulveris* (1862–63), a more difficult work, defines value as the power of anything to sustain and enhance life. Though Ruskin was an art expert and not an economist, his writings had a wide influence, notably on J. A. Hobson and on socialist thought.

# S

**Michael T. Sadler**
*English Writer and Politician*      *1780–1835*

Sadler was born at Snelston, Derbyshire. In *The Law of Population, a Treatise in Six Books; in Disproof of the Superfecundity of Human Beings, and Developing the Real Principle of Their Increases* (1830) Sadler used statistics to try to refute Malthus' notion of the geometric progression of population growth. Prolificacy varies inversely with numbers, he said, the controlling forces being space and the character of the land. Sadler's efforts in economic policy matters contributed to the passing of the Factory Act of 1833, which has been called the first blow to laissez-faire.

**Claude Henri de Rouvroy, Comte de Saint-Simon**
*French Social Philosopher*      *1760–1825*

Saint-Simon, born in Paris to a poor branch of a famous French family, was educated privately. In 1777–82 he was an army officer and served in the American Revolution. He was involved in a number of unsuccessful promotional schemes, including one to build a canal from the Atlantic to the Pacific. As a nobleman, he was imprisoned in 1793–94 during the Reign of Terror. Released, he made a fortune in land speculation and set up a salon in Paris, entertaining the leading scientists and intellectuals of his day. He began writing on social reform in 1802; by 1804 he had used up his money, and he spent the end of his life writing in near-poverty.

Called the father of French socialism, Saint-Simon was not himself a socialist. In editing and writing for such publications as his *L'Industrie* (1816–18) and *Du Système industriel* (1821–22) he envisioned peaceful transition to a planned industrial economy run by an educated elite. He did not want to socialize property, but he hoped to see owners use it in the public interest. He stood for equal opportunities and rewards based on merit. In his last work, *Le Nouveau christianisme* (1825), he advocated a modernized spiritual revival (with scientists replacing priests) in order to weld society together in a spirit of association rather than antagonism, with the goal of improving the lot of the poor. He was one of the first to see the social implications of industrialization, a term which he coined, and he formulated the idea of the organic evolution of society later used by Marx and others. He suggested that a rational science of society would be of use in reconstructing the social order, thus influencing the birth of sociology, and also Comte's positivist philosophy.

It was his followers, like Enfantin, Bazard, and Leroux, who from 1825–33 reworked his ideas into an early form of socialism, adding the socialization of property, a condemnation of capitalist exploitation, abolition of inheritance, and emancipation of women to the doctrine. Saint-Simonism attracted many, including Blanc, Chevalier, Carlyle, and J. S. Mill.

### Salerno
see Giuseppe *Ricca-Salerno*

### Friedrich Georg Sartorius, Freiherr von Waltershausen
*German Economist*      *1765–1828*

Sartorius was born in Kassel and studied theology and history at the University of Göttingen. He became professor there, expanding his lectures to political science and economics. He participated as a political expert at the Congress of Vienna. He published selections of Adam Smith's works and propagated Smith's doctrines but also offered original ideas, including a value theory based on the consumption of goods, on the need for restricting free competition through state intervention, on limitations of capital investment, and on the role of savings. His chief work is *Abhandlungen, die Elemente des National-Reichtums* (1806).

### Friedrich Karl von Savigny
*German Jurist*      *1779–1861*

Savigny, born at Frankfurt-Main, studied law at Marburg. He became professor of law at the University of Berlin. He was the founder of the German historical school of law and stimulated German economists to follow his lead by applying the historical method to economics. Savigny had made extensive studies in legal history and his publications were inspiring. To this extent it may be said that he contributed to the development of the "historical school" of political economy in Germany.

### Emil Sax
*Austrian Economist*      *1845–1927*

Sax was born in Jauering, studied at Vienna, and taught at the University of Prague but resigned because little attention was given to his work and his publications. He retired to Italy. Sax applied the marginal theory of value to the fields of public finance and transportation and found that identical laws regulate individual and public economic activities and motivations. His principal works are *Grundlegung der theoretischen Staatswissenschaft* (1887), *Der Kapitalzins* (1916), and *Die Verkehrs-*

*mittel in Volkswirtschaft und Staatswirtschaft* (3 vols., 1918–22). The last-mentioned was perhaps his greatest contribution, for it is still recognized as a classic in the field of transportation.

**Jean-Baptiste Say**
*1767–1832*

*French Economist*

Say was born in Lyons, raised in Geneva, and served a business apprenticeship in England. Returning to France, he started work in a life-insurance office, and when his employer, Clavière, became finance minister, Say became his secretary. Appointed to a post in Napoleon's government in 1799, Say resigned in 1804 in opposition to certain of its measures. For 10 years he owned a cotton-spinning mill and was not involved in politics. But after Napoleon's fall in 1814, the French government sent Say to England to study business conditions. Say published his observations in *De l'Angleterre et des Anglais* (1816). In 1819 he began to teach at the Conservatoire National des Arts et Métiers and from 1830 he was professor of political economy at the Collège de France.

Say edited the journal *La Décade*, in which he wrote many articles promoting the ideas of Adam Smith. He championed laissez-faire and had a great influence on the development of economic theory in France. Say's Law, the law of markets, whereby supply creates its own demand and aggregate supply of goods equals aggregate demand for goods, went unchallenged for a long time. Say felt that the desire for commodities is infinite and the ability to purchase is assured. His extensive writings include *Traité d'économie politique* (1803; English trans. 1821), his first major book; *Catéchisme d'économie politique* (1815); and *Cours complet d'économie politique pratique* (1828).

**Louis Auguste Say**
*1774–1840*

*French Businessman and Economist*

Louis Auguste, born in Lyons, was the brother of Jean-Baptiste Say, with whom he went to England as business apprentice. He founded sugar refineries at Nantes and Paris. He was especially interested in the utility notion and stated that anything is wealth only insofar as it has a degree of utility. He criticized Smith and Ricardo as vague in their definitions and use of terms, and said that Smith's way of thinking was that of a merchant and that his theory of value has done more harm than good. Among his writings, the following should be mentioned: *Principales causes de la richesse* (1818), *Traité élémentaire de la richesse individuelle et de la richesse publique* (1827), and *Études sur la richesse des nations et réfutation des principales erreurs en économie politique* (1836).

Albert Eberhard Friedrich Schäffle

*German Economist and Sociologist*                    *1831–1903*

Schäffle, born in Nürtingen, studied at the University of Tübingen, where he later taught political economy. In 1871 he became for a short time Austrian minister of commerce. Afterwards he devoted himself to journalism and writing.

Schäffle was affiliated with the historical school, but stressed the concept of society as an organic system which can be analyzed like the biological organism of the human body. He stood for government intervention, and was opposed to the so-called purely individualistic, atomistic system, which with a few slogans like liberty, exchange, self-interest, competition, and a state which only serves as security and safety bureau, tries to characterize an economic system. But he was also critical of socialism. His most noted work is *Die Quintessenz des Sozialismus* (1875), which was for a short time banned in Prussia. In his *Die nationalökonomische Theorie der ausschliessenden Absatzverhältnisse* (1867) he described in an original way the function of rent.

**Johann August Schlettwein**

*German Physiocrat*                    *1731–1802*

Born in Weimar, Schlettwein became professor at Basel and Giessen and advised Margrave Karl Friedrich of Baden. He unsuccessfully tried to introduce the single tax on the agricultural net product. His overenthusiasm for physiocracy did more harm to the new ideas than good. His many writings include *Grundfeste der Staaten oder die politische Ökonomie* (1778).

**Theodor Schmalz**

*German Physiocrat*                    *1760–1831*

Schmalz, born in Hanover, studied at Göttingen. He taught law at Königsberg and Halle and became the first rector of the University of Berlin in 1810. Schmalz has been called the last of the physiocrats. He remained convinced that the doctrines of Quesnay would triumph. He wrote *Staatswirtschaftslehre in Briefen an einen teutschen Erbprinzen* (1818).

**Schmidt**
see Max *Stirner*

**Gustav von Schmoller**

*German Economist*                    *1838–1917*

Born in Heilbronn, Schmoller studied at the University of Tübingen. He was professor at the universities of Halle and Strassburg, and for 35 years at Berlin. Remembered as a great teacher, writer, and economist, he was the leader of the so-called younger historical school and a founder of the Verein für Sozialpolitik. Outstanding among his many writings is *Grundriss der allgemeinen Volkswirtschaftslehre* (2 vols., 1900–1904). Here he dealt with the elements of political economy, its social nature and origin, the social process of the exchange of goods, and, finally, with the development of economic life as a whole. With Karl Menger he conducted the famous "Methodenstreit" (quarrel about methodology), which was furious and unpleasant.

**Erich Schneider**
*German Economist*     *1900–*

Born in Siegen, Schneider studied at the universities of Göttingen (Ph.D.) and Frankfurt and taught at Bonn, Aarhus (Denmark), and Kiel, where he was professor and director of the Institute of World Economics from 1946. He was visiting professor in the U.S. and received honorary degrees at Berlin, Stockholm, Paris, and Helsinki. His remarkable publications make him one of the German leaders in modern economics. He wrote *Reine Theorie monopolistischer Wirtschaftsformen* (1932), *Theorie der Produktion* (1934), *Einführung in die Wirtschaftstheorie* (1947), *Wirtschaftlichkeitsrechnung* (1951), *Industrielles Rechnungswesen* (1939), *Wirtschaftspläne und Wirtschaftliches Gleichgewicht* (1952), *Geld, Kredit, Volkseinkommen und Beschäftigung* (1962). His *Introduction to Economic Theory* (1947), which has seen many editions, deals with the interdependence of the whole economy, micro- and macro-analysis, price theory, and theory of production and general equilibrium.

**Freiherr Wilhelm von Schröder**
*Austrian Cameralist*     *1640–1688*

Schröder (spelled Schroetter in Keynes' *General Theory*) was born at Königsberg and studied law at the University of Jena. He became adviser to Emperor Leopold I of Austria and thus came to great political influence. Schröder wrote *Fürstliche Schatz und Rentkammer* (1686). Basically he followed the ideas of Thomas Mun, even though he declared, as Keynes stated, that "he would wish that display in clothing and the like were even greater." He believed that the prince stands above the law and that the people should not expect to be informed about the affairs of the state. He found that money circulation is more important than the amount of money available, since it is money circulation which brings income to people. Schröder proposed a bank system that could expand money supply through notes and drafts.

**Schuckburgh**
see Sir George Augustus W. Schuckburgh-*Evelyn*

**Franz Hermann Schulze-Delitzsch**
*German Jurist and Cooperative Founder*                    *1808–1883*

Schulze was born in Delitzsch, and in 1848 became a member of the Prussian National Assembly. He was a member of the Prussian Chamber of Deputies (1861–75) and of the German Reichstag (1881–83). He believed in free trade, unrestricted competition, and self-help rather than assistance from the state. Coming to the conclusion that only private, voluntary organizations could bring workers real relief from their miseries, he started such organizations for sick relief and soon added consumer cooperatives for small artisans. In 1850 he helped establish loan banks and credit cooperatives, the success of which led to a central organization for all cooperatives. Schulze was instrumental in 1867 in getting the Prussian government to pass a new law permitting limited liability for cooperatives. This became a German law in 1889. His writings and speeches are collected in *Schriften und Reden* (5 vols., 1909–13).

**Gerhart von Schulze-Gävernitz**
*German Economist*                                          *1864–1943*

Born in Breslau, Schulze-Gävernitz was for 30 years professor at the University of Freiburg and also served in the German Reichstag. He was a man of vision and ideals but not really interested in the technical aspects of economics. He wrote *Zum sozialen Frieden* (1890) and *Der Grossbetrieb, ein wirtschaftlicher und sozialer Fortschsritt* (1892). In both books he made enlightening statements about the social and economic problems of large firms.

**Hermann Schumacher**
*German Economist*                                          *1868–1952*

Schumacher was born in Bremen and became a professor at the University of Berlin. His teaching capacity and extraordinary personality assured him not only great audiences but also lasting influence. He was the teacher of Eucken. In all his works he tried to show the world-wide interrelationship among the economic problems of the time and to expose the fundamentals of the developments. His books include *Weltwirtschaftliche Studien* (1911) and *Die Wirtschaft in Leben und Lehre* (1934).

**Joseph Alois Schumpeter**
*American Economist*                                        *1883–1950*

Born in Trietsch, Moravia (Austria), Schumpeter studied law at the University of Vienna and attended the economics seminars of Wieser, Böhm-Bawerk, and Philippovich. He taught at the universities of Czernowitz, Graz, and Bonn and came to Harvard University in 1932.

He was president of the American Economic Association (1948) and of the Econometric Society (1939–41). Outstanding among his many publications are *The Theory of Economic Development* (1934), *Capitalism, Socialism and Democracy* (1942), *Business Cycles* (1939), *Ten Great Economists* (1951), and his greatest contribution, *History of Economic Analysis* (1954, edited posthumously by his wife). Far more than an economist, he was not only versed in all fields of economic theory, but also in mathematics, social philosophy, statistics, and in the practical problems of the time. His writings contain concepts of the whole economic process: the equilibrium situation, business-cycle theory, and challenging statements and questions about the survival of capitalism (which he questioned not because of social difficulties but on account of super-success). Although Schumpeter's reputation was international, he did not intend to propagate any new economic system, or combine his many followers into a "school"; for him it was more important to offer his message for what it was worth and to enter it into the flow of ideas to be used by those for whom his interpretations had meaning.

**William Robert Scott**
*British Economist*     *1868–1940*

Scott has been called an economist, economic historian, and econometrician. He was professor at the University of Glasgow and a Fellow of the British Academy. About Glasgow's famous economist he wrote *Adam Smith as Student and Professor* (1937). In his book *Economic Problems of Peace after War* (2 vols., 1917–1918) he discussed international and national communication and problems of finance, including the question of war debts. He also wrote some historical works.

**Scotus**
see John *Duns Scotus*

**George Poulett Scrope**
*English Geologist and Economist*     *1797–1876*

George Thomson adopted the name Scrope after marrying the heiress of the Scrope family. He was born in London, studied at Oxford and Cambridge, and became a member of the House of Commons (1833–68), where he exposed his economic ideas. He also propagated them in the press and in a great number of pamphlets (for which he has been called "the Pamphlet Scrope"). While his social philosophy was liberal, he argued in favor of institutional control and against laissez-faire. He believed that "rules for guidance" of men are essential. He analyzed the term "profit" and had a notion of equilibrium. His tracts deal with money and banking, the conditions of agricultural labor, the poor laws, and many other subjects. His principal books are *Principles of Political Economy* (1833) and *Political Economy for Plain People* (1873).

**Veit Ludwig von Seckendorff**
*German Historian and Statesman* — *1626–1692*

The leading German Cameralist, Seckendorff was born in Erlangen and educated at the University of Strassburg. He became chancellor of the University of Halle in 1663. In the service of several German states and princes, he wrote *Der Deutsche Fürstenstaat* (1656), which saw 8 editions and was read in German universities for more than a century. An apology for the quasi-absolute state of 17th-century Germany, this work gives not only a rationalization of the power and efficiency of the state but also a definite vision and policy. Given a numerous and well-employed populace as the goal of government, Seckendorff proposed 12 measures to accomplish it, such as compulsory education, protection and internal freedom of industry which would eliminate the monopolies of craft guilds, special attention to the production of necessary goods, and exchange of surplus for useful goods from other countries. He also wrote *Der Christen Staat* (1685).

**Secondat**
see Charles de Secondat, Baron de la Brède et de *Montesquieu*

**Henri Eugène Sée**
*French Historian* — *1864–1936*

Born at Saint-Brice (Seine-et-Oise), Sée was educated at the Sorbonne. Sée believed that the most important factors in the evolution of societies are the economic needs. His writings include *Matérialisme historique et interprétation économique de l'histoire* (1929), *Histoire économique de la France* (2 vols., 1939–42), and *Les Origines du capitalisme* (1926).

**Edwin Robert Anderson Seligman**
*American Economist* — *1861–1939*

Born in New York City, Seligman studied at Columbia University (Ph.D.) and abroad at the universities of Berlin, Heidelberg, Geneva, and Paris. He taught at Columbia University. He also served on many committees and commissions during the Roosevelt administration and in 1902 was president of the American Economic Association, of which he had been a founder. Later he became the editor of the *Encyclopedia of the Social Sciences*, to which he himself contributed. He was a recognized authority on taxation, having written *Essays in Taxation* (1895) and *Studies in Public Finance* (1925). Also well known are his *The Economic Interpretation of History* (1902), *Principles of Economics* (1905), and *Essays in Economics* (1925).

**Lucius Annaeus Seneca**
*Roman Philosopher and Statesman*     *ca. 3 B.C.–65 A.D.*

Seneca was born in Córdoba, Spain, and brought to Rome for his education in rhetoric and philosophy. Exiled through the influence of Claudius I's first wife, he returned to Rome when Claudius remarried and became the tutor of Nero, the emperor's son. When Nero became emperor, Seneca enjoyed 5 years as the virtual ruler of Rome, but then fell into disfavor and was forced by Nero to commit suicide. Celebrated for his 9 tragic dramas and his philosophical writings expounding Stoicism, Seneca also put forth economic ideas. He saw money as the root of most evils, and greed and envy as the source of all injustice. Seeing the interrelationship of the nations of the world, he observed that various regions having been differently endowed, commercial intercourse is necessary for the mutual satisfaction of the needs of all.

**Seneuil**
see Jean Gustave *Courcelle-Seneuil*

**Nassau William Senior**
*English Economist*     *1790–1864*

Born in Berkshire, Senior studied at Magdalen College, Oxford, and at Lincoln's Inn and was the first to occupy the chair of political economy at Oxford (1825–32 and after 1847). He served as Master in Chancery and on governmental commissions inquiring into contemporary economic conditions. He advocated government support and regulations for housing and health and took an active interest in the poor laws and in national education. His activities in public affairs in fact overshadowed his great contributions to economic science, until 1937, when Marian Bowley uncovered his place in economic theory.

A brilliant and systematic thinker, he produced many original ideas. Perhaps best known is his abstinence theory of capital accumulation, but significant also are his contributions to value theory and his explanation of the relationship between value and cost. He expanded the rent theory but was less successful in regard to wage theory. He also wrote about wages, value and money, population, and the theory of wealth. Senior was often critical of the classics. He treated economics purely as a deductive science and took the deductions as absolute facts. His only book, *An Outline of the Science of Political Economy* (1836), does not do full justice to his knowledge and capacity, being a poorly arranged, hasty compilation of lecture notes; much more representative are his articles in the *Edinburgh Review*.

**Antonio Serra**
*Italian Mercantilist*     *1580–1650*

Serra was born in Cosenza, Calabria. Nothing is known of his education save that he called himself "Doctor" on the title page of the book he wrote in prison while serving a term for conspiring to free Naples from Spanish rule and establish a republic there. The book, published in 1613 but little noticed at the time, has been called the first mercantilist publication. Entitled *Brief Treatise on the Causes Which Can Make Gold and Silver Plentiful in Kingdoms where There Are No Mines*, it outlines a program of how the desired wealth can be obtained, under a capable government or a good administration, by an industrious and energetic population. Serra saw the most important sources of wealth to be agriculture and the trade in manufactured goods.

**Anthony Ashley Cooper, 3rd Earl of Shaftesbury**
*English Philosopher*                    *1671–1713*

Born in London, Shaftesbury was educated under the supervision of Locke, who remained his personal friend. He became a leading deist and exerted a great influence on the age of the Enlightenment, and in particular on Adam Smith, with a philosophy of nature as a harmonious order. He stressed a theory of "moral sense" and the idea of "balance of the passions" which, if all men would attend to it sufficiently, would lead to a situation in which "the balance of trade in commerce and the balance of power in politics would take care of themselves." Most of his essays are collected in *Characteristics of Men, Manners, Opinions, Times* (1711).

**Anthony Ashley Cooper, 7th Earl of Shaftesbury**
*English Conservative Social Reformer*           *1801–1885*

Shaftesbury became a member of Parliament in 1826 and introduced legislation prohibiting employment of women and children in coal mines and establishing a ten-hour day for factory workers. He also submitted legislation providing care for the insane and promoted building of model tenements.

**George Bernard Shaw**
*British Writer*                    *1856–1950*

Born in Dublin, Shaw went to London, where he wrote music and drama criticism and many brilliant plays, for which he won the Nobel Prize in literature in 1925. Highly interested in socialism and economic problems, he was a member of the Fabian Society, a friend of Sidney and Beatrice Webb, a founder of the London School of Economics and Political Science (1895), and editor of the Fabian Essays. His social and economic ideas, which pervade his dramas, are given more systematic treatment in his *The Intelligent Woman's Guide to Socialism and Capitalism* (1928).

Henry Sidgwick
*English Economist and Social Philosopher*                    *1838–1900*

Sidgwick was born at Skipton, Yorkshire, was educated at Cambridge, and became a professor of moral philosophy at Cambridge. He wrote on ethics and politics but also published *Principles of Political Economy* (1883). He was a convinced utilitarian who tried to reconcile utilitarianism with the rational concepts of Kant. While he accepted laissez-faire, he permitted exceptions and qualifications and found it is rationally not justified to rely exclusively on men as the best guardians of their personal welfare. He also gave government a much wider role in economic affairs and expected an expansion of the functions of government.

Simon
see Pierre Simon, Marquis de *Laplace*

Jean Charles Leonard de Sismondi
*Swiss Economist and Historian*                    *1773–1842*

Purportedly the son of an aristocratic Italian family, Sismondi was born in Geneva, Switzerland, whither the family had fled from France. But they had to move to England when the influence of the French Revolution also reached Geneva. Sismondi, always inclined toward business, had here an excellent chance to study English business behavior and political institutions. Returned to the Continent, he lived on a farm in Tuscany and set down his observations in *Tableau de l'agriculture toscane* (1801). In 1803 he published *De la Richesse commerciale*, closely following the ideas of Adam Smith. After receiving an invitation to write an article on political economy for the *Edinburgh Encyclopaedia* he intensified his studies in economics and discovered that many of the ideas he had accepted did not conform with reality. In 1819 he published *Nouveaux principes d'économie politique*, to which his later writings added little. He felt that the classics were too concerned with the accumulation of wealth in the very narrow sense and not nearly enough with human wealth as such. Laissez-faire would only make the rich richer and all others even more miserable. Thus he changed the ultimate aim of economics, criticized the distribution of income, and tried to replace the abstract classical teaching with social ideas that included the notion of a social account, anticipating macroeconomic theories. He opined that it is the responsibility of the government to see that progress is shared by all members of the society, since inequality and unevenness in wealth and property do not produce identity of interests of the individual and society.

**Sumner Hubert Slichter**
*American Economist*                                              *1892–1959*

Slichter was born in Madison, Wisconsin, and studied at the University of Wisconsin, the University of Munich (Germany), and the University of Chicago (Ph.D.). He taught at Princeton, Cornell, and Harvard universities. Labor economics was his first field of interest; his dissertation was published as *The Turnover of Factory Labor* (1919). He stressed the need for labor organizations and was in favor of a greater voice of labor in industrial enterprises. In a similar way he was interested in consumer economics, and came to the conclusion that consumers do not have sufficient influence on production; herein he found the major cause of industrial waste. In his *Modern Economic Society* (1931) he opined that economic planning would be advantageous for the economy. Planning, now a tool in large corporations, he felt should be spread over a wider area. Slichter also wrote *Union Politics and Industrial Management* (1940) and *The American Economy* (1949). In 1941 he was president of the American Economic Association.

**Eugen Slutsky**
*Russian Economist*                                              *1880–1948*

In an article, "Sulla teoria del bilancio del consumatore," in the Italian *Giornale degli economisti* in 1915, Slutsky made a remarkable contribution to modern indifference curve analyses. Only later was this article rediscovered by Hicks and Allen and only 15 years after Slutsky's death was a translation into Russian language completed.

**Albion Woodbury Small**
*American Educator*                                              *1854–1926*

Born in Buckfield, Maine, Small studied at Colby College, the Newton Theological Institute, abroad at the universities of Berlin and Leipzig, and at Johns Hopkins University (Ph.D.). He became professor of history and political economy and later president at Colby College, and at the University of Chicago, where he went in 1892 to occupy the chair of sociology, he became vice-president and graduate dean. Small wrote outstanding works on sociology but also enriched economic science with his remarkable book *The Cameralists* (1909) and his English translations of the works of Karl Menger. His other important books include *The Meaning of Social Science* (1910) and *Between Eras: From Capitalism to Democracy* (1913).

**William Smart**
*Scottish Economist*                                              *1853–1915*

Smart was born in Renfrewshire and studied at the University of Glasgow. He was an industrialist who became a professor at the University

College in Dundee, Queen Margaret College, and the University of Glasgow. In 1905 he became a member of the Royal Commission on Poor Laws. He translated works of Böhm-Bawerk and Wieser and thus opened the way for the Austrian School in English-speaking countries. He admired Carlyle and Ruskin. His works include *An Introduction to the Theory of Value* (1891), *Studies in Economics* (1895), *The Distribution of Income* (1899), *Taxation of Land Value and the Single Tax* (1900), *The Return to Protectionism* (1904), *Second Thoughts of an Economist* (1915), and *Economic Annals of the Nineteenth Century*, of which unfortunately only 2 volumes appeared (1910 and 1917).

**Smith**
see Richmond *Mayo-Smith*
John *Prince-Smith*

**Adam Smith**
*Scottish Economist*
*1723–1790*

Smith was born in Kirkcaldy, near Edinburgh. He studied at Glasgow University and at Balliol College, Oxford, concentrating on mathematics, philosophy, the Latin and Greek classics, and the Italian and French languages. In 1762 he received the doctor of law degree at Glasgow. Eschewing an earlier ambition to become an Episcopal clergyman, he became a teacher of English literature at the University of Edinburgh and in 1750–51 also gave lectures on political economy there. Shortly after, he was offered the chair of logic at Glasgow and a year later the chair of moral philosophy. His lectures became very popular and in 1759 he published his *Theory of Moral Sentiments*. In 1764–66 he was traveling tutor to the young Duke of Buccleuch, whom he accompanied to Switzerland and France; there he met many eminent people, including the leading Physiocrats. By 1764, Smith had begun his famous *Inquiry into the Nature and Causes of the Wealth of Nations*, which he completed in Kirkcaldy after his return, supported by a lifelong pension granted in connection with the tutorship. Published in 2 volumes in 1776, the book had extraordinary success and was translated into many languages. In recognition of the fame Smith brought to England, the king appointed him commissioner of customs in Scotland (1778), a position which was very lucrative. Much of the income he used, however, for secret charities. In 1787 he was elected Lord Rector of the University of Glasgow, but he continued to live in Edinburgh, where he died. In his *Wealth of Nations* he postulated the theory of laissez-faire, examined value, the division of labor, the process of production, free trade, institutional developments, natural liberty, the function of government, and the role of capital. He attacked the mercantilists and rejected the theory of the Physiocrats that land alone is the basis of wealth. Adam Smith has often been called the father of economics.

**Erasmus Peshine Smith**
*American Economist*                                    *1814–1882*

Born in New York City, Smith studied at Columbia College and Harvard Law School. In 1871–76 he was in Japan as special adviser in international law to the Mikado. Smith was a disciple of Henry Carey, and his main purpose was to provide a truly American outlook on political economy. His *Manual of Political Economy* (1853) was later translated into French.

**Carl Snyder**
*American Statistician*                                    *1869–1946*

Snyder was born in Cedar Falls, Iowa. He joined the Federal Reserve Bank, New York, as an economist and became president of the American Statistical Association in 1928 and a member of the American Academy of Arts and Sciences. He wrote many articles, of which "A New Index of the General Price Level from 1875" (*Journal of the American Statistical Association*, 1924) is of particular importance. In *Capital, the Creator: The Economic Foundation of Modern Industrial Society* (1940) he insisted that labor has done next to nothing to assist in the tremendous changes created by capital. Snyder praised invention and saving for the success of the industrial economy.

**Socrates**
*Greek Philosopher*                                    *469–399 B.C.*

It has been said that Socrates was the wisest man who ever lived. He himself said that wisdom consists of knowing that nothing is known finally. At about age 30 Socrates gathered in Athens a small group of young men to discuss philosophy and the art of living. He spoke about truth, virtue, justice and, it seems, according to Plato, about community property. This may have been one of the reasons that he was condemned to death because it was feared that he would mislead the youth. As far as is known, he himself did not write anything, but his life and work has been described by his greatest pupils, Plato and Xenophon.

**Friedrich Julius Heinrich Reichgraf von Soden**
*German Civil Servant*                                    *1754–1831*

Soden was born in Ansbach. He studied law in Erlangen and Jena and was employed in the justice department of Bayreuth, but retired in 1796 to his estates. Inspired by Margrave Karl Friedrich von Baden, the physiocrat, he started to devote himself to the study of political economy. Soden arranged for a German translation of Smith's *Wealth of Nations* and wrote *Die National-Ökonomie* (9 vols., 1803–24), which he planned as a complete work on economics and administrative science. He leaned heavily on Adam Smith, whose ideas he tried to combine with those of the Cameralists.

**Ernest Solvay**
*Belgian Industrialist and Inventor*                                    *1838–1922*

Solvay was born near Brussels and became, through his inventions, a famous scientist and industrialist. His papers and some lectures appeared in *Annales de l'Institut Solvay* (1900), a research institute funded by Solvay's enterprises. Solvay developed a system of "social accounting," introducing what he thought would be a more perfect payment system. Checks and clearing-houses would replace bank notes and other forms of money. The state would supply the checkbooks and would thus be able to exercise control; thereby it could remove inequality of opportunity and increase productivity to its maximum. He was opposed to the amassing of inherited wealth.

**Werner Sombart**
*German Economist*                                    *1863–1941*

Sombart, born in Ermsleben, studied at Pisa, Breslau, and Berlin and taught at Breslau and Berlin. He was a specialist in Marxian socialism but was not a socialist himself, though he expressed radical views in many of his books. Here should be listed *Sozialismus und soziale Bewegung im 19. Jahrhundert* (1896, translated into English as *Socialism and the Social Movement*, 1909), *Die Juden und das Wirtschaftsleben* (1913), *Deutscher Sozialismus* (1934, translated as *A New Social Philosophy*, 1937). In *Der moderne Kapitalismus* (1902–27) Sombart offered a systematic historical picture of economic development in Europe from the beginning to 1927, to which he added *Das Wirtschaftsleben im Zeitalter des Hochkapitalismus* (1927). All his books make stimulating reading even if professional historians did not hesitate with their criticism. Sombart was influenced by the Historical School. He believed that political economy should try to understand the past in order to prepare properly for the future and that quantitative, mathematical economics, which only concentrates on the analysis of the present, is inadequate.

**Joseph von Sonnenfels**
*Austrian Neomercantilist*                                    *1732–1817*

Sonnenfels, born in Nikolsburg, Moravia, the son of a rabbi, was professor of finance and cameralistics at the University of Vienna and adviser to Maria Theresa, Joseph II, and Leopold II. Roscher said, "For more than two generations the Austrian national economy was dominated by Sonnenfels." In favor of enlightened absolutism, he was in many ways still deeply rooted in mercantilist ideas. Yet he also advocated a guaranteed minimum subsistence income and proposed that the state should take care of the sick. Sonnenfels disliked state enterprises and the guild system and was against monopolies of any kind. He favored import restriction (except for raw materials), stimulation of export, indirect taxes, and the abolition of capital punishment. His ideas and policies remind one often of Justi. Sonnenfels expressed his thought in *Grundsätze der Polizey, Handlung und Finanzwissenschaft* (1765–67).

## Georges Sorel
*French Syndicalist*     *1847–1922*

Born in Cherbourg, Sorel studied engineering at the Ecole Polytechnique in Paris. In 1882 he became an active Syndicalist, propagating the emancipation of the working class through seizure and control of industry, and devoted himself to organizing labor movements. His best-known book, *Réflexions sur la violence* (1908, English trans. 1914), contains, it seems, many contradictions. Sorel admired both fascism and bolshevism—in fact any movement that planned to remove the ruling bourgeoisie. He had strong anti-intellectual attitudes. He attacked finance capital, but favored industrial capitalism; he was in favor of heroism in the social war, but was not interested in fighting for higher wages. He had contempt for parliamentary democracy, but in spite of all exercised a remarkable influence on the average Frenchman and on some leaders.

## George Soule
*American Economist*     *1887–1970*

Soule was born in Stamford, Connecticut, and studied at Yale University. He taught at Rutgers University, Bennington College, and Colgate and Columbia universities. His books include *Ideas of the Great Economists* (1952) and *Planning U.S.A.* (1967). Soule was director-at-large of the National Bureau of Economic Research and editor of *The New Republic*.

## Othmar Spann
*Austrian Economist*     *1878–1950*

Born in Altmansdorf, Spann studied at Vienna, Zürich, Bern, and Tübingen. Spann developed a system he called "Universalism," which seems to be related to the Romantic nationalism of Fichte and Müller. He bitterly attacked the atomistic individualism of the classics, particularly Adam Smith, stating that their view of wealth is too narrow, that self-interest is overemphasized, and that idealism is entirely replaced by materialism. Spann saw in the nation an organic whole in which the individual played a subordinate part. His economics deals mostly with the means to a social end and with the final goals of life. His main works are *Fundament der Volkswirtschaftslehre* (1918) and *Die Haupttheorien der Volkswirtschaftslehre* (1911), which latter book saw 25 editions.

**William Spence**

*English Physiocrat*  
*1783–1860*

Spence was born at Hull. Disenchanted with the industrial system, which he attacked, Spence pleaded for the old economic society and stated in two tracts (1807, 1808) that capital investment in the new system creates instability and insecurity, whereas an agricultural society offers the desired security and stability. He proposed limiting land property rights.

**Herbert Spencer**

*English Philosopher*  
*1820–1903*

Spencer was born in Derby, Derbyshire. He was educated by his father and uncle and started to work for a railway at the age of 17. He became an engineer but also a sub-editor of the *Economist* (1848). His *Social Statics* appeared in 1850, followed by some philosophical and sociological works. In 1898 he published *What Is Social Revolution?*

Spencer applied the ideas of organic evolution, which he had formulated before Darwin, to the social organism. He refused to include the "unknowable" in his studies. For him government was a necessary evil which has only the duty to protect and enforce economic contracts. His ideas on the "survival of the fittest" became a powerful influence.

**Arthur Spiethoff**

*German Economist*  
*1873–1957*

Spiethoff, born at Düsseldorf, studied at Berlin and Geneva and became professor at the universities of Berlin, Prague, and Bonn, has been called the leading modern German business-cycle theorist. An assistant and friend of Schmoller, he edited Schmoller's *Jahrbuch* for 20 years. Spiethoff distinguished 2 types of theoretical economic studies: the pure theory (Quesnay, Ricardo, Thünen, Menger, Walras, Jevons, Clark, Pareto, and Keynes) and the realistic, empirical, concrete theory (List, Schmoller, Sombart, Max Weber). To this second group he added his own name. Among his writings are *Anschauliche und reine wirtschaftliche Theorie* (1949), *Die allgemeine Volkswirtschaftslehre als geschichtliche Theorie* (1933), and his masterpiece *Die wirtschaftlichen Wechsellagen* (2 vols., 1955), in which he presented his fluctuation theory.

**Piero Sraffa**
*English Economist*                                    *1898–*

Sraffa, born in Italy, was a student of Marshall and taught at Trinity College, Cambridge. He wrote "The Law of Returns under Competitive Conditions" (*Economic Journal*, 1926), arguing that the law of returns should be expressed in terms related to conditions that are not purely competitive. He drew attention to the monopolistic forces in the economy and with his views opened the way to the study of imperfect competition. Sraffa also made outstanding contributions to the understanding of Ricardo and the classics.

**Heinrich Freiherr von Stackelberg**
*German Economist*                                    *1905–1946*

Stackelberg was born at Kudinow (Russia) of a German father and an Argentine mother. The family moved to Cologne, Germany, in 1917. He studied at Bonn, became professor at Berlin (1935) and at Bonn (1941). In 1943 he became guest-professor in Madrid, where he died.

Besides articles in learned journals, he published *Grundlagen einer reinen Kostentheorie* (1932), *Marktform und Gleichgewicht* (1934), and *Grundzüge der theoretischen Nationalökonomie* (1943). The last-named book was hardly on the market when the whole edition was destroyed in the air attacks on Stuttgart. Stackelberg completed a second enlarged edition, which appeared under the title *Grundlagen der theoretischen Volkswirtschaftslehre* (1948). Stackelberg's studies of markets are comparable to Joan Robinson's and Chamberlin's, which were written at the same time. They deal extensively with the problems of oligopoly. Stackelberg defended the use of mathematical analysis in economic theory, seeing it as a tool of a disciplined and exact method, forcing the researcher to eliminate any form of "phantasy."

**Joseph Stalin**
*Russian Communist*                                    *1879–1953*

Born in Gori, Georgia, his real name was Dzhugashvili but he named himself Stalin ("made of steel"). The son of a shoemaker, he became a Marxist while studying for the priesthood. He joined the Bolsheviks, was arrested 6 times and exiled for life to Siberia. Amnestied in 1917, he became a member of Lenin's cabinet and came to power after Lenin's death (1924), becoming sole leader in 1927. In 1928 he ended Lenin's "New Economic Policy" and inaugurated the first "Five Year Plan" for industrialization and collectivization. He continued to rule Russia until his death in 1953.

**Sir Josiah Charles Stamp**
*English Economist and Banker* — *1880–1941*

Stamp was born at Bexley, Kent. He died with his wife and eldest son during an air attack on London. Stamp was director of the Bank of England and of leading industrial enterprises. He was made an adviser to the government and a member of the Dawes Plan and the Young Plan commissions. Stamp was a recognized tax expert. In 1915 he published his study *British Incomes and a Statistical Study of Capital and Property.* He also wrote *Fundamental Principles of Taxation* (1919) and *Wealth and Taxable Capacity* (1922). Other papers and essays on national income and public finance he wrote with Arthur Lyon Bowley.

**Lorenz von Stein**
*German Social Philosopher* — *1815–1890*

Von Stein was born in Schleswig and studied law at the University of Kiel. He went to Paris for further studies and there met Blanc and Cabet. Returned, he taught at Kiel, but was dismissed because of propagating independence for Schleswig, a German province. For a short while he was at the University of Munich. In 1855 Stein was appointed professor at Vienna, where he remained for the rest of his life. His major work was *Die Geschichte der sozialen Bewegung in Frankreich von 1789 bis auf unsere Tage* (1850). Here he showed the development of the social movements in France and also expressed his own ideas. Stein felt that the state has the responsibility for assisting the lower classes. A reform from above would in his mind bring about a conservative socialism which would make for social harmony. Equal opportunities should be given to all, and individual freedom should be protected. In other works, von Stein dealt with public finance, administration theories and policies, and economic analysis.

**Sir Leslie Stephen**
*English Writer* — *1832–1904*

Born in London, Stephen studied at King's College, London, and Trinity Hall, Cambridge, where he later taught until he resigned for personal reasons and devoted himself exclusively to writing. Stephen was well known for his book *History of English Thought in the Eighteenth Century* (1876). He also wrote *The English Utilitarians* (3 vols., 1900), some biographical works, and *Social Rights and Duties* (1896). Stephen was knighted in 1902.

**Sternegg**
see Karl Theodor von *Inama-Sternegg*

**Sir James Denham Steuart**
*Scottish Mercantilist*                                      *1712–1780*

Born in Edinburgh, Steuart studied law at Edinburgh University. After being admitted to the Faculty of Advocates he spent 5 years traveling on the European continent. In 1745 he was sent on a mission to France but, until 1763, was forbidden to return home because he was a supporter of the Stuarts. He was also the first economic advisor to the government of India. While abroad he wrote several treatises, the most important being *An Inquiry into the Principles of Political Economy* (1767). Although its purely mercantilist concepts were soon to be replaced by the liberal ideas of Adam Smith and others, this work remains a comprehensive and systematic exposition of the older economic theory. Steuart's other writings were collected, published, and edited by his son in 1805. Steuart has been called the "last of the Mercantilists."

**Dugald Stewart**
*Scottish Philosopher and Economist*                         *1753–1828*

Stewart was born in Edinburgh and studied at Edinburgh and briefly at Glasgow before he was called home to take his ailing father's classes in mathematics. Soon Stewart started to teach moral philosophy and political economy at the University of Edinburgh; he continued for 25 years. He wrote extensively on philosophy but here it is of interest that he became a biographer of Adam Smith: *Memoirs of Adam Smith, LL.D.* (1793) and *Account of the Life and Writings of Adam Smith, LL.D.* (1795). As a teacher, Stewart followed Smith's ideas closely although personally he inclined toward Physiocracy. His *Lectures on Political Economy* are collected notes from a course he gave at Edinburgh in 1800.

**Max Stirner**
*German Anarchist*                                           *1806–1856*

Stirner's real name was Caspar Schmidt. Born in Bayreuth, he studied philosophy and theology at Berlin and Erlangen and became a teacher. Stirner was the most outspoken individualist, for whom the ego is everything, property is anything the individual can put his hand on, and might is right. He drove individualism and laissez-faire to the extreme. His major work is *Der Einzige und sein Eigentum* (1845); it is the purest demonstration of egocentric attitudes. He died in extreme poverty.

**Adolf Stöcker**
*German Leader of Social Protestantism*                      *1835–1909*

A Lutheran pastor and military chaplain, in 1874 Stöcker became court preacher in Berlin and had great influence on Prince William (later Emperor William II). A great orator, Stöcker appealed more to the middle classes and educated people than to the working classes. In 1878 he helped form the Christlichsoziale Arbeiterpartei (Christian Social Workingmen's Party) which was strictly monarchist, more paternalist than anti-capitalist, and anti-Semitic. Influenced by members of the court, the emperor dismissed his pastor in 1890 and thus the party lost support and status. Stöcker's speeches and writings were published as *Gesammelte Schriften* (2 vols., 1890–93).

### Heinrich Friedrich von Storch
*Russian Economist*       *1766–1835*

Von Storch was born in Riga and studied at Jena and Heidelberg before entering the Russian civil service. Storch wrote (in German) a 9-volume work on Russia at the end of the 18th century, offering a historical and statistical picture. He also published *Cours d'économie politique* (1815) and an income analysis in *Considérations sur la nature du revenu national* (1824). He closely followed Adam Smith but did not believe that universal economic laws could be formulated, nor did he accept Smith's "unproductivity" of professionals.

### Stanislaus Gustavovich Strumilin
*Russian Economist and Statistician*       *1877–*

Strumilin has been called the best-known economist in the Soviet Union. He was chairman of the Central Economic Accounting Board, professor at Moscow University and the Plekhanov Institute of National Economy, and deputy chairman of the Council for the Study of the Productive Forces in the U.S.S.R.

Strumilin was also professor of political economy at the Academy of Sciences Institute of Economics, the leading Soviet economic research organization, which publishes the journal on theoretical economics, *Vofrosy Ekonomiki* (*Problems of Economics*). His many publications include *Wealth and Labor* (1905), *Outline of Soviet Economics* (1928), *Problems of Planning in the U.S.S.R.* (1932), *The Industrial Revolution in Russia* (1944), *Outline of Statistical Economics* (1959), and *Outline of Socialist Economy* (1959).

### Südenhorst
see Otto von *Zwiedineck-Südenhorst*

### Maximilien de Béthune, Duc de Sully
*French Statesman*       *1560–1641*

Sully was born in Rosny, studied in Paris, joined the court of Henry of Navarre as a boy, became a member of the king's council of finance, and finally was named minister and sole superintendent (1598). His success in state financial matters increased his reputation. Sully encouraged agriculture and said "Le labourage et le pastourage, voilà les deux mamelles dont la France est alimentée." He relied on labor and agriculture in his policies. Fiscal policy was, as he saw it, a part of the general economic policy. His *Mémoires des sages et royales oeconomies, d'éstat, domestiques, politiques, et militaires de Henri le Grand* (1638) is a most enlightening contribution to the understanding of his time. Even after the assassination of Henry IV it was recognized that Sully had done much for the recovery of France. The baton of Marshal of France was conferred upon him in 1634.

**William Graham Sumner**

*American Sociologist and Economist*                                    *1840–1910*

Born in Paterson, New Jersey, Sumner graduated from Yale University and studied abroad at Geneva, Göttingen, and Oxford. He became an Episcopal clergyman but in 1872 returned to Yale as professor of social sciences. Sumner propagated the philosophy of individualism, though he recognized that the individual rises or falls with and within the social system. All that could interfere with natural law and the law of supply and demand was to him unacceptable, and he condemned socialism, trade unions, and most state interference in economic affairs, including interstate commerce laws. Blunt and uncompromising, he ridiculed humanitarian sentiments. As a sociologist he believed reform useless in the face of solidly entrenched human customs. He is remembered for his books *What Social Classes Owe to Each Other* (1883), *Folkways* (1907), and *Science of Society* (with A. G. Keller, 4 vols., 1927).

**Camillo Supino**

*Italian Economist*                                                             *1860–1931*

Supino, born at Pisa, had no formal training in economics but gained such a high reputation in this field that he was appointed professor of economics at the Istituto Tecnico, Genoa. Later he was professor at Messina, Siena, and Pavia. His *La Navigazione dal punto di vista economico* (1890) is an important contribution to the economic study of transportation. Interested in economic theory and money and banking, he also wrote *Storia della circolazione bancaria in Italia* (1895), *Il Mercato monetario internazionale* (1910), and *Il Capitale immaginario* (1932). Of interest, too, is his *Il Chrisi economiche* (1907), which has been called a kind of seismology of business cycles. He opposed the marginal utility theory. Supino has been admired as a man of vision and imagination.

**Theo Suranyi-Unger**
*American Economist*                                    *1898–*

Suranyi-Unger was born in Budapest and studied at the University of Graz, Palatine Joseph Technical College, and Pazmany University. He taught at various universities in Austria and Hungary and in the U.S. at Syracuse University from 1946. He wrote *Philosophie der Volkswirtschaft* (2 vols., 1923–26), translated into English as *Economics in the 20th Century* (1931); *Private Enterprise and Government Planning* (1950); and *Comparative Economic Systems* (1952).

**Johann Peter Süssmilch**
*German Writer*                                    *1707–1767*

Süssmilch was born in Berlin where he became a pastor. Süssmilch has been called a mercantilist population statistician. His treatise *Die göttliche Ordnung in den Veränderungen des menschilichen Geschlechts* (1741) gives statistical material on birth and death rates and on age combinations of the population. Süssmilch saw in the population changes a divinely ordered harmony between individual and public interests. He knew about Petty's writings and was read by Sonnenfels, whose works were studied by Malthus.

# T

## Frank William Taussig
*American Economist*                                                    *1859–1940*

Born in St. Louis, Missouri, Taussig studied at Harvard University (Ph.D. and LL.B.), St. Louis University, and the University of Berlin. Active in both academic and public affairs, he was professor of political economy at Harvard until retiring in 1935, chairman of the U.S. Tariff Commission (1917–19), and a member of President Wilson's Advisory Committee on Peace. In 1904 he was elected president of the American Economic Association. He enjoyed an international reputation, receiving 4 honorary doctorates (one from the University of Bonn, Germany) and being elected a Fellow of the American Academy of Arts and Sciences. He was editor of the *Quarterly Journal of Economics* from 1896–1935.

His writings show a sense of realism. In the field of international trade and finance he proved himself neither a free-trader nor a protectionist. His dissertation, *The Tariff History of the United States*, was published in 1892 and saw 8 editions. His many other books include *The Silver Question in the United States* (1892); *Wages and Capital* (1896); *Principles of Economics* (1911); *Some Phases of the Tariff Question* (1915); *Inventors and Money Makers* (1915); *Free Trade, the Tariff and Reciprocity* (1920); his outstanding contribution, *International Trade* (1920); and *Social Origins of American Business Leaders* (1932).

## Richard Henry Tawney
*English Economist*                                                    *1880–1962*

Born in Calcutta, India, Tawney was educated at Rugby and at Balliol College, Oxford. After graduating he worked first in the University Settlement in the east end of London, then for the newly founded Worker's Educational Association. In 1913 he was appointed director of the Ratan Tata Foundation for the study of poverty at the London School of Economics. He enlisted in the infantry in 1915 and was severely wounded in 1916. Tawney was elected fellow of Balliol in 1918 but moved to the London School of Economics where he taught economic history. He served on governmental committees, and was economic advisor to the British Embassy in Washington in 1942.

He was a member of the Fabian Society and has been called a Guild Socialist. He attacked industrialism for failing to produce freedom. He deplored the loss of community solidarity and was concerned about people becoming mere tools of production, exclaiming: "Man is not a thing." Among his many successful books are *The Acquisitive Society* (1920); *Religion and the Rise of Capitalism* (1926), which brought him international fame; and *Equality* (1931).

**Fred Manville Taylor**
*American Economist*                                                  *1855–1932*

Taylor, born in Northville, Michigan, was educated at Northwestern University. He taught history and politics at Albion College for 12 years but moved in 1892 to the University of Michigan (where he had received the Ph.D. degree in 1888), taught political economy there, and in 1904 became professor. In 1928 he was president of the American Economic Association. He published *Some Chapters on Money* (1906) and the highly successful *Principles of Economics* (1911). He followed the neo-classical school and tried to adjust the teachings of the Austrians to the reality of his time as he saw it. His ultimate interest, however, centered on problems of social justice and on the conditions affecting general welfare; with Oskar Lange he wrote *On the Economic Theory of Socialism* (1938).

**William Temple**
*English Mercantilist*                                                  *born ca. 1720*

Temple wrote *A Vindication of Commerce and the Arts* (1758) in which he did not hesitate to suggest that children at four years of age be sent to the workhouse so that they could earn their living, working 12 hours a day, and thus learn to be useful.

**Louis Adolphe Thiers**
*French Statesman, Journalist, and Historian*                          *1797–1877*

Born in Marseilles, Thiers became an incomparable orator, politician, and prime minister under Louis Philippe. From 1871–73 he was president of the republic. His historical works, particularly *L'Histoire de la révolution française* (1823–27), are outstanding. Of even greater interest is his *De la Propriété* (1848), with which he hoped to correct the errors of the socialists.

**Thomas Aquinas**
see St. Thomas *Aquinas*

**William Thompson**
*Irish Socialist*                                                       *1775–1833*

Thompson was born at Cork, County Cork, as the son of well-to-do parents who sent him to college. There he was attracted by the works of Bentham and Owen, and he began to develop his ideas on social reform and socialism. Long before Marx, Thompson had the notions of surplus value, of value created by labor alone, and of excessive capital accumulation. In 1824 he published *An Inquiry into the Principles of the Distribution of Wealth Most Conducive to Human Happiness,* in which he attacked private property and unearned income. Following Owen, Thompson saw the cooperative movement as the solution to social problems. He was an active member of the London Cooperative Society and frequently wrote articles in the *Cooperative Magazine.* His *Labour Rewarded* was published in 1827.

### Henry David Thoreau
*American Essayist, Poet, and Naturalist*               1817–1862

Born in Concord, Massachusetts, Thoreau became one of the literary critics of materialism and wealth who, together with Emerson, Carlyle, Kingsley, and others, left a deep impression on social thought in English-speaking countries. He was a powerful social critic with a wide and lasting influence; his essay "Civil Disobedience" inspired many social reformers, including Gandhi. With his good friend Emerson and fellow transcendentalists Thoreau was a supporter of Brook Farm, a short-lived venture in communal living which toward its close was based on the ideas of Fourier. Thoreau's experiment in living alone and as self-sufficiently as possible is recounted in *Walden* (1854), his most famous book.

### Henry Thornton
*English Merchant and Banker*               1760–1815

Thornton, born into a well-to-do banker's family in Clapham, did not care for schooling. He became an active member of the banking house Down, Thornton and Free and was director of the Bank of England. For 30 years he was a member of Parliament (serving on the Bullion Committee) and belonged to the "Clapham Sect," which stood for the abolition of the slave trade and similar philanthropic goals. In 1802 he published *An Inquiry into the Nature and Effects of Paper Credit of Great Britain* and *Serious Reflections on Paper Money in General.* His philanthropic attitudes were impressive. When he died the *Gentleman's Magazine* reported, "He was so active to glorify God and benefit man that a near view of him is a most humbling lesson."

Thornton developed ideas that came close to a theory of forced capital accumulation. Excessive savings would supply more investment funds than demanded, and the interest rate would fall. This would stimulate new investment and would discourage further savings until both were equalized. Total spending on consumption and investment would then be adequate to purchase the industrial output.

**William Thomas Thornton**
*English Economic Author*                                    *1813–1880*

Born in Burnham, Thornton became a clerk in the East India Company and in 1858 secretary for public works in the India Office. He was a friend of John Stuart Mill. In 1869 he wrote *On Labour, Its Wrongful Claims and Rightful Dues, Its Actual Present and Possible Future.* He found that wages are paid by the employer out of the capital investment; therefore it is the employer's decision how much he is willing to pay. He criticized the wage-fund theory and opposed the use of the term "average wages." The guide for the producer's decisions is the consumer's demand. Later he wrote also about peasant proprietors and advocated what may be called a land reform.

**Johann Heinrich von Thünen**
*German Landowner and Economist*                            *1783–1850*

Thünen, born in Oldenburg, became one of the most outstanding figures in political economy. After studying at an agricultural college near Hamburg and briefly at the University of Göttingen, he bought an estate in Mecklenburg-Schwerin and spent his life farming it. His drive for explanations and truth was connected with painstaking research and empirical experience in the writing of his famed *Der Isolierte Staat in Beziehung auf Landwirtschaft und Nationalökonomie* (3 vols., 1826–63). It took nearly 20 years before the first volume was recognized as a challenging contribution. Then he was induced to publish a second volume; the third was published posthumously by friends and followers.

In volume 1 Thünen developed a location theory in relation to rent and price problems. Volume 2 deals with the natural wage related to interest and rent; and volume 3 treats the determination of rent, periods of land rotation, and forest management. Thünen did not hesitate to consider ethical aspects; he was highly interested in social justice and was alarmed by the conditions he observed around him. In his concept of wages, he protests the treating of labor wages like a price for an inanimate commodity. The mathematical wage formula, which he asked to be engraved on his tombstone, proved to be incorrect, but the idea behind it survived. For his arguments Thünen used material carefully collected by himself over many years. In this sense it may be said that he was one of the first to attempt to make economics an exact science.

**Count Leo Tolstoy**
*Russian Writer*                                            *1828–1910*

Born in Yasnaya Polyana, the estate of his noble family, Leo Tolstoy became obsessed with the desire for social reform and attempted to establish schools for the peasantry. Tolstoy was educated at Kazan University, studying law and oriental languages. He was an officer defending besieged Sevastopol (1855) before he retired to his country estate. From 1876 on he became more and more of a mystic, following Christ, trying to give up all his property and to live a simple life with a philosophy of nonviolence. Gandhi, with whom he had an exchange of letters, adopted this idea. Tolstoy's many works, read ever since, have exercised a deep influence and describe modern civilization in a unique way.

*English Merchant and Economist*  **Thomas Tooke**  *1774–1858*

Born in Russia, Tooke throughout life was associated with English-Russian trade. He became, with Ricardo and Torrens, one of the founders of the Political Economy Club, in which he played a dominant role and was recognized as an expert on finance and banking. He was called before several Parliament committees to give evidence on questions of foreign trade and on the Bank Act. He served as governor of the Royal Assurance Corporation from 1840–52.

Tooke was one of the early advocates of free trade and contributed to monetary theory by introducing the notion of price fluctuation as the cause of changes in demand and supply. He denied that banks can sufficiently affect the quantity of money in circulation or prices as such. His writings include *Merchant's Petition* (1819), which is a call for free trade, *Thoughts and Details on High and Low Prices* (1823), *An Inquiry into the Currency Principle* (1844), and *A History of Price and of the State of the Circulation from 1793 to 1856*, a comprehensive, 6-volume work written with William Newmarch during 1838–57. It was the first work of this type in which facts are not only presented but also explained.

*English Economist*  **Colonel Robert Torrens**  *1780–1864*

Torrens, born in Ireland, served in the Royal Marines from 1797–1834. In 1826 he was elected a member of Parliament. Torrens was a founder of the Political Economy Club and was in the chair at the opening meeting. His writings, which demonstrate great knowledge and understanding of economic matters, include *Essay on the Production of Wealth* (1821), *Letters on Commercial Policy* (1833), *On Wages and Combinations* (1834), *On the Colonization of South Africa* (1835), and *The Budget* (1844). Torrens was one of the first to state that international trade does not depend upon absolute cost differentiations only. He developed the idea of comparative costs and contributed new notions on wealth, the law of diminishing returns, and the cooperation of land, labor, and capital in production. He also made original contributions to the theories of rent, wages, and money. For a long time after his death Torrens was forgotten until Lionel Robbins in 1958 published a penetrating study of his ideas and activities.

**Arnold Toynbee**
*English Economic Historian and Reformer* *1852–1883*

Toynbee, born in London, studied at Pembroke College, Oxford, and later at Balliol College, Oxford, where he was appointed tutor. His only extant work is *Lectures on the Industrial Revolution of the 18th Century in England*, published posthumously in 1884. Describing the new commercial policies and the rise of the laissez-faire doctrine, Toynbee concluded that it was the change in economic thought and attitudes rather than in the industrial institutions themselves that produced these great developments of the industrial revolution. His interest in social reform and adult education was expressed in his lecturing to the working classes at large industrial centers.

**Tracy**
see Antoine Louis Claude *Destutt, Comte de Tracy*

**Trosne**
see Guillaume Francis *Le Trosne*

**George Tucker**
*American Economist* *1775–1861*

Tucker was born in Bermuda and studied law at William and Mary College. He was active in Virginia politics, became a member of the U.S. House of Representatives and, in 1825, professor of moral philosophy and political economy at the University of Virginia. He wrote *Laws of Wages, Profits and Rent Investigated* (1837), *The Theory of Money and Banks Investigated* (1839), and *Political Economy for the People* (1859), but his greatest contributions to economics are found in his *Progress in the United States in Population and Wealth in Fifty Years* (1843). Tucker also published works on politics and American history.

**Josiah Tucker**
*English Neo-Mercantilist* *1712–1799*

Tucker was born at Laugharne, Carmarthenshire. He became dean of Gloucester. He wrote many essays and tracts on contemporary economic problems and strongly defended free trade as beneficial to the country. Some of his writings were translated into French and appeared in the *Journal économique*. In his *Elements of Commerce and Theory of Taxes* (1755) Tucker said that freedom, correctly applied, is nothing else than understanding the divine rule and divine order. Acting according to this precept will lead to harmony everywhere.

Russian Economist
**Mikhail Ivanovich Tugan-Baranovsky**
*1865–1919*

Tugan, born in Solyonoye, Ukraine, originally studied natural science and mathematics at Kharkov University but soon turned to economics, which he taught until the October Revolution of 1917, when he was made finance minister in the Ukraine. Influenced by Dühring, Tugan wrote *Soziale Theorie der Verteilung* (1913), in which he stated that the theory of distribution must first of all explain the dependence among the various classes (and has nothing to do with value or price theories). He opined that only through well-organized labor could exploitation by employers be restricted. The higher wages labor would thereby receive would have to be paid out of the profits of the employers, and not be shifted to the consumer in the form of higher prices. His other works deal with the theoretical foundations of Marxism, the history of Russian industrialism, and the historical view of modern socialism. Tugan believed that Say's law of markets could be applied only to conditions in which small producers were dominating, and only when these producers were well-informed about the sales opportunities for their products. In regard to business fluctuation, Tugan followed the so-called organic cycle theory, whereby the cause of a crisis is found to be the disproportional use of resource allocation in the production of capital and consumer goods.

American Economist and Political Scientist
**Rexford Guy Tugwell**
*1891–*

Born in Sinclairville, New York, and educated at the University of Pennsylvania (Ph.D.), Tugwell became under-secretary of Agriculture, chairman of the planning department of the city of New York, and governor of Puerto Rico. He taught at Pennsylvania, Washington, Chicago, Columbia, and Howard universities and the London School of Economics, and later became chancellor of the University of Puerto Rico. Tugwell was a prominent member of President Roosevelt's "Brain Trust" and exerted great influence on the New Deal legislation. Of his writings should be noted *The Economic Basis of Public Interest* (1922), *Industry's Coming of Age* (1927), *The Place of Planning in Society* (1954).

French Economist and Statesman
**Anne Robert Jacques Turgot**
*1727–1781*

Turgot, born in Paris the son of a Norman merchant, studied at the Sorbonne and entered public service. A man of exceptional ability, he rose to high governmental position and was appointed controller-general of France by Louis XVI in 1774. In this capacity he tried to put some of the physiocratic ideas into practice. In many instances he was successful, but his famous "six édits" reform plan met with the strong opposition of those whose vested interests would have been hurt. The king was forced to dismiss him in 1776. Ended was Turgot's dream that a benevolent monarch would initiate the economic and financial reforms so urgently needed in France. The last opportunity for reform from above was missed, and the only way that remained open was a revolution from below, which occurred a few years later. In this sense Turgot was a failure. But his brilliant mind presented economics with *Réflexions sur la formation et la distribution des richesses* (1769), making him the first to outline a complete system of economic theory treating value and distribution, division of labor, the origin and use of money, the nature of capital and interest, and the role of agriculture. Turgot is considered also to be the first economist to give a clear definition of the law of diminishing returns. In spite of the fact that he was a Physiocrat, he proved himself an independent scholar who did not hesitate to go his own way when he found it necessary. He did not agree with Quesnay that land alone was productive, but accepted the idea of a single tax on the "produit net."

**Turroni**
see Constantino *Bresciani-Turroni*

**Charles Augustus Tuttle**
*American Economist*                                           *1863–1935*

Tuttle was born at Hadley, Massachusetts. He studied at Amherst College and the University of Heidelberg (Ph.D.). He taught at Amherst, Wabash College, and Wesleyan University, where he was professor of economics and head of the department of social sciences. He published *Outline of Course in Economic Theory* (1894), *Principles of Economics* (1919), and *A Functional Theory of Economic Profit* (1927) in addition to articles in the *American Economic Review* and the *Journal of Political Economy*.

# U

**Unger**
see Theo *Suranyi-Unger*

**George Unwin**
*English Economic Historian*                              *1870–1925*

Born at Stockport, Unwin left school at the early age of 13. His employer, a hatmaker, encouraged him to continue with readings. He won a scholarship to the College of Cardiff, and later to Oxford. He studied briefly under Schmoller in Berlin and later at the London School of Economics. Unwin became private secretary to Lord Leonard Courtney and later occupied the first chair of economic history in Britain at the University of Manchester. Noted should be his *Industrial Organization in the Sixteenth and Seventeenth Centuries* (1904) and *Guilds and Companies of London* (1908). In his view voluntary communities, families, trade unions, churches and schools are more fundamental to the development and growth of society than economic changes and the actions of the state.

**Andrew Ure**
*Scottish Philosopher and Chemist*                          *1778–1857*

Ure, born in Glasgow, where he was also educated, held the chair of natural philosophy at the Andersonian University, Glasgow. In his *Philosophy of Manufactures* (1835) he rendered a shocking picture, with detailed statistical material, of the employment of women and children in the English textile industry.

**Gerónimo De Uztariz**
*Spanish Statesman*                                        *1670–1732*

Uztariz was a high-ranking, policy-making public official at the time of Philip V and Cardinal Alberoni. He was an author of international reputation, and a member of the Trade Council and the Council of the Indies. His book *Theórica y práctica de comercio y de marina* (1724) not only deals with international trade, but also gives a detailed and comprehensive description of the tax system, monopoly system, and population problem of his time, making it a valuable source book. In addition to keen observation of contemporary conditions, it offers excellent analysis and critical evaluation of the institutions of the day.

# V

### Jacob Vanderlint
*English Mercantilist*                                    *?–1740*

Vanderlint, of Dutch extraction, was one of the first writers to propagate the idea that increased flow of money stimulates trade. He was also one of the first to argue for freedom in economic transactions, because of the wisdom found in the natural order set by a benevolent providence. These ideas were expressed in his book *Money Answers All Things* (1734).

### Evgeny Samuilovich Varga
*Russian Economist*                                    *1879–1964*

Varga, born in Budapest, studied at the universities of Budapest, Paris, and Berlin and taught political economy at the University of Budapest. Later he became commissar of finance and chairman of the Supreme Soviet of National Economy. He was also professor of political economy at the U.S.S.R. Academy of Sciences and at the Institute of World Economics and International Relations in the U.S.S.R. Varga has been called the senior Soviet expert on the economics of capitalism. Important among his many writings are *New Phenomena in World Economic Crises* (1934), *Twentieth Century Capitalism* (1961), and *Contemporary Capitalism and Economic Crises* (1962).

### Marcus Terentius Varro
*Roman Scholar and Writer*                                    *116–27 B.C.*

Varro, the son of a large landowner, enjoyed the best education available in his days, studying in Rome and Athens and becoming a scholar well versed in Latin and Greek literature. He also served under Pompey as a soldier and was a friend of Octavian. For political reasons he lived much of his life in retirement, devoting himself to studies and writing. Prolific, he wrote books covering all fields of human endeavor, but only *Rerum rusticarum* survives. Here he stated that successful and profitable use of agricultural land depends upon the distance to the consumption center. This notion suggests location theory, which was developed much later.

### Sébastien Le Prestre, Seigneur de Vauban
*Marshal of France*                                    *1633–1707*

Born into poverty in St.-Léger, Vauban was trained as an engineer and served Louis XIV in nearly all of his wars. He became governor of Lille

(1668), commissioner of fortifications (1678), and marshal of France (1703). A brilliant engineer, he built France a cordon of fortresses.

Also a sharp observer and independent thinker, toward the end of his life he became interested in the country's political and economic problems and discovered many faults. In particular he was concerned with the plight of a large part of the population of France. He submitted many proposals for socioeconomic improvements. Waiting in vain for a favorable reaction, Vauban decided in 1707 to publish *Projet de dîme royale*, putting forth the idea that every citizen without exception has the duty to support the state in proportion to his means. Half of the revenue needed should come from a 5 percent tax (in kind) on the gross produce of the soil. In addition, Vauban proposed a 5 to 10 percent income tax on house rents and wages, including governmental salaries, and suggested a small salt tax, a profit tax for commercial and industrial enterprises, and an excise tax on coffee, tea, tobacco, and liquor. The king ordered the whole edition of Vauban's treatise burned, and Vauban died on the day this order was executed.

*American Economist*  **Thornstein Bunde Veblen**
                     *1857–1929*

Veblen, born in Wisconsin as the son of a Norwegian immigrant farmer, studied under J. B. Clark at Carleton College, and also at Johns Hopkins University and Yale University (Ph.D.). His views and attitudes prevented him at first from obtaining an academic position but he finally received a postgraduate fellowship at Cornell University and later at the University of Chicago, where he also taught and became the editor of the *Journal of Political Economy*. He never reached the rank of professor and had to move from college to college: from Stanford University to the University of Missouri and the New School for Social Research. He was an ineffective teacher, indifferent to most of his students, and a skeptical, bitter, and pessimistic man somehow endowed with an appeal for women. In his later years he was aided financially by one of his former students. He died alone, just a few months before the stock-market crash, which he had predicted. Nevertheless, Veblen's genius has been internationally recognized. The king of Norway paid him a visit while in the U.S., and the American Economic Association offered him its presidency, which he declined.

A severe critic of Bentham, Veblen was the founder of the Institutional school of economics. He stressed the need for studying the economy as a whole and emphasized the role of institutions in economic activities. Drawing analogies to Darwinian evolution, Veblen showed the constancy of change in society and economic institutions; instead of searching for equilibrium, he studied the motion of the economy and found that maladjustments are normal and not exceptional occurrences. Conflicts of interests were to him of much greater importance than the so-called harmony of interests that had been so widely preached. Veblen replaced the pleasure-and-pain psychology of the classics with a psychological analysis of the bases of social institutions, thus challenging the assumptions on which Ricardian economics was based. He also de-emphasized abstract theorizing in favor of a more inductive, factual approach. His analyses of business, the price system, and the role of the technician have been widely influential. A critic of the existing order, he suggested liberal reforms to effect a more equal distribution of wealth.

Veblen's many books found an international audience. His most famous, *The Theory of the Leisure Class* (1899), attacked the unequal distribution of wealth and introduced the concept of "conspicuous consumption." Noteworthy also are his *The Theory of Business Enterprise* (1904), *The Instinct of Workmanship and the State of the Industrial Arts* (1914), *Imperial Germany and the Industrial Revolution* (1915), *An Inquiry into the Nature of Peace* (1919), *Vested Interests and the State of the Industrial Arts* (1920), *Engineers and the Price System* (1921), and *Absentee Ownership and Business Enterprise in Recent Times: The Case of America* (1923).


**Vecchio**
see Gustavo *Del Vecchio*


**Count Pietro Verri**
*Italian Economist and Statesman*                    *1728–1797*

Verri was born in Milan and studied in Milan, Rome, and at the College of Nobles in Parma. He was a captain in the Seven Years War and later an officer in the Austrian and also in the French administration in Milan. An economist of the first rank, Verri produced some independent and original ideas and made important recommendations in policy matters. He had a clear notion of economic equilibrium and took what would today be called an econometric approach. He calculated a balance of payments and demonstrated the constant-outlay demand curve. He anticipated the theory of shifting of taxes, stating that taxes are paid finally by consumers and therefore reduce spending and consumption. He supported liberalism and laissez-faire, and saw the true wealth of a nation to be in the growth of its industry and commerce.

His numerous publications, many of which were translated into German and French, include *Elementi del commercio* (1760); *Commercio de' grani* (1769), on the laws of trade, mainly of grains; and *Meditazioni sull'economia politica* (1771). His posthumously published *Memorie storiche* shows his notable ability to relate facts to theory and to back his arguments with historical material. Many of his articles appeared in *Il caffe* (The Coffeehouse), a magazine founded by him and his friends.

**Henry Vethake**
*American Mathematician and Economist*  1792–1866

Vethake, born in British Guiana, was educated at Columbia College. He taught mathematics and physics there and at other institutions until becoming president of Washington College, Virginia, in 1835. In 1836 he accepted a call to the University of Pennsylvania as professor of mathematics and provost. He became increasingly interested in moral philosophy and political economy, and in 1838 he published *Principles of Political Economy*. Here he included a few "innovations," as he himself called them, defining immaterial and intellectual matters as part of capital and wealth.

**Giovanni Battista Vico**
*Italian Lawyer and Philosopher*  1668–1744

Vico, born in Naples, and professor at Naples, proclaimed he taught "all the knowable." His real field was philosophy of history or historical sociology, which he called a "new science." It was an evolutionary science, stressing the changes in social institutions. This had a great effect on the development of economic thought, especially through Galiani, who accepted Vico's ideas.

**Vicomte Alban de Villeneuve-Bargemont**
*French Social Reformer*  1784–1850

Villeneuve was born at Château St. Alban. One of the Catholic critics of economic liberalism, he became a central figure in the movement for social reform. Among his works are *Economie politique chrétienne* (1834), and *Histoire d'économie politique* (1840).

**Louis René Villermé**
*French Social Researcher*  1782–1863

Villermé, born in Paris, is noted for his celebrated work *Tableau de l'état physique et moral des ouvriers employés dans les manufactures de coton, de laine, et de soie* (1840), which describes wretched working conditions in the textile industry. The research was sponsored by the Academie des Sciences Morales et Politiques. Villermé reported: "in some establishments in Normandy the thong used for the punishment of children appears as an instrument of production in the spinner's trade."

**Jacob Viner**
*American Economist*  1892–1970

Born in Montreal, Canada, Viner studied at McGill University and Harvard University (Ph.D.). He taught at the University of Chicago and at Princeton University. He published *Studies in the Theory of*

*International Trade* (1937), *International Economics* (1951), and *The Long View and the Short* (1958). Viner edited the *Journal of Political Economy* for 18 years, was president of the American Economic Association in 1939, and served as a consultant to the Treasury from 1939–42. An authority on international trade, he dealt with topics like purchasing power parity, trade restrictions, devaluation of currencies, and exchange controls. Of special interest are his studies, supported with excellent statistical material, on the effects of price restrictions.

**Simon Vissering**
*Dutch Economist*                                               *1818–1897*

Vissering, born at Amsterdam, studied at Leyden and became professor at Leyden University (which had many Japanese students). Vissering gained his reputation through his influence on economic studies in Japan, particularly in regard to statistics and international economics. His books, translated into Japanese, were the first on economics available in Japan. His principal work is *Handboek voor practische Staathuishoudkunde* (*Manual for Practical Economy*) (1860).

**François Marie Arouet de Voltaire**
*French Philosopher and Writer*                                 *1694–1778*

Born in Paris, François Marie Arouet later assumed the name Voltaire. He traveled in England and Prussia, where he befriended King Frederick II. Amassing a fortune through speculation, he purchased an estate near Lake Geneva, where he spent his later years. He was twice imprisoned in the Bastille, and became a lifelong foe of religious and political persecution and an admirer of the liberalism of English political institutions. The author of more than 50 volumes of philosophy, history, criticism, tales, tragic dramas, poems, and brilliant letters, he was the central figure of the French Enlightenment and had enormous influence.

Voltaire bitterly attacked the doctrines of the physiocrats, particularly their ideas of a natural order and the single tax. His friendship with Turgot later did much to modify his views on physiocracy, though he continued to quarrel with Mirabeau. In his historical writings Voltaire introduced an emphasis on economic and cultural developments.

# W

**Ernst Wagemann**
*German Statistician*       *1884–1956*

Born in Charnalcillo, Chile, Wagemann studied at Göttingen, Berlin, and Hamburg. Wagemann was professor at Berlin and director of the German Statistical Office. He related his statistical research to economics and sociology and contributed much to population studies. In *Menschenzahl und Völkerschicksal* (1948) he evolved a population theory which he called "demodynamics" and stated that business cycles are connected with population fluctuations. Wagemann also coined the term "sociometrics" for statistical measurements of social values; "econometrics" is that part of sociometrics concerned with economic objects alone.

**Adolf Heinrich Gotthilf Wagner**
*German Economist*       *1835–1917*

Wagner, born in Erlangen, taught at various German universities before his 46-year career as professor of economics at the University of Berlin. He was a founder of the "Verein für Sozialpolitik" and a member of the Christian Socialist party and the Protestant Social Congress. He was elected to the Prussian Diet and later appointed to the Prussian House of Lords (1910). Wagner was an influential teacher and made great contributions in the field of public finance, stressing a broad national and social viewpoint. His *Finanzwissenschaft* (4 vols., 1877) became a standard work. In his opinion, the science of finance should serve as guidance in the policy of redistribution of income, in taxation, and in the elimination of unearned increment which, for him, actually belonged to society and not to individuals. His *Grundlegung der politischen Ökonomie* (1876) also found wide acceptance. In it, he combined the historical, evolutionary approach with the more abstract outlook of the Austrians. While these two books may represent his main works, a long list of additional publications could be added.

**Daniel Wakefield**
*English Barrister*       *1776–1846*

Wakefield was a follower of Steuart but added original ideas about rent, interest, and positive and relative costs. He also dwelt on value in his writings, which dealt mainly with fiscal policy and theory. He was in favor of protectionism and wrote *An Essay upon Political Economy, Being an Inquiry into the Truth of Two Positions of the French Econ-*

*omists that Labour Employed in Manufactures is Unproductive, and that All Taxes Ultimately Fall upon or Settle in the Surplus Produce of Land* (1799).

**Abraham Wald**
*German Economist*                                              *1902–1950*

Wald, born at Cluj, Rumania, and self-schooled, went in 1927 to Vienna and worked with Karl Menger in geometry and later at the Austrian Institute for Business Cycle Research on econometrics. In 1938 he accepted an invitation from the Cowles Commission and was brought by professor Hoteling to Columbia, where he remained. He died in an airplane crash on a lecture tour. Wald, a leader in econometrics, published many articles. Of special interest are "Über einige Gleichungssysteme der Mathematischen Ökonomie" (1936; translated and published in 1951 in *Econometrica,* where other of his articles were also published), and "The Approximate Determination of Indifference Surfaces by Means of Engel Curves" (*Econometrica*, 1940).

**Amasa Walker**
*American Businessman and Economist*                             *1799–1875*

Born in Woodstock, Connecticut, Walker became a merchant and enjoyed a very successful life. Starting as a schoolteacher, he became a merchant in Boston, took part in public life, presided over peace conferences abroad, and helped found Oberlin College, where he taught political economy. He also lectured at Amherst College. He helped form the Free Soil Party and favored railroad development. He served as secretary of state in Massachusetts, was a member of the state legislature, and was elected to Congress. In 1857 he started to publish articles in *Hunt's Merchant* and also published a pamphlet, *The Nature and Uses of Money and Mixed Currency*. With his son, Francis A. Walker, he wrote the widely-read *Science of Wealth* (1866). Walker was well versed in financial and currency matters. He favored free trade and followed the classics except that he rejected Malthus' population theory.

**Francis Amasa Walker**
*American Economist and Soldier*                                 *1840–1897*

Born in Boston, Walker studied for a year at Amherst College, joined the army, and became a brigadier general in the Civil War. He served the government as chief of the Bureau of Statistics, superintendent of the census (1870, 1880), and commissioner of Indian affairs. He taught political economy at Yale University and became president of the Massachusetts Institute of Technology. He was a member of the National Academy of Sciences, a founder of the American Economic Association, of which he was the first president, serving for 7 years, and was president of the American Statistical Association for 15 years. He published *The Wage Question* (1876), in which he stated that wages are paid out of the product and not out of the capital and rejected the wage-fund theory. He also wrote *Money* (1878), *Land and Its Rent* (1883), and *Political Economy* (1883). General Walker was a remarkable man, highly respected in economics, education, and public life. He saw economics as a science rather than an art.

**Robert Wallace**

*Scottish Clergyman and Statistician*                    *1697–1771*

Wallace was educated at Edinburgh University and became a Presbyterian clergyman. In 1753 he published *Dissertation on the Numbers of Mankind in Ancient and Modern Times*, in which he opined that the world's population was larger in ancient times. In 1761 he wrote *Various Prospects of Mankind, Nature and Providence*, in which he described egalitarian communism as the most perfect form of government. This work was criticized by Godwin. Since Malthus' work started from a criticism of Godwin's ideas, Wallace may have had more influence on Malthus than any of the other writers who anticipated his principles.

**Graham Wallas**

*English Economist and Writer*                    *1858–1932*

Born in Sunderland, Wallas studied at Shrewsbury and at Corpus Christi College and became a schoolteacher, until he started to lecture at university extension courses. He joined the Fabian Society in 1886, but resigned when the society supported Joseph Chamberlain's tariff policy in 1904. He held public office on school boards, public committees, and Royal commissions. From 1895–1923 he was on the faculty of the London School of Economics. Among his writings are *Human Nature in Politics* (1908), *The Great Society* (1914), and *The Art of Thought* (1926). He did not believe that man is directed by enlightened self-interest, which he called an intellectualist assumption, and he felt that too much weight was being given to institutions and systems instead of to the human being.

**Antoine-Auguste Walras**

*French Economist*                    *1801–1866*

Walras, born at Montpellier, was at first professor of philosophy at the Royal College of Caën, but later turned to economics. He published *De la Nature de la richesse et de l'origine de la valeur* (1831), which stated that the origin of value is found in the scarceness of goods. He introduced the term "rarity" in the sense that supply is not sufficient to cover the needs of demand. He was the father of Léon Walras.

## Marie Ésprit Léon Walras
*French Economist*  1834–1910

Léon Walras was born in Evreux, the son of A. A. Walras. The first part of his life was one of great disappointment. He graduated from the lycée at Douai, failed the entrance examination to the Ecole Polytechnique twice, withdrew from the Ecole des Mines, wrote a novel which was a failure, and worked briefly for the *Journal des économistes* and *La Presse*. With Léon Say he founded a bank for producers' cooperatives which soon failed. He could not obtain an academic position, and manuscripts of articles were returned to him unpublished.

Walras had been stimulated by his father and his father's teacher, Cournot, to try political economy. At the International Congress in Lausanne (1860) the canton of Vaud offered a prize for the best paper on its fiscal problems. Walras submitted a paper advocating the nationalization of land and was awarded only 4th prize. But in 1870 he was appointed professor of political economy at the Académie at Lausanne, where he taught until 1892, when ill health forced him to resign.

Walras is considered the founder of the Lausanne School of economics. He was the first economist to apply mathematical analysis to the study of the general equilibrium. He produced a new system of equations and discussed price determination under 4 partial theories: exchange, production, capitalization, and circulation. His many outstanding contributions to economics include *Eléments d' économie politique pure* (1874), *Theorie mathématique de la richesse sociale* (1883), and *Études d' économie sociale* (1896), in which he addressed himself to social ethics and advocated a land-nationalization scheme. His *Études d' économie politique appliquée* (1898) discusses practical problems in monetary economics, markets, banking and credit, and the stock market.

## Waltershausen
see Friedrich Georg *Sartorius, Freiherr von Waltershausen*

## Warville
see Jacques Pierre *Brissot de Warville*

## Francis Wayland
*American Writer and Economist*  1796–1865

Wayland was born in New York City and studied at Union College, where he later became a professor of mathematics and philosophy. From 1827–55 he was president of Brown University. He published many works on religion and political science; to economics he gave *Elements of Political Economy* (1837) and *The Moral Laws of Accumulation* (also 1837). A courageous man and an excellent teacher and administrator, he had a great impact on his students and colleagues. Wayland saw in economics a science for finding the divinely established laws.

**Beatrice Potter Webb**
*English Fabian Socialist*                                    *1858–1943*

Beatrice Potter was born in Gloucester and educated privately. An able social worker and investigator into economic and social conditions, she took a large part in research that led to a revision of the English Poor Laws. She was an early advocate of minimum wage legislation. With her husband, Sidney Webb, she helped build the Fabian Society and British Labour Party. Together they wrote many books, including *Methods of Social Study* (1932). Her own works include *The Co-operative Movement in Great Britain* (1891).

**Sidney Webb**
*English Fabian Socialist*                                    *1859–1947*

Webb was born in London and educated in Switzerland and Germany. Returned, he went to City of London College and attended evening school at Birkbeck Institute. In 1891 he became a member of the London County Council. He served on many committees and commissions and was professor of public administration at London University. A leading supporter of the British Labour Party, he entered Parliament, was secretary of state for colonies and dominions in the Labour cabinet of 1929, and is credited with writing the Labour platform advocating a minimum living standard for all. In order to give the Labour Party a seat in the House of Lords, in 1929 he was made Baron Passfield, a title which his wife, Beatrice Potter Webb, never accepted.

Often called the father of the British socialist movement, Webb was a founder of the Fabian Society and wrote up much of its platform. Throughout his life he was possessed by a strong passion for social justice. His many publications include *Socialism in England* (1890), *Social Democracy* (1916), *The Decay of Capitalist Civilization* (1923), and *Soviet Communism: A New Civilization* (1935). Webb founded the *New Statesman* in 1913.

**Adolf Weber**
*German Economist*                                           *1876–1963*

Adolf Weber, born at Mechernich, near Bonn, taught at Cologne, Breslau, Frankfurt, and Munich. His writings enjoyed wide attention, especially *Allgemeine Volkswirtschaftslehre* (1928), *Weltwirtschaft* (1932), and *Geld, Banken, Börsen* (1935), which all went through numerous editions.

**Alfred Weber**
*German Economist*                                      *1868–1958*

The brother of Max Weber, Alfred Weber was born in Erfurt and studied at Berlin. A professor at the University of Prague and, after 1907, at the University of Heidelberg, he was one of the first economists to concentrate on the industrial location problem. He wrote *Über den Standort der Industrien* (1909). Later he stressed cultural and sociological aspects in economics.

**Max Weber**
*German Economist and Sociologist*                     *1864–1920*

Max Weber, born in Erfurt, studied law at Heidelberg, Berlin, and Göttingen, but his interest centered on economics, of which he became a professor at Freiburg and later at Heidelberg. A man of great drive, he overworked himself; ill-health forced him to reduce his scholarly activities and finally to give up his position. He traveled to Rome and there was inspired to study the economic activities of medieval monasteries. In 1904 he visited the U.S. and participated in the Congress of Arts and Sciences at St. Louis. In later life he was visiting professor at Vienna and Munich, where he died of pneumonia. The University of Heidelberg established the Max Weber Institute in his honor.

Though Weber was highly interested in a comprehensive study of society in its sociological aspects, his main field of interest remained economics. He rejected Marx's theory of economic determinism, and stressed the importance of ethical and religious factors in the formation of capitalism, notably in his famous work, *Die Protestantische Ethik under der Geist des Kapitalismus* (1904). *Grundriss der Sozialokonomik* (1911), *Gesammelte Aufsätze zur Wissenschaftslehre* (1922), and *Wirtschaft und Gesellschaft* (2 vols., 1925, posthumous) are among his other writings.

**Wilhelm Weitling**
*German Social Reformer*                               *1808–1871*

Weitling was born at Magdeburg. As a young man he spent some years in France and came under the influence of French socialists, especially Fourier and Cabet. In his *Die Menschheit, wie sie ist und wie sie sein sollte* (1838) he projected a hierarchical structure of society. In *Garantein der Harmonie und Freiheit* (1842) he discussed the relationship between freedom and human desires and stressed the need for the individual's voluntary fulfillment of his duties toward society. He believed that a just social order must be based on the development of spiritual and  mental forces in all men. Weitling accepted property as such, but stated that private property would become a curse if free, unoccupied land were no longer readily available. Though he saw private ownership of land as the root of all evil, he did not oppose private ownership of the means of production.

**David Ames Wells**
*American Geologist and Economist*                    *1828–1898*

Born in Springfield, Massachusetts, Wells studied geology and chemistry at Williams College and Lawrence Scientific School, where he became a member of the faculty. During the Civil War he turned to economics. His essay *Our Burden and Our Strength* (1864), dealing with national debt, brought him appointment as chairman of the National Revenue Commission (1865). Later he was made special commissioner of revenue, and chairman of the New York State Tax Commission. His reports are not only of historical value but include contributions to fiscal theory. Wells remained a strong individualist and supporter of laissez-faire. He wrote *A Primer of Tariff Reform* (1884), *Practical Economics* (1885), *The Relation of the Tariff to Wages* (1888), *Recent Economic Changes* (1889), and *The Theory and Practice of Taxation* (1900).

**Siegfried Wendt**
*German Economist*                    *1901–1966*

Born in Hamburg, Wendt studied at Berlin and Freiburg and taught at Mannheim, Heidelberg, Göttingen and Giessen. He was visiting professor in Istanbul. He published *Die Währungssysteme* (1947), *Die Entwicklung des deutschen Geldwesens* (1950), and *Geschichte der Volkswirtschaftslehre* (1961).

**Sir Edward West**
*English Economist*                    *1782–1828*

West, born at St. Marylebone, Middlesex, became a lawyer and was sent to India as a judge for some time. West opposed the wage-fund theory, tried to clear up the confusion over the statement "profits depend on wages," got into an argument with Malthus over rent, and wrote *Essay on the Application of Capital to Land* (8 vols., 1815). He joined the pessimists in regard to population pressure, failing industrial returns, and ever-increasing land rents.

**Richard Whately**
*English Writer and Archbishop*                    *1787–1863*

Whately was born in London and studied at Oriel College, Oxford. He occupied the Drummond Chair of Political Economy at Oxford from 1830–31 and afterward became Archbishop of Dublin. In 1832 he established the chair for political economy at Trinity College, Dublin. In his *Introductory Lectures on Political Economy* (1831) he suggested that economics be called "catallactics," or the science of exchange, and

defined man as the only animal that makes exchanges. For him, utility
and wealth were relative and subjective.

**John Wheeler**
*English Lawyer*                                     *approx. 1560–1630*

Wheeler was secretary of the Society of Merchant Adventurers. In its
defense he wrote *Treatise on Commerce* (1601), showing that well-
organized and orderly trade is superior to unorganized trade.

   Wheeler submitted a survey of the trade with Holland and the North-
German Hansa.

**William Whewell**
*English Scientist*                                     *1794–1866*

Born in Lancaster, Whewell's whole life centered in Cambridge, where
he studied mathematics and became, in turn, a Fellow of Trinity College, professor of mineralogy, professor of moral philosophy, master of
the college, and vice-chancellor of the university. He came late to economics, but proved himself well versed in this field. His contributions
were mainly in methodology. He wrote a series of papers giving a
mathematical exposition of certain economic doctrines (1829, 1831,
1850). His *Six Lectures on Political Economy* (1862), originally prepared and delivered in Cambridge for the Prince of Wales, is of peren-
nial interest.

**White**
see Charles *Dupont-White*

**Horace White**
*American Journalist*                                     *1834–1910*

White was born at Colebrook, New Hampshire, and was educated at
Beloit College, Wisconsin. Interested in journalism, he joined the staff
of the Chicago *Tribune*, where he became chief editor in 1874. Soon he
left to become co-editor and later chief editor of the New York *Evening
News*. In 1895 White published his *Money and Banking, Illustrated by
American History*. In 1908, New York's governor, Charles E. Hughes,
appointed White chairman of the Commission on Speculation in Securities and Commodities.

**Johan Gustav Knut Wicksell**
*Swedish Economist*                                     *1851–1926*

Wicksell, born in Stockholm, studied mathematics and philosophy at
the University of Uppsala (Ph.D.) and expanded his studies in England, Germany, France, and Austria. He came to economics at the age
of 40 and became professor at the University of Lund (1900–16).

He was well versed in the economics of Böhm-Bawerk, Pareto, and Marshall, and followed Walras closely. He leaned heavily also on Wicksteed and Edgeworth. He took the best ideas and elements of these outstanding economists and successfully integrated their greatest contributions. He published *Value, Capital and Rent* (1893), *Finance Theory* (1896), and *Interest and Prices* (1898). Most of his books appeared in German and were later translated into English. In 1901 his *Lectures on Political Economy* was published in Swedish. A second volume appeared in 1906 and contained his famous theory concerning the relation between money, rate of interest, and general level of prices. Wicksell was the founder of the so-called Swedish School and was an early leader in dynamic economics.

**Philip Henry Wicksteed**
*English Economist*                                        *1844–1927*

Born in Leeds, Wicksteed studied at University College, London. For 20 years he was a Unitarian minister at Little Portland Street Chapel, London. His philosophical interests were in ethics but he became more and more concerned with sociology and economics, partly because of reading Henry George's *Progress and Poverty*. He left the chapel and became university extension lecturer. Among his many writings are *Alphabet of Economic Science* (1888), *Essays on Coordination of the Laws of Distribution* (1894), and *Common Sense of the Political Economy* (1910). The last is one of the most comprehensive nonmathematical expositions of the marginal utility concept which Wicksteed explained with "proportional utility", comparing the utility of one commodity with another. He also succeeded in correlating value and distribution and in demonstrating the reversibility of the market supply curve.

**Friedrich Freiherr von Wieser**
*Austrian Economist*                                        *1851–1926*

Born in Vienna, Wieser studied at the University of Vienna, and was mainly interested in history. Reading *Grundsätze*, by Menger, his father-in-law, he became curious about economics and proceeded to study further at Heidelberg, Jena, and Leipzig. He taught at the University of Prague but returned to Vienna in 1903 as Karl Menger's successor. In 1917 he was appointed to the Austrian Upper House and served as minister of commerce in the last two cabinets of the Austro-Hungarian Empire. In three books he made original and important contributions to economics: *Ursprung der Hauptgesetze des wirtschaftlichen Güterverkehrs* (1884), *Der natürliche Wert* (1889), and *Theorie der gesellschaftlichen Wirtschaft* (1914). Wieser exposed the theory of "Grenznutzen" (marginal utility), and explained indirect utility. His works brought him international recognition. With Menger and Böhm-

Bawerk he represents the Austrian School. He developed the theory of subjective value.

**James Wilson**
*English Businessman and Civil Servant*     *1805–1860*

Wilson was a member of Parliament, secretary of the Board of Control, financial secretary, vice-president of the Board of Trade, and finally financial minister in India. In order to propagate free-trade ideas he founded the *Economist*. When Wilson went to India, Bagehot, his son-in-law, became the editor. Wilson wrote *Influences of the Corn Laws* (1839), *Fluctuation of Currency* (1840), and *Capital, Currency, and Banking* (1845). A man of the practical world, Wilson saw political economy as the science of buying and selling, the study of the ordinary bargains of men.

**Thomas Wilson**
*English Statesman*     *1525–1581*

Born at Harwick, Roxburghshire, and educated at Eton and Cambridge, Wilson was a member of Parliament and served under Elizabeth I as master of bequests and secretary of state (1577). Here he confirmed his view, expressed in Parliament in 1571, opposing all interest payment. Though a bill had been passed permitting interest up to 10 percent, it was not enforceable. Only Wilson and one other member opposed it. Wilson became dean of Durham in 1579 and wrote *Discourse upon Usurie* (1584).

**Karl Georg Winkelblech**
*German Scientist and Social Reformer*     *1810–1865*

Winkelblech, born in Mainz, studied chemistry at Giessen. He became a professor of natural science at Marburg and Kassel and published his socialist views under the name of Karl Marlo. Of special interest is his *Untersuchungen über die Organisation der Arbeit oder System der Weltökonomie* (4 vols., 1850–52). He spoke about "panpolism" (the opposite of monopolism) and declared that every man has a right to work and the freedom to dispose of his earned income according to his own wishes. He proposed a form of guild collectivism.

**Gerrard Winstanley**
*English Reformer*     *1609–1660*

Winstanley was the inspirer and spokesman of the Diggers, an action group that in 1649–50 settled on uncultivated land near London and started to farm it. They practiced a form of egalitarian communism and believed that God gave land for the use of all men. After the overthrow of Charles I they stated that former landlords no longer had any claim to the land. The Diggers who, being pacifists, did not offer resistance, were dispersed by soldiers and mob violence in 1650. Several of Winstanley's pamphlets are still known: *A Watchword to the City of London and the Army* (1649) and *The Law of Freedom in a Platform, or True Magistracy Restored* (1652).

**Albert Benedict Wolfe**

*American Economist*                                                    *1876–1967*

Wolfe, born in Arlington, Illinois, studied at Harvard University (Ph.D.) and taught at Oberlin College, the University of Texas, and Ohio State University. His main interest was in value theories. He wrote *Readings in Social Problems* (1916) and notable articles such as "Full Utilization, Equilibrium, and Expansion of Production" (*Quarterly Journal of Economics,* 1940), "Economics and Democracy" (*American Economic Review,* 1944), and "Neurophysical Economics" (*Journal of Political Economy,* 1950).

**Barbara Frances Wootton**

*English Economist*                                                      *1897–*

Born at Cambridge, Barbara Adam married John Wesley Wootton, who was killed in the war in 1917. In 1935 she married George P. Wright.

She studied at Girton College, Cambridge, where she became lecturer in economics. Later she became principal of Morley College for Working Men and Women, and professor at the University of London in 1948. She was made a life peer and baroness in 1958. In her book *Freedom under Planning* (1945) she investigated the nature of economic freedom and found, contrary to Marx's expectations, that freedom of individuals occurs in many systems, including the unplanned, individualistic ones. Among Lady Wootton's many other writings, *Social Foundations of Wage Policy* (1955) is of special interest.

**Carroll D. Wright**

*American Economist*                                                    *1840–1909*

Born in Dunbarton, New Hampshire, Wright studied at Tufts and Dartmouth. He became chief of the Massachusetts Bureau of Labor Statistics and later U.S. commissioner of labor (1885). In 1902 Wright was appointed president of Clark College. His fields of interest were statistics, economic history, labor economics, and social economics in general. He wrote *Factory System of the United States* (1880), *Industrial Depressions* (1886), *History of Wages and Prices in Massachusetts 1752–1883* (1895), and *The Battle of Labor* (1906). Wright felt that a better understanding of labor conditions would serve the interests of all, and he worked to establish harmony between labor and capital.

# X

**Xenophon**

*Greek Historian, Philosopher, and Soldier*          *ca. 430–355 B.C.*

Xenophon, born near Athens, became a pupil of Socrates, about whom he wrote in *Memorabilia*. He fought with Cyrus the Younger in Persia and when Cyrus was killed was chosen to command the Greek soldiers in their march homeward. His book the *Anabasis* is the famous account of this adventure. Later he fought for Sparta against Athens and Thebes and was banished by the Athenians. His many writings include the *Cyropaedia*, in which he offered interesting ideas on the division of labor, and the *Oeconomicus*, in which he outlined ways of increasing the revenue of Athens. He advocated agriculture and the promotion of manufacture and trade. He recommended the forming of joint-stock companies and proposed making silver mining a state enterprise.

# Y

**Allyn Abbott Young**

*American Economist*      *1876–1929*

Young, born in Kenton, Ohio, studied at Hiram College and the University of Wisconsin (Ph.D). He taught at Western Reserve University; Dartmouth College; the University of Wisconsin; Stanford, Washington (St. Louis), Cornell, and Harvard universities; and at the London School of Economics. He was also chief of the U.S. Economic and Statistics Commission to negotiate peace after World War I.

An excellent mathematician and statistician, he sought to combine the older neo-classic with the new Walrasian economics. He was highly interested in the problems of the aged and poor in Massachusetts, in farm relief, and in the depreciation allowances by firms. His wide education and knowledge made him also well versed in many fields related to economics. Among his works are "Increasing Returns and Economic Progress" (*Economic Journal,* 1913), *An Analysis of Bank Statistics of the United States* (1924), and *Economic Problems: New and Old* (1927).

**Arthur Young**

*English Agricultural Economist*      *1741–1820*

Young, born in London, was the first secretary of the Board of Agriculture. He became blind in 1811. His numerous books deal with agricultural problems and with travels during which he investigated agricultural conditions. Of historical interest are *A Six Months Tour Through the North of England* (1771) and *Travels in France* (1787–89). In 1784 Young founded the *Annals of Agriculture*, to which George III contributed under the name Ralph Robinson. Young advocated the employment of new methods on large-scale farms, careful treatment of the soil, and the use of hired labor rather than tenant farmers.

# Z

**Frederik Zeuthen**
*Danish Economist*                                    *1888–1959*

Zeuthen's article "Monopoly and Competition" appeared in the *Nationaloekonomisk Tidsskrift* in 1929. He made himself a name with *Problems of Monopoly and Economic Warfare* (1930), successfully integrating theoretical and statistical material with historical and legal aspects.

**Georg Heinrich Zincke**
*German Cameralist*                                   *1692–1769*

Zincke was born in Naumburg. A civil servant, Zincke affords an example of how much the Cameralists were interested in administrative problems, even to a degree that they could be called forerunners in the science of business administration. In 1742 Zincke published *Grundriss einer Einleitung zu den Cameralwissenschaften*.

**Ferdinand Zweig**
*Polish Economist*                                    *1896–*

Zweig was born in Cracow and studied at the universities of Cracow (L.L.D.) and Vienna and later at the London School of Economics. He worked at the Central Statistical Office in Poland and became professor at the University of Cracow. In 1939 he escaped to England and served as economic adviser to the exiled Polish prime minister. He was Simon Research Fellow at Manchester University and visiting professor at the Hebrew University, Jerusalem, and at Tel-Aviv University. Zweig published a series of studies on the British working classes. Among his other writings, many of which were translated into several languages, are *Planning of Free Societies* (1942), *Economic Ideas* (1950), and *The Israeli Worker* (1959).

**Otto von Zwiedineck-Südenhorst**
*German Economist*                                    *1871–1958*

Zwiedineck was born in Graz, studied at Graz, Heidelberg, and Leipzig and worked for some years at the chamber of commerce at Graz and Vienna. Later he taught at Karlsruhe and Munich. With Wicksell he was one of the first to relate the total nominal income in an economy to changes in the value of money (*Schmollers Jahrbuch*, 1909). In 1952 he published *Von der älteren zur neueren Theorie der politischen Ökonomie*.

**Ulrich Zwingli**
*Swiss Reformer*
*1484–1531*

Zwingli was born at Wildhaus, in the Toggenburg Valley. In spite of his reformational religious attitudes, Zwingli remained so deeply rooted in the socioeconomic doctrines of the Scholastics that he approved the death sentence for a leading businessman accused of charging excessive interest rates.

# APPENDIX I

# On the Present Generation

# Of Economists

# APPENDIX I
# On the Present Generation
# Of Economists

In our "Age of the Economist," the economic literature has mush-roomed. Countless academic writers and economic politicians are trying to analyze, explain, and solve the multitude of problems produced by rapidly increasing economic activities in all parts of the world. Tech-nological breakthroughs greater than at any time in history, growing international economic interrelationships, and added knowledge about all phases of human behavior have created both a wealth of economic pro-duction and a confusion of fundamental values. The struggle for the rights and dignity of the individual and also for the rights of the society as a whole has intensified. Policy controversies have divided contemporary economists not only into many groups—groups representing ideological attitudes that run the gamut from the rebirth of Adam Smith's liberalism to the projecting of a new world structure, from conservative dissent to the New Left's revival of Marxism. Economists are suggesting a laissez-faire free market economy, a regulated market economy, and a planned economy; socialistic economic institutions, plain communism, and pure anarchism. They believe in a glorious future of new supermen living in abundant affluence—and warn about the approaching energy crisis and the self-destruction of mankind through pollution and the interruption of the natural cycle. Which of the theoretical findings, normative propo-sitions, pragmatic experiments, and trials will still have the attention of students of economic affairs fifty years from now can hardly be predicted.

Present-day economists are so numerous that it is impossible to list all the names of those who have lately made outstanding contributions to economic theory and policy; neither is this the purpose of this book. Still, at the risk of unfairness, I would like to mention a few who at present enjoy international recognition. Naming these people does not require going into biographical details, which may be found easily in many current directories and handbooks of professional organizations, but I would like to list a few books of theirs which have found wide attention and appreciably influenced economic theory or policy.

Although economics, like the arts and natural sciences, is international in concept and the search for truth, these contemporary economists are here listed by nation. It seems that the lead in these studies has shifted from Great Britain and the European continent to the United States, but the following list shows nevertheless that there have been extraordinary achievements in many countries, with remarkable developments in such non-European nations as Japan, Argentina, and Brazil.

## ARGENTINA

Raul Prebish (1901–    ). Secretary-general of the U.N. Conference on Trade and Development from 1964. Wrote *Introduccion a Keynes* (1947).

## AUSTRIA

Friedrich August von Hayek (1899–    ). Taught at the universities of London and Chicago as well as Vienna and Freiburg. Wrote *The Road to Serfdom* (1944), *The Pure Theory of Capital* (1946), *Capitalism and the Historians* (1954), *The Constitution of Liberty* (1960).

Anton Tautscher (1906–    ). Wrote *Ernst Ludwig Carl der Begründer der Volkswirtschaftslehre* (1939), *Geschichte der Volkswirtschaftslehre* (1950), *Wirtschaftgeschichte Österreichs* (1973).

## BRAZIL

Robert de Oliveiro Campos (1917–    ). Wrote on the responsibility of private enterprise for economic growth and social improvement.

## CANADA

Anthony Dalton Scott (1923–    ). Wrote *National Resources: The Economics of Conservation* (1955).

## FRANCE

Maurice Allais (1911–    ). *Économie et Interêt* (1947).
Robert Gibrat (1904–    ). *Les Inégalités économiques* (1931).
François Perroux (1903–    ). *L'Économie du XXe siècle* (1961).

## GERMANY

Hans Albert (1921–    ). *Ökonomische Ideologie und politische Theorie* (1954).

Herbert Giersch (1921–    ). *Multiplikator Theorie* (1954) and *Das Handelsoptimum* (1956).

Elisabeth Lauschmann (1920–    ). *Grundlagen einer Theorie der Regionalpolitik* (1972).

Erich Preiser (1900–    ). *Grundzüge der Konjunkturlehre* (1933).

Hans Ritschl (1897–    ). *Grundlagen und Ordnungen der Volkswirtschaftslehre* (2 vol. 1947–48), *Die Grundlagen der Wirtschaftsordnung* (1954), *Marktwirtschaft und Gemeinwirtschaft* (1973).

## GREAT BRITAIN

R. G. D. Allen (1906–    ). *Mathematical Analysis for Economists* (1938).

Colin G. Clark (1905–    ). *The Conditions of Economic Progress* (1940).

Maurice Herbert Dobb (1900–    ). *Capital Enterprise and Social Progress* (1925), *Economic Growth and Planning* (1960).

Sir Roy Forbes Harrod (1900–    ). *Toward a Dynamic Economics* (1948), *The Life of J. M. Keynes* (1951), *The Dollar* (1953), *Reforming the World's Monetary System* (1965).

Sir John Richard Hicks (1904–    ). *The Theory of Wages* (1932), *Value and Capital* (1939), *A Revision of the Demand Theory* (1956), *Essays in World Economics* (1959).

John Jewkes (1902–    ). *Public and Private Enterprise* (1965).

Richard P. Kahn (1905–    ), a friend of Keynes, introduced the concept of the multiplier (*Economic Journal,* 1931).

Nicholas Kaldor (1908–    ). *Essays on Value and Distribution* (1960), *Essays on Economic Policy* (1962).

Sir William A. Lewis (1915–    ). *The Principle of Economic Planning* (1949).

James Edward Meade (1907–    ). *The Theory of International Economic Policy* (2 vol. 1951–52), *Principles of Political Economy* (2 vols. 1965–68).

Edward Joshua Mishan (1917–    ). *The Costs of Economic Growth* (1967), *Welfare Economics* (1969).

## ITALY

Amintore Fanfani (1900–    ). *Storia delle dottrine economiche* (2 vols. 1938–45).

## JAPAN

Joichi Itazaki (1908–    ). *Methods of Political Economy* (1960).

Ryokichi Minobe (1904–    ). *The Economy of Japan* (1962).

Shigeto Tsuru (1912–    ). *Keynes versus Marx* (1956).

Yuzo Yamada (1902–    ). *Theory of Planned Economy* (1950).

## NETHERLANDS

Mark Blaug (1927–      ). *Economic Theory in Retrospect* (1962).
Jacques J. Polak (1914–      ). *An International Economic System* (1954).
Jan Tinbergen (1903–      ). *Econometrics* (1961), *Shaping the World Economy* (1963).

## NORWAY

Ragnar A. K. Frisch (1895–      ). *Maxima and Minima* (1960), *Theory of Production* (1962).
Trygve Haavelmo (1911–      ). *A Study in the Theory of Economic Evolution* (1954).

## SPAIN

Gabriel Franco (1915–      ). *Historia de la economia por los grandes maestros* (1965).

## SWEDEN

Sune Carlson (1909–      ). *A Study on the Pure Theory of Production* (1939).
Bent Hansen (1920–      ). *A Study in the Theory of Inflation* (1951).

## SWITZERLAND

Emil Küng (1914–      ). *Wirtschaft und Gerechtigkeit* (1967).
Friedrich August Lutz (1901–      ). *Zinstheorie* (1956).

## RUSSIA

A. A. Arzumanyan (1904–      ). *The Great October Revolution and the Crises of Capitalism* (1957).
S. V. Kantorovich (1912–      ). *The Best Use of Economic Resources* (English translation 1965).
N. D. Kondratieff (1892–      ). Wrote on long cycles, employing statistics. Deported to Siberia 1930.
E. G. Liberman (1897–      ). Suggested using market economy techniques for economic reform.

## UNITED STATES

Lawrence Abbott (1902–      ). *Quality and Competition* (1955), *Economics and the Modern World* (1960).

Kenneth J. Arrow (1921–     ). *Social Choice and Individual Values* (1951).

William Jack Baumol (1922–     ). *Economic Dynamics* (1957), *Business Behavior, Value and Growth* (1959), *Economic Theory and Operations Analysis* (1960).

Abram Bergson (1914–     ). *Essays in Normative Economics* (1966).

Kenneth Ewart Boulding (1910–     ). *A Reconstruction of Economics* (1950), *Principles of Economic Policy* (1958), *Economic Analysis* (1966), *The Meaning of the Twentieth Century* (1964).

Arthur F. Burns (1904–     ). *Frontier of Economic Knowledge* (1954), *Prosperity without Inflation* (1957).

Dudley Dillard (1913–     ). *The Economics of John Maynard Keynes* (1948).

Evsey David Domar (1914–     ). *Essays in the Theory of Economic Growth* (1957).

Robert Dorfman (1916–     ). *Linear Programming and Economic Analysis* (1958), *The Price System* (1964).

Milton Friedman (1912–     ), the leader of the Chicago School, wrote *Essays in Positive Economics* (1953), *Inflation, Causes and Consequences* (1963), *The Optimum Quantity of Money and other Essays* (1969).

Daniel R. Fusfeld (1922–     ). *The Age of the Economist* (1966), *Economics* (1972).

John Kenneth Galbraith (1908–     ). *The Affluent Society* (1958), *The New Industrial State* (1968), *Economics and the Public Purpose* (1973).

Eli Ginsberg (1911–     ). *The Pluralistic Economy* (1965 with others).

Gottfried von Haberler (1900–     ). *The Theory of International Trade* (1935).

Seymour E. Harris (1897–     ). *The Assignats* (1926).

Robert L. Heilbroner (1919–     ). *The Worldly Philosophers* (1953), *The Making of Economic Society* (1962), *The Limits of American Capitalism* (1967), *The Human Prospect* (1974).

Walter Wolfgang Heller (1915–     ). *New Dimensions of Political Economy* (1968).

Lawrence Robert Klein (1920–     ). *The Keynesian Revolution* (1947).

T. Charles Koopmans (1910–     ). *Activity Analysis of Production and Allocation* (1951).

Simon Smith Kuznets (1901–     ). *Modern Economic Growth* (1966).

Robert Lekachman (1920–     ). *A History of Economic Ideas* (1959), *The Age of Keynes* (1966).

Richard H. Leftwich (1920–     ). *The Price System and Resource*

*Allocation* (1968), *An Introduction to Economic Thinking* (1969).

Wassily Leontief (1906–    ). *Studies in the Structure of the American Economy* (1953).

Abba P. Lerner (1903–    ). *The Economics of Control* (1944), *Essays in Economic Analysis* (1953).

Fritz Machlup (1902–    ). *Essays in Economic Semantics* (1963), *Economics of Seller's Competition* (1952).

Gardiner Colt Means (1896–    ). *The Corporate Revolution in America* (1962), *Pricing Power and the Public Interest* (1962).

Geoffrey Moore (1914–    ). *Business Cycle Indicators* (1961).

Oskar Morgenstern (1910–    ). *Theory of Games and Economic Behavior* (1944 with von Neumann), *On the Accuracy of Economic Observations* (1950).

Richard Abel Musgrave (1910–    ). *The Theory of Public Finance* (1959).

Paul Anthony Samuelson (1915–    ), a Nobel Prize Winner, wrote *Foundations of Economic Analysis* (1947), *Economics* (1948), *Collected Scientific Papers* (1966).

Henry William Spiegel (1911–    ). *The Rise of American Economic Thought* (1960), *The Growth of Economic Thought* (1971).

George Joseph Stigler (1911–    ). *Production and Distribution Theory* (1947), *The Organization of Industry* (1967), *Essays in the History of Economics* (1964).

Paul M. Sweezy (1910–    ). *The Theory of Capitalist Development* (1942), *The Present as History* (1953).

Robert Triffin (1911–    ). *The World Money Maze* (1966), *Europe and the Money Muddle* (1957).

Walter Albert Weisskopf (1904–    ). *The Psychology of Economics* (1955), *The Psychology of Abundance* (1966).

# APPENDIX II

## An Outline of Periods and Schools in Economic Thought

# APPENDIX II

# An Outline of Periods and
# Schools in Economic Thought

The outline that follows arranges the names of the economists and social thinkers listed in this book according to their viewpoints and trends in time. The names are given in alphabetical order. Some are listed under more than one heading. The names with an asterisk * are not listed in the main text but are discussed briefly in the Appendix "The Present Generation of Economists."

A. *Toward the Formation of Political Economy* (450 B.C.-1750)

 1) *The Ancient Age.* Early economic thoughts and attitudes.
 The Greeks: Economic problems as part of political philosophy.
  Aristotle, Epicurus, Plato, Socrates, Xenophon.
 The Romans: Legal aspects and the role of agriculture. Cato, Cicero, Columella, Diocletian, Justinian, Pliny the Elder, Seneca, Varro.

 2) *The Middle Ages.* The theological-philosophical doctrine of an organized economy.
 Early writers: Ambrosius, Augustine.
 The Scholastics: Albertus Magnus, Antonine, Aquinas, Bacon (Roger), Bernadin of Siena, Biel, Buridan, Duns Scotus, Lugo, Molina, Navarrus, Oresme.
 Heralds of a changing time: Bodin, Calvin, Copernicus, Descartes, Hobbes, Luther, Machiavelli, Malebranche, Zwingli.
 Other writers and personalities of distinction: Agricola, Armstrong, Aylesbury, Bacon (Francis), Botero, Campanelli, Carafa, Cecil, Cromwell, Culpeper (father), Dumoulin, Gresham, Hales, More, Potter, Sully, Wheeler, Wilson (Thomas).

 3) *The Age of Mercantilism.* The politically regulated economy of national states.

British Mercantilists: Child, Coke, Davenant, Fortrey, Gee, Malynes, Manley, Massie, Misselden, Mun, Petty, Steuart, Vanderlint.

French Mercantilists: Colbert, Laffemas, Melon, Montchrétien.

German and Austrian Mercantilists (called Cameralists): Becher, Besold, Bornitz, Conring, Darjes, Hornigk, Justi, Klock, Lau, Schröder, Seckendorff, Sonnenfels, Süssmilch, Zincke.

Italian Mercantilists: Davanzati, Broggia, Serra.

Reform Mercantilists (pleading for free trade and greater money supply): Asgill, Barbon, Briscoe, Cantillon, Ganilh, Genovesi, Gournay, Necker, North (Dudley), Ortes, Tucker (Josiah).

Other writers and personalities of distinction:

In Britain: Baxter (Richard), Bellers, Berkeley, Chamberlen, Culpeper (son), Defoe, Fauquier, Gervaise, Gould, Graunt, Hale, Harrington, Harris (Joseph), Hutcheson, King (Gregory), Law, Locke, Newton, North (Roger), Paterson, Pollexfen, Postlethwayt, Shaftesbury (3rd Earl), Temple, Wallace, Winstanley.

In France: Boisguillebert, Montesquieu.

In Germany: Obrecht, Pufendorf.

In Holland: Graswinkel, Grotius, Mandeville.

In Italy: Ceva, Montanari, Vico.

In Spain: Campomanes, Uztariz.

B. *The Foundation of Political Economy* (1750–1870)
The rise of individualism and economic liberalism.

1) *Forerunners.*
Anderson (James), Argenson, Beccaria, Boisguillebert, Butel-Dumont, Cantillon, Carl, Gournay, Hume, Locke, Montesquieu, Morellet, Petty, Rousseau, Vauban.

2) *The Physiocrats.* The search for causality and an economy based on natural law. The laissez faire doctrine.
Baudeau, Dupont de Nemours, Iselin, Karl Friedrich of Baden, Le Trosne, Mercier, Mirabeau, Quesnay, Schlettwein, Schmalz, Spence, Turgot.
Critics of the Physiocrats: Forbonnais, Galiani, Graslin, Linguet, Mably, Voltaire.

3) *Adam Smith and the English Classical School.* The quest for freedom of action and individual initiative. The acceptance of the profit motive in an environment of free competition.
Bentham, Cairnes, Chalmers, Everett, Fawcett, Malthus, McCulloch, Mill (James), Mill (John Stuart), Place, Ricardo, Smith (Adam), Tooke, Torrens, Senior.

Expansion to the European continent: Boccardo, Buguoy, Dunoyer, Hermann, Hufeland, Jakob, Kraus, Mangoldt, Nazzani, Nebenius, Rau, Sartorius, Say (Jean-Baptiste), Soden, Vissering.

The Paris Group: Block, Courcelle-Seneuil, Leroy-Beaulieu, Molinari.

The Manchester Group: Bright, Cobden, Faucher, Prince-Smith.

Critics of the Classics: Alison, Bailey, Barton, Bastiat, Bowen, Buchanan, Cardozo, Carey (Henry Charles), Carey (Matthew), Dühring, Ensor, Ferrara, Hazlitt, Jones, Lauderdale, List, Rae, Raymond, Say (Louis Auguste), West.

Other writers and personalities of distinction:

In Britain: Attwood, Babbage, Bain, Banfield, Brand, Cobbett, Craig, De Quincey, Doubleday, Eden, Evelyn, Fullarton, Horner, Marcet, Martineau, Price, Ramsay, Ravenstone, Read, Rooke, Sadler, Scrope, Stewart, Thornton (Henry), Ure, Wakefield, Whateley, Whewell, Wilson (James).

In France: Blanqui (J. A.), Canard, Condillac, Condorcet, Daire, Dupin, Garnier, Villermé.

In Germany: Braun, Dieterici.

In Italy: Custodi, Gioja, Rossi, Verri.

In Switzerland: Cherbuliez, Herrenschwand.

In the U.S.S.R.: Storch.

In the United States: Franklin, Hamilton, Jefferson, Perry, Walker (F. A.), Wells.

4) *Anarchism.* The ultimate individualism, rejecting any state authority and legal regulations.
Bakunin, Godwin, Grave, Kropotkin, Proudhon, Reclus, Stirner.

C. *Socio-Economic Movements* (from 1800 on)

Turning from abstract and deductive studies to sociological, historical, evolutionary and behavioral aspects, stressing socio-economic problems.

1) *Associationists and the Co-operative Movement.* Seeking to solve socio-economic problems through cooperation in various forms.
Blanc, Brisbane, Cabet, Considérant, Fourier, Gide, Laidler, Owen, Raiffeisen, Saint-Simon, Schulze-Delitzsch, Sismondi, Thompson.

2) *The Romantics.* Stressing moral law and the importance of society and state.
Baader, Carlyle, Gentz, Müller (Adam), Ruskin. Universalism: Spann.

3) *Social Reformers.* Emphasizing the dignity of man and measures for assistance to the poor and underpriviled.

> Beveridge, Brissot, Godin, Le Play, Solvay, Stein, Toynbee.

> Christian Social Reformers and Solidarism: Brants, Bourgeois, Huet, John XXIII, Ketteler, Leo XIII, Nell-Breuning, Paul VI, Pius XI, Pesch, Stöcker, Tolstoy, Villeneuve-Bargemont.

> Land Reformers: Boisguillebert, Damaschke, Flürscheim, George, Gesell, Gossen, Hertzka, Huet, Mill (J. S.), Ogilvie, Morelly, Paine, Spence, Thornton (W. T.), Walras (Léon), Weitling, Winstanley.

4) *The Historical School.* An attempt to explain economic life and behavior as results of cultural development.

> Forerunners: Droz, Jones, Savigny.

> German Historical School: Brentano, Bücher, Hildebrand, Knapp, Knies, Roscher, Schmoller, Wagner.

> Historical Sociological School: Brinkmann, Gottl-Ottlilienfeld, Schumacher, Sombart, Spiethoff, Weber (Max).

> British Historical School: Ashley, Ashton, Bagehot, Clapham, Cunningham, Foxwell, Ingram, Leslie, Rogers, Stephen, Toynbee, Unwin.

> Other followers of the Historical School: Beer, Cusumano, Heeren, Held, Inama-Sternegg, Juglar, Laveleye, Levasseur, Maine, Martiis, Meitzen, Schulze-Gävernitz, Small.

5) *The American Institutionalists.* The evolution and interdependence of institutions within a society.

> Anderson (B. M.), Atkins, Ayres, Clark (J. M.), Commons, Ely, Hamilton (W. H.), Hoxie, Means,* Mitchell, Slichter, Taussig, Veblen, Wolfe.

6) *Welfare Economics.* Economic activities as means to the welfare of the people.

> Clark (J. M.), Clay, Dobb,* Hicks,* Hawtrey, Hobson, Kaldor,* Mishan,* Myrdal, Pareto, Patten, Pigou, Schäffle, Sidgwick, Tawney, Taylor.

7) *Conservative Social Reformers.* Social reforms for political and humanitarian reasons.

> Bismarck, Shaftesbury (7th Earl), Stein.

8) *Social Market Economy.* A liberal economy for social purposes.

> Erhard, Müller-Armack, Röpke.

> Other writers and personalities of distinction:

> In Belgium: Denis.

> In Britain: Booth, Hammond (J. L.), Hammond (Barbara), Scott, Smart.

> In France: Buret, Cauwès, Demolins, Durkheim, Gibrat,* Mantoux, Sée.

In Germany: Conrad, Diehl, Engel, Gesell, Oncken, Oppenheimer.

In Italy: Einaudi, Graziani, Mazzola.

In Sweden: Hecksher.

In the United States: Adams (C. F.), Atkinson, Bascom, Colwell, Carlton, Carver, Graham, Groat, Hollander, Knight, McVickar, Monroe, Perlman, Phillips, Seligman, Smith (E. P.), Tucker (George), Vethake, Wayland, White, Wright.

D. *The Growth of Socialism* (from 1820 on)
Centrally planned economy with limitation or elimination of private property and/or competition.

1) *Utopian Socialism.* Hopes and dreams for a better society and future.
Bellamy, Cabet, Campanella, Fichte, Harrington, Hertzka, Huxley, Morris, Plato.

2) *Early Socialists.* Demand for collective actions.
Babeuf, Bazard, Blanqui (L. A.), Buchez, Chevalier, Enfantin, Fix, Gray (John), Hodgskin, Lamennais, Leroux, Thompson.

3) *Marxian Socialism.* Collectivism and central planning as the solution to economic problems.
Bukharin, Engels, Hilferding, Kautsky, Lange, Lederer, Lenin, Luxemburg, Mao, Marx, Plekhanov, Stalin.

4) *Reform Socialism.* Democratic development to a socialistic end.
Bray, Bernstein, Tugan-Baranovsky.

5) *Variations of Socialist Ideas and Forms.*
The Chartists: O'Brien (Bronterre).
The Christian Socialists: Heimann, Hitze, Hughes, Kingsley, Maurice, Ritschl,* Wagner.
The Fabian Socialists: Laski, Shaw, Tawney, Wallas, Webb (Beatrice), Webb (Sidney).
Guild Socialism: Cole, Tawney, Winkelblech.
Land Socialism: Dove, Hall, Loria, O'Brien (G. A. T.), Oppenheimer.
Rational Socialism: Colins.
State Socialism: Blanc, Cusumano, Dupont-White, Lassalle, Menger (Anton), Rodbertus.
Syndicalism: Sorel.

E. *The Revival of Economic Theory* (from 1870 on)
New developments in economic theories.

1) *New Aspects and Contributions to Economic Theory.*
   Marginal concepts: Cournot, Dupuit, Gossen, Jevons, Lloyd, Longfield, Thünen, Whately.
   The Austrian Group of the Psychological School: Böhm-Bawerk, Clark (J. B.), Fetter, Menger (Karl), Meyer, Mises, Philippovich, Sax, Wieser.
   The Lausanne Group: Antonelli, Barone, Bresciani-Turroni, Pantaleoni, Pareto, Walras (A. A.), Walras (Léon).
   The Cambridge Neoclassics: Flux, Marshall, Pigou, Robertson, Robinson (Austin).
   The Swedish School: Cassel, Hansen (Bent),* Lindahl, Lundberg, Myrdal, Ohlin, Wicksell.

2) *The Functional Approach to Economics.*
   The Indifference Curve: Allen (R. G. D.),* Edgeworth, Fisher, Hicks,* Pareto, Schneider, Slutsky.
   Markets and Prices: Abbott,* Auspitz, Berle, Bowley, Chamberlin, Cournot, Davenport, Eucken, Guyot, Jewkes,* Kaplan, Kemmerer, Leftwich,* Levy (H.), Lieben, Liefmann, Lösch, Machlup,* McCracken, Means,* Miksch, Robinson (Joan), Stackelberg, Supino, Weber (Alfred), Zeuthen.
   Money and Business Cycles: Äkerman, Aftalion, Anderson (B. M.), Biddle, Bendixen, Bolles, Bullock, Cannan, Cassel, Conant, Davidson, Del Mar, Del Vecchio, Dunbar, Ferraris, Fisher, Foville, Friedman,* Frisch,* Giffen, Goschen, Hahn, Hansen (Alvin), Hawtrey, Hayek,* Helfferich, Hicks,* Hobson, Juglar, Keynes (J. M.), Lederer, Lindahl, Lundberg, MacLeod, Mises, Mitchell, Moore (G.),* Musgrave,* Myrdal, Nasse, Nicholson, Ohlin, Overstone, Palgrave, Pohle, Preiser,* Rist, Schumpeter, Spiethoff, Tinbergen,* Triffin,* Tugan-Baranovsky, Wagemann, Wicksell, Zwiedineck-Südenhorst.
   Econometrics: Baxter (R. D.), Cheysson, Fisher, Launhardt, Moor (H. L.), Allais,* Divisia, Frisch,* Haavelmo,* King (Wilford), Klein,* Mayo-Smith, Tinbergen,* Wald.
   Value-Free Economics: Cassel, Dietzel, Gottl-Ottlilienfeld, Liefmann, Robbins, Weber (Adolf), Weber (Max).

3) *Other Contributions to New Theoretical Developments, and Contemporary Writers.*
   In Australia: Hearn.
   In Austria: Amonn, Tautscher,* Polanyi.
   In Britain: Bastable, Bonar, Jenkin, Jennings, Keynes (J. Neville), Levy (L.), Longe, Meade,* Sraffa, Stamp, Wicksteed.
   In France: Baudrillart, Bourguin, Colson, Neymarck, Passy, Pirou.

In Germany: Ammon, Bortkiewicz, Cohn (G.), Dietzel (K. A.), Ehrenberg, Giersch,* Lauschmann,* Lexis, Wendt.

In Holland: Blaug,* Pierson, Polak.*

In Italy: Conigliani, Cossa, Croce, Fanfani,* Messedaglia, Ricca-Salerno, Ricci.

In Japan: Itazaki,* Minobe,* Tsuru.*

In Norway: Aarum, Haavelmo.*

In Spain: Franco.*

In Sweden: Carlson,* Hansen (Bent).*

In Switzerland: Küng,* Lutz.*

In the U.S.S.R.: Arzumanyan,* Kantorovich,* Kondratieff,* Liberman.*

In the United States: Bergson,* Boulding,* Briefs, Burns (A. F.),* Fusfeld,* Galbraith,* Ginsberg,* Haberler,* Hadley, Haley, Haney, Harris (S. E.),* Heilbroner,* Heller,* Homan, Lekachman,* Lerner,* Lowe, Nurske, Ripley, Soule, Spiegel,* Stigler,* Sweezy,* Tugwell, Tuttle, Viner, Weisskopf,* Young (Allyn A.).

4) *The Keynesian Revolution.* Macroeconomics.
Dillard,* Föhl, Hansen (Alvin), Harrod,* Keynes (J. M.), Kahn,* Lerner,* Robinson (Austin), Samuelson,* Schneider.

5) *After Keynes.* Later developments.
Economic Growth, Development and Planning: Clark (Colin),* Domar,* Ellis, Hansen (Bent),* Harrod,* Landauer, Lauschmann,* Lewis,* Kuznets,* Myrdal, Nurske, Preiser,* Ritschl,* Schumpeter, Strumilin, Wootton, Yamada,* Zweig.
Some Special Contributions to Economic Analysis:
Activity Analysis: Koopmans.*
Game Theory: Morgenstern,* Neumann.
Input-Output Analysis: Leontief.*
Linear Programming: Dorfman.*
Multiplier Effect: Kahn.*
Operations Analysis: Baumol.*

# APPENDIX III

## Bibliography

# APPENDIX III
# Bibliography

Bell, John Fred. *A History of Economic Thought.* New York, 1953.

Blaug, Mark. *Economic Theory in Retrospect.* Homewood, Ill., 1962.

Cannan, Edwin. *A Review of Economic Theory.* London, 1929.

Fellner, William. *Emergence and Content of Modern Economic Analysis.* New York, 1960.

Ferguson, John M. *Landmarks of Economic Thought.* New York, 1938.

Fusfeld, Daniel R. *The Age of the Economist.* Glenview, Ill., 1966.

Gill, Richard T. *Evolution of Modern Economics.* Englewood Cliffs, N.J., 1967.

Gray, Alexander. *The Development of Economic Doctrine.* New York, 1931.

Haney, Lewis. *History of Economic Thought.* New York, 1911.

Heilbroner, Robert L. *The Worldly Philosophers.* New York, 1953.

Heimann, Eduard. *History of Economic Doctrines.* New York, 1945.

Kuhn, W. E. *The Evolution of Economic Thought.* Chicago, 1963.

Lekachman, Robert. *A History of Economic Ideas.* New York, 1959.

Marshall, Howard D. *The Great Economists.* New York, 1967.

Mitchell, Broadus. *Great Economists in Their Times.* Totowa, N.J., 1966.

Neff, Frank Amandus. *Economic Doctrines.* New York, 1950.

Newman, Philip Charles. *The Development of Economic Thought.* New York, 1952.

Oser, Jacob. *The Evolution of Economic Thought.* New York, 1963.

Palgrave, Robert H. Inglis. *Dictionary of Political Economy.* London, 1894–1899.

Rima, I. H. *Development of Economic Analysis.* Homewood, Ill., 1967.

Roll, Eric. *A History of Economic Thought.* London, 1938.

Schumpeter, Joseph A. *History of Economic Analysis.* New York, 1954.

Seligman, Ben B. *Main Currents in Modern Economics.* Glencoe, Ill., 1962.

Soule, George. *Ideas of the Great Economists.* New York, 1955.

Spiegel, Henry W. *The Growth of Economic Thought.* Englewood Cliffs, N.J., 1971.

Taylor, Overton H. *A History of Economic Thought.* New York, 1960.

Whittaker, Edmund. *Schools and Streams of Economic Thought.* Chicago, 1960.

Zweig, Ferdinand. *Economic Ideas.* New York, 1950.

Äkerman, Johan. *Nationalekonomiens utveckling.* Lund, 1951.

Amoroso, Luigi. *Lezioni sulle dottrine economiche.* Rome, 1927.

Chevalier, Jean. *Doctrines économiques.* Paris, 1945.

Gide, Charles, and Charles Rist. *Histoire des doctrines économiques.* Paris, 1909.

Graziani, A. *Storia delle dottrine economiche.* Naples, 1949.

Kruse, Alfred. *Geschichte der volkswirtschaftlichen Theorien.* Munich, 1948.

Lluch y Capdevila, Pedro. *Historia de las doctrinas economicas.* Barcelona, 1935.

Mombert, Paul. *Geschichte der Nationalökonomie.* Jena, 1927.

Muhs, Karl. *Kurzgefasste Geschichte der Volkswirtschaftslehre.* Wiesbaden, 1955.

Salin, Edgar. *Geschichte der Volkswirtschaftslehre.* Bern, 1923.

Schmolders, Günter. *Geschichte der Volkswirtschaftslehre.* Wiesbaden, 1961.

Tautscher, Anton. *Geschichte der Volkswirtschaftslehre.* Vienna, 1950.

Villey, Daniel. *Petite histoire des grandes doctrines économiques.* Paris, 1944.

Wendt, Siegfried. *Geschichte der Volkswirtschaftslehre.* Berlin, 1961.